GOD'S ACTION IN NATURE'S WORLD

In 1981 Robert John Russell founded what would become the leading center of research at the interface of science and religion, the Center for Theology and the Natural Sciences. Throughout its twenty-five year history, CTNS under Russell's leadership has continued to guide and further the dialogue between science and theology. Russell has been an articulate spokesperson in calling for 'creative mutual interaction' between the two fields.

God's Action in Nature's World brings together sixteen internationally-recognized scholars to assess Robert Russell's impact on the discipline of science and religion. Focusing on three areas of Russell's work – methodology, cosmology, and divine action in quantum physics – this book celebrates Robert John Russell's contribution to the interdisciplinary engagement between the natural sciences and theology.

Ashgate Science and Religion Series

Series Editors:

Roger Trigg, *Department of Philosophy, University of Warwick, UK*

J. Wentzel van Huyssteen, *James I. McCord Professor of Theology and Science, Princeton Theological Seminary, USA*

Science and religion have often been thought to be at loggerheads but much contemporary work in this flourishing interdisciplinary field suggests this is far from the case. *The Ashgate Science and Religion Series* presents exciting new work to advance interdisciplinary study, research and debate across key themes in science and religion, exploring the philosophical relations between the physical and social sciences on the one hand and religious belief on the other. Contemporary issues in philosophy and theology are debated, as are prevailing cultural assumptions arising from the 'post-modernist' distaste for many forms of reasoning. The series enables leading international authors from a range of different disciplinary perspectives to apply the insights of the various sciences, theology and philosophy and look at the relations between the different disciplines and the rational connections that can be made between them. These accessible, stimulating new contributions to key topics across science and religion will appeal particularly to individual academics and researchers, graduates, postgraduates and upper-undergraduate students.

God's Action in Nature's World

Essays in Honour of Robert John Russell

Edited by

TED PETERS
and
NATHAN HALLANGER

ASHGATE

Published by
Ashgate Publishing Limited
Gower House
Croft Road
Aldershot
Hampshire GU11 3HR
England

Ashgate Publishing Company
Suite 420
101 Cherry Street
Vermont, 05401-4405
USA

Ashgate website: http://www.ashgate.com

British Library Cataloguing in Publication Data
God's Action in Nature's World: Essays in Honour of Robert John Russell. –
(Ashgate Science and Religion Series)
1. Religion and science. 2. Natural theology. I. Peters, Ted, 1941– .
Hallanger, Nathan.
III. Russell, Robert J.
261.5'5

US Library of Congress Cataloging in Publication Data
God's Action in Nature's World: Essays in Honour of Robert John Russell /
edited by Ted Peters and Nathan Hallanger.
    p.   cm. – (Ashgate Science and Religion Series)
Includes bibliographical references and index.
1. Religion and science. 2. Russell, Robert J. I. Russell, Robert J. II. Peters,
Ted, 1941– . III. Hallanger, Nathan. IV. Series.
BL241.G62 2006
215–dc22   2005020702

ISBN 0 7546 5556 3 (hardback)

This book is printed on acid-free paper.

Printed and bound in Great Britain by Antony Rowe Ltd, Chippenham, Wiltshire

This book is dedicated to Robert John Russell, who continues to challenge and inspire those interested in the creative mutual interaction between theology and the natural sciences.

Contents

List of Contributors

Ian G. Barbour, Emeritus Professor of Physics and Religion, Emeritus Bean Professor of Science, Technology and Society, Carleton College, Northfield, Minnesota, USA.

Philip Clayton, Ingraham Chair, Claremont School of Theology and Professor of Philosophy at the Claremont Graduate University, Claremont, California, USA.

George V. Coyne, SJ, Director, Vatican Observatory, University of Arizona, Tucson, Arizona, USA, and Castel Gandolfo, Italy.

Paul Davies, Professor of Natural Philosophy in the Australian Centre for Astrobiology, Macquarie University, Sidney, Australia.

Noreen Herzfeld, Professor of Computer Science, St John's University and the College of St Benedict, and Director of the Koch Chair in Catholic Thought and Culture for the College of St Benedict, Collegeville, Minnesota, USA.

Heup Young Kim, Professor of Systematic Theology, Kangnam University, Korea.

Nancey Murphy, Professor of Christian Philosophy, Fuller Theological Seminary, Pasadena, California, USA.

Arthur Peacocke, founding director, Ian Ramsey Centre at St Cross College, Oxford, and former Dean of Clare College, Cambridge, United Kingdom.

Ted Peters, Professor of Systematic Theology, Pacific Lutheran Theological Seminary and the Graduate Theological Union, Berkeley, California, USA.

John Polkinghorne, former Professor of Mathematical Physics at Cambridge University and President of Queens College, Cambridge, United Kingdom.

William R. Stoeger, SJ, Staff Astrophysicist and Adjunct Associate Professor of Astronomy, Vatican Observatory, Vatican Observatory Research Group, Steward Observatory, University of Arizona, Tucson, Arizona, USA.

Charles H. Townes, Professor in the Graduate School at the University of California at Berkeley, USA.

Lou Ann Trost, former Program Director, the Center for Theology and the Natural Sciences, Berkeley, California, USA, and former Associate Director for Parliament Program, the Council for a Parliament of the World's Religions, Chicago, Illinois, USA.

J. Wentzel van Huyssteen, James I. McCord Professor of Theology and Science, Princeton Theological Seminary, Princeton, New Jersey, USA.

Kirk Wegter-McNelly, Assistant Professor of Theology, Boston University School of Theology, Boston, Massachusetts, USA.

Wesley J. Wildman, Associate Professor of Theology and Ethics, Boston University School of Theology, Boston, Massachusetts, USA.

Preface

Nathan Hallanger

Since 1981 the Center for Theology and the Natural Sciences (CTNS) in Berkeley, California, has guided, supported, and enabled a wide range of scholars – philosophers, theologians, historians, and scientists, among others – to join in interdisciplinary dialogue. CTNS has been engaged in a quest for meaning and truth not limited by disciplinary boundaries, thereby venturing forth into the unknown, posing complicated questions without knowing exactly where they might lead. In the process CTNS has created an intellectual space in which scientists and theologians can question, challenge, and support one another in critical and honest dialogue. This is no small feat. Facing the challenging obstacles to dialogue between theology and science has required tireless effort, innovative vision, and boundless enthusiasm, all of which have been provided by CTNS's founder and director, Robert John Russell.

For many who seek this mutually enriching engagement between theology and the natural sciences, Russell's contributions have offered invaluable guidance. As a theologian and a physicist, Russell has provided unparalleled insight into the ways in which theology and science can be mutually beneficial. Building on earlier efforts to move beyond models of conflict between science and religion, Russell not only examines how theology and science should relate, but also enacts his proposals in addressing specific research questions. Russell's recent efforts show that he is committed to pressing the dialogue to its limits by addressing 'worst case scenario' questions where one finds dissonance rather than consonance between scientific theories and theological commitments.

One recent example focuses on understanding resurrection in theology and science. For Russell the questions framing his contribution are the following: (1) 'How are we to understand the Christian notions of bodily resurrection and eschatology in light of the far-future of the universe?' and (2) 'Can Christian commitments to resurrection and eschatology influence new scientific research programs?' Such questions require scholars to examine the relevant data from theology *and* from the natural sciences in developing theological proposals as well as influencing scientific research programs. Myopic notions of science or of theology do not do justice to the complexity of the issues at hand.

Russell has developed a vision for theology–science interaction, developed toughest case scenarios to test his vision, and provided glimpses of how one might respond to such scenarios. Like Russell, many others in the field would like to see the discussion advance beyond the conflict model and the two-languages approach. With his introduction of the 'creative mutual interaction model', Russell offers perhaps the most ambitious alternative, one that challenges both scientists and theologians to leap forward together. The chapters in this volume reflect the impact of Robert John Russell's invitation to take that leap toward honest and challenging engagement between theology and science.

Among Russell's many contributions to the burgeoning field of science and theology are his efforts at describing how it is that science and theology should relate to one another; his project of developing an understanding of God's action in the natural world; and his vision of the universe and its laws as the realm of God's ongoing presence. The chapters are organized around these three broad themes, though, as the essays make clear, Russell's contributions cover a wide swath in the theology–science dialogue.

Ted Peters's essay, 'Robert John Russell's Contribution to the Theology & Science Dialogue', surveys Russell's influence on the ongoing dialogue between theology and science through the lens of what Peters calls 'Bobisms', phrases that are uniquely Russell's. He identifies five: 'creative mutual interaction'; 'non-interventionist objective divine action'; 'atoms may be small, but they're everywhere'; 'if it's true, then it must be possible'; and 'first instantiation of a new law of nature'. Peters argues that Russell and the Center for Theology and the Natural Sciences that he founded represent a move toward 'hypothetical consonance' between theology and science. Russell's vision of 'creative mutual interaction', Peters concludes, represents Russell's most valuable contribution to the field of science and theology.

Part I: Creative Mutual Interaction between Science and Theology

William R. Stoeger, SJ, assesses Russell's contributions to methodology. He builds upon and expands Russell's paths for relating science and theology while evaluating the possibilities for ensuring positive and creative interaction. Stoeger proposes a system of levels to describe how science and theology relate and then compares his schema to Russell's description of paths between science and theology. Stoeger argues that his levels can encompass Russell's paths since Stoeger's description includes unreflective dimensions of interaction. Finally, Stoeger examines the common foundation of both proposals, critical realism, and the key issues of applying a critical realist epistemology to theology.

Nancey Murphy also analyzes Russell's contributions to the methodology of science–theology interaction, and asks whether Russell's paths of interaction between science and theology include all the possibilities and whether the paths he does include are legitimate descriptions. Murphy pays special attention to Russell's description of ways that theology can influence science. In examining Russell's contributions to the field, Murphy assesses the degree to which Russell's own writings fit the schema of paths relating science and theology that Russell has provided. Using Russell's work on quantum cosmology, Murphy shows how Russell's methodological proposal can be used to describe the actual work being done when theology and science engage in creative mutual interaction, and concludes by suggesting further developments of the role of philosophy in science–theology dialogue.

Like Murphy, Philip Clayton evaluates Russell's notion of creative mutual interaction. Clayton argues that creative mutual interaction (CMI) is the most ambitious proposal for dialogue between theology and science; in fact, creative mutual interaction is more challenging than a unification of the two fields because it requires that one examine the other field from the perspective of that field. Yet CMI has yet to achieve the status of a Lakatosian 'progressive research program', Clayton argues, since it has not produced successes in actual test cases. The role CMI plays in theology and science dialogue, Clayton concludes, can be understood as a regulative ideal, just as for Immanuel Kant the idea of God functions as the regulative ideal for reason. Other typologies for understanding how one relates the two fields serve as sub-goals for specific periods even while creative mutual interaction remains the final goal.

J. Wentzel van Huyssteen examines Russell's work as a particularly successful example of – and model for – interdisciplinary dialogue. Van Huyssteen then identifies the affinities between Russell's recent work and van Huyssteen's own work on postfoundational rationality. Creative mutual interaction would be enhanced, van Huyssteen believes, by postfoundationalist notions of rationality that create liminal epistemic spaces for interdisciplinary dialogue. Rather than universal methods for engagement, we should seek contextual and transversal rationality to engage specific problems within specific disciplines. The plurality of rationalities allows for new interconnected webs to be woven between fields such as theology and science. For van Huyssteen, Russell's creative mutual interaction points clearly in this direction.

In Chapter 6 Heup Young Kim provides a critical perspective on the dialogue between science and religion, arguing that it suffers from a strong Western bias that fails to account for the plurality of the world's religions. Taking up the work of Russell's mentor Ian Barbour, Kim explores the limitations of Barbour's typology for ways of relating science and religion, and argues that Barbour is more prescriptive than descriptive. Instead of typologies and bridge metaphors, Kim suggests using the concept of the *Tao* of life as a key to interactions between sciences and religions (not between science and religion). He suggests further that taking account of interreligious dialogue and incorporating other East Asian insights – such as notions of nothingness and the significance of space – might be where the sciences truly meet the religions.

Part II: Quantum Physics and Divine Action

Kirk Wegter-McNelly focuses his chapter on Russell's work on quantum physics. He begins by surveying Russell's early writings on theology and quantum physics, in which Russell's key concerns are complementarity and quantum indeterminacy. As Wegter-McNelly points out, Russell's concern early on is to use quantum physics as a tool for re-imagining Christian concepts of creation. Wegter-McNelly charts Russell's early work on divine action, leading into his contributions to the CTNS/Vatican Observatory series on the subject, before examining a crucial component of Russell's hypothesis: the meaning of 'event' in quantum physics. An 'event' is important for Russell if he is to argue for the pervasiveness of God's non-interventionist objective divine action at the quantum level. Wegter-McNelly concludes by exploring the implications of three recent attempts by physicists to understand the nature of quantum 'events'.

In Chapter 8, 'Indeterminacy, Holism, and God's Action', Ian G. Barbour describes the points of agreement and disagreement between Russell's work and his own. Barbour critiques Russell's assertion that God acted in all quantum events prior to the advent of life, but has acted selectively after the advent of life to allow for creativity and freedom. For Barbour, process thought provides a more adequate lens through which to view divine action than does Russell's model, for it describes how God might act at higher levels in a 'top–down' fashion.

In his chapter 'Basic Puzzles in Science and Religion', Charles H. Townes argues that a clear articulation of problems in the dialogue between science and religion can serve as a catalyst for creative discussion. He then delineates five key problems involving creation, divine action, free will, consciousness, and the human spirit. As in scientific discovery, Townes believes that research into these five areas can lead to revolutionary findings that expand our understanding while leaving present insights at least partially intact.

John Polkinghorne picks up the conversation about Russell's contributions to dialogue between theology and physics in his chapter 'Quantum Theology'. Polkinghorne traces Russell's contributions through the CTNS/Vatican Observatory conferences (and subsequent books) on divine action, from his discussions of complementarity and quantum indeterminacy to later discussions of quantum cosmology and creation *ex nihilo*. Russell's insights in these areas, Polkinghorne concludes, exemplify his belief that theology can influence the scientific process at some level.

In Chapter 11, Wesley J. Wildman examines Russell's theory of divine action in light of its motivations and its theological context. Having placed Russell within wider discussions of divine action, Wildman finds motivations for the theory in Russell's understanding of God, his preference for concrete intelligibility in theological assertions, and his efforts to develop a theology of nature that integrates as much contemporary scientific knowledge as possible. Wildman challenges Russell to focus less on the biblical picture of a personal God who is a being among beings, and more on Christian theology's heritage in Greek philosophy.

Part III: Cosmology and God's Action in Nature's World

George V. Coyne, SJ, the head of the Vatican Observatory, provides a brief historical survey of the relationship between theology and science before turning to an examination of the current status of the dialogue. After examining Greek mythology, early Christianity, and early modern science, Coyne turns his attention to the contributions of Pope John Paul II to theology and science dialogue. Against this backdrop Coyne investigates the implications of contemporary physics for understanding humanity's quest for ultimate meaning, and notes how understanding the universe and its laws provides greater understanding of humanity and humanity's relationship to God.

Arthur Peacocke's chapter, 'Emergent Realities with Causal Efficacy – Some Philosophical and Theological Applications', explores an important context for understanding divine action in emergent phenomena. Emergence, Peacocke notes, enables one to understand an entity as embodying characteristics not logically reducible to that entity's component parts. Peacocke sees the non-reducibility of emergence as a useful guide for re-examining both philosophical issues such as mind–body interactions and theological issues surrounding prayer, worship, and divine action. Peacocke concludes that the concept of emergence may serve to connect the physical, mental, and spiritual realms, and thus overcome the barriers between science and religion.

In Chapter 14 Lou Ann Trost brings Russell's work on non-interventionist objective divine action into dialogue with the work of Wolfhart Pannenberg. Trost points to convergences in the work of Pannenberg and Russell on contingency and quantum indeterminacy; divine action as trinitarian; and the relationship between divine action and a future-oriented ontology. These convergences provide fertile ground for the development of a philosophy of nature. Trost argues that combining insights from Russell and Pannenberg may foster an understanding of the freedom of the natural world as a basis for a theological-based ecological ethics.

In 'How Many Universes?', physicist Paul Davies reviews the notion of the multiverse, the idea that our 'universe' is but one component of a much larger system. As Davies notes, the multiverse hypothesis is cited as one way of understanding why the universe we inhabit seems to exhibit particular fundamental laws of physics that have made the evolution of sentient life possible (if not inevitable). Yet Davies explains that the hypothesis might invalidate itself by leading to the conclusion that our universe is a simulation and thus that our observations have no meaning beyond the parameters of our simulation. Even though Davies believes that it is an unavoidable conclusion based on cosmology and modern physics, the multiverse hypothesis is of little use when one reaches the level of humans as reflective moral agents.

Finally, Noreen Herzfeld uses Russell's notion of creative mutual interaction to engage the world of cyberspace and video games from a theological perspective. The disembodied world of computer technology promises not simply an escape from the mundane but an escape from embodied reality itself. Video games, the internet, and other technologies increasingly foster an understanding of human selves as information. Theology should engage this fad and show how true human existence is bodily and relational. In such instances, Herzfeld argues, theology can provide a critical lens through which to uncover scientific fads and fallacies, and thus show how science can benefit from creative mutual interaction.

In sum, these chapters represent Robert John Russell's impact on theology and science dialogue. Russell has developed a method of 'creative mutual interaction'; provided insights into divine action in light of quantum physics; and examined the origin and evolution of our universe throughout its nearly 14-billion-year history. But those are by no means Russell's only contributions to the field.

Since 1981 Bob has taught students at the Graduate Theological Union and its nine member seminaries. His constructive proposal for dialogue between theology and the natural sciences has influenced hundreds of masters and doctoral students. Through his many classes, seminars, and scholarly presentations, Bob has affected not only the hallowed halls of the academy, but also the pulpits and pews of congregations across the country and around the globe. So in addition to the research, conferences, and publications he has produced through the Center for Theology and the Natural Sciences, Bob has created – and continues to create – an enduring legacy by educating future religious and theological leaders. Thus, *God's Action in Nature's World* serves as a tribute not only to a thoughtful scholar but also to an energetic teacher, a wise advisor, and a true partner in dialogue – Robert John Russell.

Acknowledgements

A number of friends and colleagues helped greatly in the preparation and production of this book. Thank you to Sarah Lloyd and Anne Keirby at Ashgate Publishing for their guidance and assistance. The Graduate Theological Union and its member seminaries and affiliates serve as the intellectual home for CTNS. Thanks to GTU President James Donahue and Dean Arthur Holder for continued support of the Center. Thanks as well to J. Wentzel van Huyssteen and Roger Trigg, editors for *Ashgate's Science and Religion Series*.

Special thanks go to Carla Jimenez, who provided invaluable aid in the early stages of the book. Everyone at CTNS provided much-needed guidance throughout the stages of production: Bonnie Johnston, Dale Loepp, Melissa Moritz, James Haag, Whitney Bauman, and Carl York.

We would like to express admiration as well as gratitude to one very special person, Rev. Charlotte Russell, Bob's spouse, companion, friend and co-worker.

CHAPTER ONE

Robert John Russell's Contribution to the Theology & Science Dialogue

Ted Peters

Over the last two-and-a-half decades, a brief yet potentially groundbreaking chapter of intellectual history has been in the writing in Berkeley, California. The larger story is the history of the relationship between faith and science. The Berkeley chapter tells of new encounters, new relationships, new insights, and new breakthroughs. Leading the way across new thresholds has been my colleague and friend Robert John Russell, who founded the Center for Theology and the Natural Sciences (CTNS) at the Graduate Theological Union (GTU) in 1981. In what follows I would like to outline briefly the *Science and Religion* story; then I would like to turn specifically to the chapter in which Bob Russell is the chief character.

We will explicate the central contributions of Robert John Russell by identifying five key concepts, which we affectionately call 'Bobisms'. These key concepts comprise: (1) CMI: the 'creative mutual interaction' between science and theology; (2) NIODA: 'non-interventionist objective divine action' in nature's world; (3) ASBE: 'atoms may be small, but they're everywhere'; (4) $t > p$ – that is, 'if it's true, then it must be possible'; and (5) FINLON, according to which the Easter resurrection of Jesus is the 'first instantiation of a new law of nature'. This last one, FINLON, has a corollary, MTLT, or 'miracle today, law tomorrow'. What is distinctive and admirable about Russell's contribution to the dialogue between science and religion is his insistence that we will not have arrived at a true interaction until the day comes when the theologian provides the scientist with a prompting that leads to progressive empirical research. Such insistence takes courage. It demonstrates that the scientific spirit of raising up a possibility, formulating it into a hypothesis, and then pursuing research to confirm or disconfirm it can become a challenge to expand the horizon of science while it enriches the life of theology and, thereby, the life of faith.

Science & Religion versus Science & Theology

The flowering of dialogue between laboratory scientists and academic theologians in Berkeley belongs in a global garden of new growth. During the final third of the twentieth century something dramatic began to blossom in the world's intellectual flower bed, namely the field of *Science & Religion*. Within this apparently spontaneously growing nosegay is a new hybrid, the field of *Science & Theology*. The soil has been enriched by a growing cultural respect for religion and the widespread sense that a conversation needs to be cultivated between the spiritual and empirical dimensions of human knowing. The dialogue between Theology & Science has blossomed within a larger garden of growing interest in Science & Religion.

What we mean by 'science' here is quite specific. By *science* we refer to natural sciences such as physics, cosmology, evolutionary biology, genetics, and the neurosciences; and it includes supporting disciplines such as history of science and philosophy of science. Although on occasion we will dip into one or another social science, for the most part the emerging field limits itself to the natural sciences.

The natural science that is relevant here is quite specifically *modern* science. Modern science is inherently and relentlessly revolutionary in spirit. Its ruthless dedication to empirically derived truth renders science brutal in its disregard for previous beliefs, even sacred beliefs. No appeal to traditional religious authority can stand in the face of repudiation by modern scientific theory or its companion, technology. This is the science which we find in a new partnership with religion.

By *religion* we refer to two regions of religious thought. The first is generically spiritual, wherein research scientists are asked to explore ways in which their understandings of nature emit evidence or lack of evidence of transcendence. The second is doctrinally conceptual, wherein Christian systematic theology, as well as the philosophical or conceptual components to traditions such as Islam, Judaism, Hinduism, Buddhism, and Chinese traditions, is placed in dialogue with the sciences to re-conceive God's relation to the world in creation, providence, moral guidance, and related interactions. Science and religion is a field of academic study that invites contributions from a variety of sciences and a variety of religious commitments. The academic field of Science & Religion is not itself a religious tradition or homogeneous school of thought.

What we know as the field of *Science & Religion* is actually the outgrowth of an originally much more specific agenda that could be called *Science & Theology* or, as the title of the CTNS journal has it, *Theology and Science*. This is the case for both conceptual and historical reasons. Conceptually, science as a human enterprise operates at the level of the human mind. Science is rational, conceptual. So also is theology. Theology is that component to the religious life that relies on the human mind to understand God's relation to the world and to ourselves. Theology is to religion what science is to nature.

In the final third of the twentieth century, it was the pioneering work of Christian theologians trained and fascinated by science that opened the door through which so many later could walk. Quite specifically, it was the trailblazing work in the mid-1960s of Ian G. Barbour, who reviewed the history of Europe's experience with scientific revolutions amidst its Jewish and Christian cultural context that provided the map of intellectual issues which needed addressing. What Barbour and his successors accomplished was the building of a conceptual bridge between reflective theology and reflective science. What would later become a broader interest in the relationship of scientific progress to religious traditions – the field of Science & Religion – traversed this initial theological bridge.

The Emergence of the Science & Religion Dialogue

As already mentioned, what we know today as the field of *Science & Religion* gained its present definition during the 1960s. There were antecedents, of course. In 1941 the American Scientific Affiliation was founded by evangelical scientists. Since the 1960s, however, an evolution in our intellectual environment has made possible lavish advances in the dialogue between natural science and religious faith.

The intellectual environment of evolutionary adaptation has witnessed three noticeable developments. The first development was an opening within science. Questions of transcendence arose during the 1960s. The confirmation of Big Bang cosmology in 1965 was perhaps the most decisive. The history of the universe as cosmologists began to describe it looked very much like the creation history described in the Bible. With the thought that perhaps the cosmos had a beginning at a certain point in time – actually the beginning of time, when $t = 0$ – provoked the question, might time have an edge, and when we peer over the edge might we be looking at eternity? Science seemed to be raising questions of transcendence and asking for religious involvement and interpretation.

The Big Bang confirmation of the 1960s led to the Anthropic Principle debate in the 1970s and 1980s. The Anthropic Principle was formulated within physics, not theology; yet it has direct theological implications. Because of the appearance of complex life-forms on planet Earth, physicists have been asking the following question: what must have been the initial conditions at the moment of the Big Bang $(t = 0)$ to eventually make life possible, or even inevitable? Such factors as the amount of mass, energy, rate of expansion, and so on could not have been different in fractions such as one to a million, or life would have been impossible. The universe seems to be fine-tuned for the appearance of life. Fine-tuning raises questions of intelligent design. The weak Anthropic Principle asks, was the universe designed to make life possible? The strong Anthropic Principle asks, was the universe designed to make life inevitable?

The debate over determinism versus indeterminism raised by quantum physics similarly opened the door to questions of transcendence. Quantum theory affirms contingency and perhaps even indeterminism at the subatomic level, giving rise to questions regarding rationality in the universe and the possibility of non-interventionist divine action in the physical realm. Newtonian or classical physics had produced a mechanistic picture of nature wherein the universe appeared like a clockwork, as a closed nexus of cause and effect. The rational structure of a clock provided the model for the rational structure of nature. If the universe is causally closed, then God's action within the world seems forbidden. Divine action would require God to intervene as an outside cause, perhaps in the form of a miracle, and this would upset the nexus.

With the advent of quantum theory, however, natural events can now be viewed as contingent. The world no longer looks like a clockwork but more like a history of natural events. Might God be acting in these unpredictable and contingent events? In sum, physics has begun to raise philosophical and theological questions that transcend what science alone can address.

A second development was the turn taken in the field of philosophy of science. For the first two-thirds of the twentieth century, strict empiricism, positivism, and reductionism had held sway. By the late 1950s and early 1960s, this approach was being challenged by a new awareness of historical relativity and the sociology of knowledge. Philosophers including Michael Polanyi, Norwood Hanson, Thomas Kuhn, Stephen Toulmin, and Imre Lakatos placed scientific knowing into historically conditioned communities of knowing. Alleged scientific objectivity underwent challenge and revision. The result was a new picture of scientific knowledge that began to look like knowledge in the humanities. Theologians had already made their peace with historical relativity in the nineteenth century, so now they could welcome twentieth-century philosophy of science into their relativistic and perspectival home.

A third intellectual development took place within the discipline of theology, namely the rise of a new breed of theologians fascinated by science and thirsty for dialogue. The reign was coming to an end for the giants of neo-Orthodox and existentialist Protestant theology – Karl Barth, Emil Brunner, Paul Tillich, Reinhold Niebuhr, H. Richard Niebuhr, Anders Nygren, Gustaf Aulén, and others. These neo-Orthodox theologians had immunized theology from science by embracing the *Two Language* model, according to which science and faith each speak a different language. Science speaks of facts, whereas religion speaks of meaning. Because the languages are untranslatable, so it was assumed, science could have no relevance for matters of faith. Science and faith are allegedly separate realms. Even so, Langdon Gilkey, a staunch disciple of Paul Tillich and Reinhold Niebuhr, pressed the theological community during the 1960s to give attention to the cultural impact of science. Science was now a theological issue because it is a cultural issue. Gilkey did not himself establish a dialogue between theology and science, but he pointed to the canyon over which a bridge of dialogue should be built.[1]

Roman Catholics were also making ready. The Second Vatican Council (1962–65) had taken *aggiornamento* as its theme – that is, opening the windows of the church so the winds of the modern world could blow through. The new mood was one of exuberant openness. This openness would soon include openness to science. With the advent of the pontificate of John Paul II in 1978, the Vatican began an aggressive program of support for dialogue between the Church and the world of natural science. 'Can we not hope that the sciences of today, along with all forms of human knowing,' asked the Pope rhetorically, 'may invigorate and inform those parts of the theological enterprise that bear on the relation of nature, humanity, and God?'[2]

Ian Barbour: The Transitional Form

What we today see as the field of *Science & Religion* evolved in this 1960s environment. For the sake of convenience, we mark the Cambrian breakthrough with the 1966 publication of *Issues in Science and Religion* by Ian G. Barbour. Born in 1923, Barbour grew up in China with a scientist father and theologian mother, and he was present the day in 1929 when Jesuit paleontologist Pierre Teilhard de Chardin arrived with the skull of what would later be called *Sinanthropus*. Barbour went on to obtain advanced degrees in both physics and theology. His first book, *Issues in Science and Religion*, defined the nascent field for four decades to follow.[3] Barbour's subsequent publications, such as *Myths, Models, and Paradigms* (1974) and *Technology, Environment, and Human Values* (1980) along with the Gifford Lectures of 1989–91, *Religion in an Age of Science* and *Ethics in an Age of Technology*, have continued to shape it.[4]

By the early 1970s centers and societies for the study of science and religion were budding around the world. At Oxford University, biologist–theologian Arthur Peacocke organized the Society of Ordained Scientists and cultivated the Ian Ramsey Centre for research in this field. The seeds for German language discussions were planted by the Karl Heim Gesellschaft, founded in 1974, which publishes an annual summary of research. At the Lutheran School of Theology in Chicago, the Zygon Center for Religion and Science was founded by Ralph Wendell Burhoe and supported by the Center for Advanced Study in Religion and Science and the Institute for Religion in an Age of Science. Philip Hefner and now Antje Jackelén succeeded Burhoe as director; and Hefner today serves as Editor of *Zygon: Journal of Religion and Science*. The European Society for the Study of Science and Theology meets biennially on the European continent. The Association of Science, Society, and Religion in India, the Australian Theological Forum, and the Center for Islam and Science in Islamabad and Edmonton are examples of centers that draw scientists and religious leaders into academic conversation and generate publications that expand the field.[5]

Since the early 1990s, the John Templeton Foundation has been granting funding to numerous individuals and organizations because its leaders believe interaction with science will facilitate 'progress in religion'. The Templeton Foundation was financial midwife at the 2002 birth of the multi-religious International Society for Science and Religion centered at Cambridge University, with physicist–theologian John Polkinghorne as its first President. The annual Templeton Prize for contributions to religion is frequently given to scholars in the field of science and religion; recipients have included physicists Charles Townes, Freeman Dyson, and Paul Davies, philosophers Seyyed Hossein Nasr and Homes Rolston III, as well as hybrid theologian–scientists Arthur Peacocke, John Polkinghorne, and Ian Barbour.

CTNS as a New Life Form

Natural selection advances evolution by accident. Engineering advances civilization by vision and design. A clever engineer perceives a need, envisions a device to meet this need, initiates the designing process, and then musters the materials for production. Robert John Russell had already perceived the need for serious engagement of faith with science as a young person. Then, while studying theology in the MDiv and MA programs at the Pacific School of Religion from 1968 to 1972, Russell began envisioning a center for research at the Graduate Theological Union in Berkeley. He was encouraged by the GTU faculty, Durwood Foster, and Andrew J. Dufner, SJ. This was followed by a PhD in physics at the University of California at Santa Cruz, where his vision broadened and deepened. Receiving his doctorate in physics and his ordination into the ministry of the United Church of Christ on the same day in 1978, he went to Northfield, Minnesota to teach physics and conduct chapel worship at Carleton College.

The design stage of what would become the Center took place at Carleton. Russell's new colleague at Carleton was Ian Barbour, who was in the middle of his near career-long professorship. The two theologian–physicists dreamed and planned for what would eventually become CTNS. Foster and Dufner visited the pair in Northfield, and the design took shape. Russell moved from Northfield, Minnesota to Berkeley in 1981 and, along with his wife, Rev. Charlotte Russell, began a now quarter-century of CTNS activities.

The Evolution from Two Languages to Dialogue, then to Hypothetical Consonance

In 1981 the broadly assumed way to relate science with religion was to keep them peacefully separate. The still-dominant model for understanding the relationship of science to theology or religion was not warfare, as many mistakenly assume; rather, it was the *Two Languages* model. Ian Barbour refers to this as the 'independence' model.[6] According to this paradigm, science is said to speak one language, the language of facts, and religion is said to speak a different language, the language of values. Science attends to objective knowledge about objects in the penultimate realm, whereas religion attends to subjective knowledge about transcendent dimensions of ultimate concern. Modern persons need both, according to Albert Einstein, who claimed the following: 'Science without religion is lame and religion without science is blind.'[7] Each of us should speak both languages, that is, so that science and religion find their separate but equal places in our wider culture.

We should not confuse this Two Language model with the classic model of the Two Books, according to which the book of Scripture and the book of nature each provides an avenue of revelation for God. The difference is that the Two Books model sees science as revealing truth about God, whereas the Two Language model sees science as revealing truth solely about the created world.[8]

While gratefully respectful toward the two languages or independence model, CTNS has sought to go beyond it. The stages beyond include dialogue, hypothetical consonance, and creative mutual interaction.

Since its founding in 1981, CTNS has regularly hosted and sponsored conferences in which laboratory scientists are invited to engage directly in dialogue with theologians (accompanied by philosophers and ethicists) regarding the implications of both scientific and theological concepts. Some of these conferences have been quite open-ended; they begin without knowing in advance where the conversation might lead. I have called this 'dice shaker' research; we place scientists and theologians in a room like placing dice in a cup, shake it up, toss it out, and see what comes out of it. Our discovery is that both scientists and theologians come with a hunger and a thirst for dialogue, believing in advance that such dialogue is important even if the end product is unknown in advance.

Why might one think dialogue is important? What we found to be inchoate and just asking for articulation is the assumption of hypothetical consonance. It is the assumption that both science and theology are concerned about the truth. And, we assume, one truth cannot contradict another truth. Somewhere in the darkness of what is not-yet-known, we assume, lies a connection between the natural world as seen through scientific glasses and as seen through the eyes of faith.

We have given this set of assumptions the label *hypothetical consonance*. Notre Dame's historian and philosopher of science Ernan McMullin gave the field the term 'consonance' for use in this context.[9] The assumption of *consonance* directs inquiry toward areas of correspondence between what can be said scientifically about the natural world and what can be said theologically about God's creation.[10] Even though consonance seems to arise in some areas, such as the apparent correspondence of Big Bang cosmology with the doctrine of creation out of nothing, consonance has not been fully confirmed in all relevant shared areas. Hence, the adjective *hypothetical* applies to theology as well as science.

Russell picked up and developed the term *consonance* in several ways. His distinctive contribution is adding, without contrasting, the notion of *dissonance*. Dissonance between a scientific model and a theological model becomes a jumping-off point for further investigation and possible alteration of one, the other, or both. Russell writes,

> I combined McMullin's idea with McFague's epistemic claim about the 'is and is not' structure of metaphor to include and thus to learn from both consonance and what I called 'dissonance' between scientific and theological theories. Rather than undercutting a coherent worldview, dissonance points to the dynamic character of our worldview, specifying where problems arise, shifts are required, and potentially greater coherence can be sought. Moreover, by recognizing that theories in both science and theology evolve and are eventually replaced, we can build change directly into the relation between science and theology rather than being threatened by it.[11]

The central hypothesis of *hypothetical consonance* is that there can be only one shared domain of truth regarding the created world, and science at its best and faith at its best both humble themselves before truth. Therefore, one can trust that consonance will eventually emerge. Hypothetical consonance provides the warrant for *dialogue* between science and theology. However, it also opens the door to a still further step in the evolving relations of science to religion, namely the 'creative mutual interaction of science and theology'. This next stage is the distinctive contribution of CTNS.

CMI: Creative Mutual Interaction

Those of us who work with Robert John Russell – 'Bob' – have noticed a most charming habit. When Bob has an insight, he mulls it over and tags it with a word or a phrase. Then, he introduces it for wider conversation and consideration. His friends have labeled these words or phrases 'Bobisms'. A number of the authors in this book have decided to focus on one or another Bobism.

The central Bobism already introduced is CMI or 'Creative Mutual Interaction', sometimes rendered 'Critical Mutual Interaction'. CMI is the answer to the following questions. Can the knowledge gained from scientific study affect what one believes theologically? For genuine dialogue to be possible, we must assume the answer is 'yes'. Can the insights of religious faith and their articulation by the theologian have an effect on natural science? Again, genuine dialogue would have to assume the answer to be 'yes'. It may not yet be clear just how one field can influence the other; still, we must assume hypothetically that mutual influence is possible.

CMI sets a goal to be achieved when scientists and theologians engage one another in dialogue. CMI tries to make clear that there are some domains of knowing where science and theology share common investment. Each brings to dialogue a given language for understanding, to be sure. Yet in many instances they occupy the same domain; and this legitimizes the pursuit of consonance. Borrowing hermeneutical language, we can expect a merging of horizons between science and faith.

However, Russell wants more. He wants to see science challenge theology; and he wants to see theology challenge science. He wants science to specify the parameters within which theologians understand the world God has created and promises to redeem. Then comes the decisive innovation of CMI: Russell asks that theology prompt science to formulate a hypothesis that will lead to a progressive research program. He asks that something theologians have learned about the world – due to their understanding of the world as God's creation – be offered to researchers as a heuristic, as a guide for further investigation. The proof, so to speak, that science and theology are actually in dialogue will be that science gains insight it could not have had without a theological prompting, and vice versa.

Russell has identified eight ways in which CMI can be pursued. The first five represent traffic moving from science toward theology; the second three reverse the direction and move from theology toward science. (1) Physical theories can provide data which place constraints on theological descriptions of the world. For example, Russell says a theology of divine action should not violate special relativity. (2) Physical theories can provide direct data to be incorporated into a theological scheme. For example, the beginning of time or $t = 0$ in Big Bang cosmology might be correlated to *creation ex nihilo*. (3) Physical theories can provide indirect data for theology – that is, following philosophical critique a scientific theory could be readied for theological input. For example, after a philosophical examination of $t = 0$ we might find that it would provide indirect testimony to the notion that the created world is contingent upon the act of a creator God. (4) Physical theories can provide indirect data for theology when filtered through a philosophy of nature, such as process philosophy or emergent monism. (5) Physical theories can function heuristically in the theological context of discovery by providing conceptual, experiential, moral, or aesthetic inspiration. Now, reversing direction, (6) theology has historically provided assumptions that underlay the development of science, such as the contingency and rationality of nature. (7) Theological theories about the created order can act as sources of inspiration in the scientific context of discovery. (8) Theological theories could provide criteria, alongside empirical adequacy, coherence, scope, and fertility, for theory choices in science, especially physics.[12]

At CTNS we employ the image of the bridge with two-way traffic to convey the CMI principle. Robert John Russell writes, 'I have expanded the methodology by analyzing how the insights of theology and philosophy influence scientists as they pursue their theoretical work. The combined methodology of "critical mutual interaction" represents a genuine "two-way" bridge between science and religion.'[13]

When formulating what would become the editorial policy for the CTNS journal, *Theology and Science*, we penned the following:

> When scientific descriptions of the natural world begin to bear the weight of undeniable truth, then we expect theologians to consider with honesty the need to incorporate scientific knowledge into religious understanding. Similarly, when theologians draw upon venerable insights regarding God, creation, human nature, or spiritual presence, then we expect scientists to consider whether such religious insights might guide a hypothesis toward a progressive research program. These expectations lead us beyond two languages toward what we at CTNS like to term, 'the creative mutual interaction of theology and science'.[14]

NIODA: Non-Interventionist Objective Divine Action

When we turn to the second Bobism, NIODA, the question becomes this: in light of modern science, how can we understand God's providential action in the natural world? Since the Enlightenment, we in the West have been given a choice between two understandings of special providence. First, God acts objectively in nature and history and we human beings respond; but these acts can only be understood as divine *interventions* into the natural and historical world, as miracles. Or, second, human subjectivity includes human action based upon God-consciousness; and what we think of as distinctively divine activity is *uniformly the same in all events* – that is, no miracles. The choice between these two is inadequate to cover the logical options, according to Russell.

'The old choice was based on classical physics and modern, reductionist philosophy', writes Russell. 'Today, because of changes in the natural sciences, including quantum physics, genetics, evolution, and the mind/brain problem, and because of changes in philosophy, including the move from reductionism to holism and the legitimacy of including whole/part and top/down analysis, *we can now understand special providence as the objective acts of God in nature and history and we can understand these acts in a non-interventionist manner consistent with science.*'[15]

During the Enlightenment and the period of classical or Newtonian physics, it appeared that we were living in a world closed within a causal nexus with no windows to transcendence. For God to act in this otherwise closed causal nexus, God would need to intervene. God would need to suspend or even violate the existing laws of nature. In short, divine action would consist of miraculous action.

Now, we are talking here about divine action *within* the world, not the creation of the world. We can assume that God acted to bring the world into existence in the first place. This is consistent with classical physics. Our concern here is special providence, or God's action within the existing natural world with its already-established laws of nature and causal network. 'If the physical world is a causally-closed, deterministic system, and if the behavior of the world as a whole is ultimately reducible to that of its physical parts, the action of a free agent – whether human or divine – must entail a violation of natural processes.'[16]

In order to avoid interventionism when describing God's action in nature's world, nineteenth-century Liberal Protestant theologians and their twentieth-century neo-Orthodox followers had turned to human subjectivity. Leaving the objective world to uniform and inviolable natural processes studied solely by science, they located God's presence in human consciousness. In order to see God's action in the world, a believer would need to see with the eyes of faith. Divine action became a subjective interpretation of an otherwise neutral or godless objective world. God's action became limited to action within the human perspective.

Neither of these two views is satisfying to Russell. 'Thus by and large the choice has been either to affirm objective special providence at the cost of an interventionist and, in some extreme cases, an anti-scientific theology, or abandon objective special providence at the cost of a scientifically irrelevant and, in many cases, a privatized theology. In this light, a third option is crucial.'[17]

The quest Russell has set out on is this: how can we conceptualize God's action in nature's world that is objective without being interventionist?

Fortunately, according to Russell, twentieth-century advances in science and the scientific worldview provide resources to aid us in this quest. During the opening decades of the twentieth century classical physics was supplemented by two new theories which drastically altered our understanding of space, time, matter, and causality. These were special relativity and quantum mechanics. In addition, revisions in thermodynamics, the arrival of chaos theory, and Big Bang cosmology with its notion of an expanding universe all present possibilities for interpreting the world as genuinely open instead of a closed causal nexus. Order is now seen as emerging from disorder. Physical reality now has an evolutionary history and a changing future. 'A case can now be made that nature, at least as understood by quantum physics and perhaps in other areas of the natural sciences, is not the closed causal mechanism of Newtonian science. Instead, it is more like an open, temporal process with the ontology of "Swiss cheese" – one in which the genuine, material effects of the human and even divine agency are at least conceivable.'[18]

The enterprise of conceiving of divine agency in objective terms leads Russell to consider various forms of postmodern holism. The essence of holism is the principle that a complex whole is greater than the sum of its parts. Applicable candidates for consideration are notions such as (a) *emergence* – that is, self-organizing evolutionary development over time leads to emerging new structures of unprecedented centered activity; (b) the *whole–part* dialectic, according to which God could act in the context of the whole while influencing all the parts, with divine action indiscernible as one cause among others; and (c) *top–down* causality or supervenience, according to which the context at the higher level determines the relation between a higher-level property and a lower-level property, suggesting that God's action could supervene lower-level causal networks and influence the course of events without intervention into those causal networks. These holistic approaches need not eliminate the (d) *bottom–up* approach, according to which God could act at a lower level of complexity to influence the processes and properties at a higher level. One of Russell's signature contributions to the dialogue is his hypothesis that God acts at the quantum level and in bottom–up fashion influences all levels of physical reality that depend on quantum activity.

Russell does not discount the possibility for non-interventionist divine action at higher, more complex levels in nature which might take the form of top–down or whole–part causality. According to whole–part or top–down models of causality, 'a localized, special event in the world is viewed as the indirect result of God acting directly in one of the two ways: either in a top–down way from a higher level in nature (using such analogies as 'mind/brain'), or in a whole–part way starting either at the physical boundaries or environment of the system (an analogy here is the formation of vortices in a liquid heated in a container), or, ultimately, at the boundary of the universe as a whole.

'[The] bottom–up approach, in contrast, views a special event in the macroscopic world as the indirect result of a direct act of God at the quantum mechanical level, amplified by a stream of secondary causes linked in a bottom–up way. This view presupposes that quantum uncertainty can be given an indeterministic ontological interpretation, while recognizing that other interpretations are also possible.'[19] Ultimately, Russell anticipates that all these forms of non-interventionist divine action would be seen to work together harmoniously.

This proposal that we search for objective divine action at the quantum level brings us to the next in our list of Bobisms, 'Atoms may be small, but they're everywhere'.

ASBE: Atoms May Be Small, But They're Everywhere

ASBE justifies Russell's giving special attention to quantum activity at the atomic level of physical reality; and it justifies a search for reconciliation of bottom–up causation with divine action. If the quantum level of physical activity is the most basic and most primitive level, then God's action here ramifies so that it might have influence on every upper level of physical and even emergent reality.

The door has been opened to this interpretation of divine action by the debate over determinism and indeterminism in quantum physics. Russell believes that the uncertainty in our knowledge of electron passage does not arise from the incompleteness of quantum mechanics as a theory as suggested by Albert Einstein nor from the influence of non-local hidden variables as suggested by David Bohm; rather, it reflects a fundamental indeterminacy in nature itself, as is held by Werner Heisenberg. Russell and others in this camp believe that quantum indeterminacy is likely to be ontological and not simply epistemological. This means that quantum systems have multiple potentialities until a measurement is made, according to which 'measurement' refers to any irreversible interaction with another system (not merely the action of an observer in a laboratory).

Here is an opportunity for a most creative proposal. Russell proposes that we think of God as acting by actualizing one among the range of potentialities in an existing quantum system. Should God act at this microlevel, that action could not be considered an intervention. Why? Because God would not be altering any existing physical laws. Instead, it is precisely the laws of quantum mechanics which make God's action non-interventionist. According to the indeterministic interpretation of quantum mechanics, there is no sufficient efficient natural cause for what happens during a measurement interaction. Therefore, if God acts in nature to bring about the result, God's action is not interventionist: it does not violate the flow of sufficient efficient natural causes, since in these cases there is no sufficient efficient natural cause.

'Our approach is *noninterventionist*', writes Russell. 'God has created the universe *ex nihilo* such that some natural processes at the quantum level are insufficiently determined by prior natural events. One could say that nature is "naturally" indeterministic. Thus God does not suspend natural causality but creates and maintains it as ontologically indeterministic. God does not violate the laws of quantum physics but acts in accordance with them.'[20] Another way to frame non-interventionism, Russell points out, is to describe the laws of nature not as ontological realities which sometimes govern nature, but rather as the faithful regular actions of God which underlie all natural processes. In this sense God's special action in bringing about a particular result of measurement is of a piece with God's general action of sustaining the world in its natural regularities.

Divine action at the quantum level would be amplified at the higher levels of physical activity. God's action at the quantum level within DNA (the making or breaking of hydrogen bonds) could lead to a genetic mutation and influence evolutionary history. God's action in the firing of a neuron could initiate system-wide changes in patterns of a person's brain activity. Russell suggests that once consciousness emerged within evolutionary history, then God increasingly refrained from determining outcomes, leaving room for top–down causality in emergent and conscious creatures.

God's non-interventionist bottom–up action here would be invisible to the laboratory scientist. Russell wants to protect the integrity of scientific research as a secular enterprise and to avoid reversion to the dreaded God-of-the-gaps arguments. So he affirms 'that science is characterized by methodological naturalism, and thus it abstains from viewing God as an explanation within science. Instead, God's direct action at the quantum level is hidden in principle from science, supporting the integrity of science and yet allowing science to be integrated fruitfully into constructive theology.'[21]

The constructive theology to which his theory of non-interventionist divine action would provide building-blocks has identifiable features. These features provide theological warrants for developing a non-interventionist under-standing of God's activity in the natural world. Russell's first concern is this. He wants what he says about objective divine providence to cohere with what theologians generally assume about general providence. If, according to the doctrine of general providence, God lays down the laws of nature at the point of creation and sustains the regularities of the natural world, then these special acts at the quantum level are consistent with the primary act of creation and with general providence. Russell's second concern is to affirm that our creator God is responsible not only for the whole of creation but also for its parts. 'God as the transcendent creator *ex nihilo* of the universe as a whole is the immanent on-going creator of each part (*creatio continua*).'[22] His third concern has to do with revelation, namely we ought to see God's intentions disclosed in what we know, not in what we do not know. Number four on his list deals with the problem of theological credibility in a cultural context imbued by science as the standard for human knowing. Non-interventionist objective special divine action, says Russell, 'offers a robust response to atheistic challenges to the intelligibility and credibility of Christian faith, since the presence of "chance" in nature does not imply an absent God and a "pointless" world but an ever-present God acting with purpose in the world.'[23]

$T > P$: If It's True, Then It Must Be Possible

This Bobism may appear to be a redundancy. Yet, to say $t > p$ is an important redundancy; because it helps to combat reductionism. Whenever we investigate a natural phenomenon, we should try to explain it according to physical processes. But we should not try to explain it away. This is Russell's way of defending theology against what Alfred North Whitehead labeled the 'fallacy of misplaced concreteness'. Whitehead says, 'this fallacy consists in neglecting the degree of abstraction involved when an actual entity is considered merely so far as it exemplifies certain categories of thought. There are aspects of actualities which are simply ignored so long as we restrict thought to these categories.'[24]

What happens in nature is not merely a collection of instances that exemplify already-existing universal laws. Nature has a history; and this history includes contingent and previously unpredictable events. Once the Newtonian clock-work cosmos has been opened up like Swiss cheese is opened up, then the uniqueness and specificity of actual occasions come to the fore. Actual natural events should be the first order of business for the scientist. Induction, not deduction, is the method of reasoning scientists should employ.

FINLON: The First Instantiation of a New Law of Nature

This recognition of contingency and openness to nature's history leads us to the next Bobism, FINLON, or 'the first instantiation of a new law of nature'. Because Christian theology posits an eschatology complete with a promised new creation yet to come, theologians can conceive of a world guided by laws of nature different from the ones we currently have. Should a new law of nature suddenly appear, it might tell us something about our creation that we could not have known previously. Anticipating a new creation, theologians are in a position to provide perspectives and suggestions that could open scientists to recognize what might be unprecedented.

The context within which Russell developed FINLON was an analysis of the concept of contingency, with special reference to the theory of the resurrection developed by Wolfhart Pannenberg.[25] Russell proposes a threefold typology of (1) global contingency; (2) local contingency; and (3) nomological contingency. Each of these has subtypes. The first, global contingency, yields (1a) global ontological contingency, which asks: why does the universe exist *per se*? Why is there something and not nothing? Or, (1b) global existential contingency, which asks: why does the universe have such global characteristics as the fundamental laws of physics and the constants of nature? Or, why this particular universe and not another one? The second, local contingency, yields (2a) local ontological contingency, which asks: why does this particular thing exist and continue to exist? Or, (2b) local existential contingency, which asks: why does this particular thing have the characteristics it has? When Russell turns to the third, nomological contingency, he locates the contingency of nature's laws. He asks, could the first instance of a new natural process inaugurate a new law of nature?

An obvious example of the inauguration of a new natural process is the onset of biological processes well into the history of the cosmos. Many aeons since the Big Bang 13.7 billion years ago had to pass lifelessly before the first sign of life on planet Earth, only 3.8 billion years ago. With the arrival of life-forms, so also came the arrival of life processes and the first instantiation of biological laws of nature. Nature has a history, and new chapters are genuinely new.

Might the Easter resurrection of Jesus fit this paradigm? Could we think of what happened to Jesus on Easter as the first instantiation of a new natural process which we can expect to become universal at some point in the future? Within the category of nomological contingency Russell places the resurrection as a *first instantiation contingency*.

We need to place FINLON in the context of a larger discussion, the discussion of consonance versus dissonance. When it comes to the concept of resurrection, we must admit that, instead of consonance, we see dissonance between science and theology. To put it crudely, any self-respecting scientist is likely to assume that it is a law of nature that dead people stay dead. Because every dead person we have seen remains dead, we would argue by analogy that Jesus must have remained dead – that is, there was no Easter.

In addition, the divinely promised new creation anticipated by theologians seems to be dissonant with the far future of the universe anticipated by physical cosmologists. Big Bang cosmology and correlative projections into the far future of the universe predict an eventual end to life and even an end to the material world as we know it. Scientists assume that the laws of nature presently in effect will determine what will happen to our universe a hundred billion years from now, perhaps forever. This could be interpreted as dissonant with Christian eschatology, because Bible-reading theologians work with a divine promise that this world will undergo a transformation, that this creation will be renewed and redeemed. The scientific future appears irreconcilable with the theological future.

Here is why. Since the Big Bang 13.7 billion years ago, the universe has been steadily expanding. A key scientific question is this: is the universe open or closed? If it is open – that is, if the amount of mass is insufficient to stop the process – then it will continue to expand and continue to cool following the law of entropy. All the original heat will dissipate, and any remaining matter will fall into a state of equilibrium. In short, it will freeze out of existence. However, if the universe is closed – that is, if the amount of mass is above the relevant threshold – then at some point expansion will stop. Gravity will cause its motion to reverse, and all matter will reconverge on a central point, heating up on the way toward its doom in an unfathomably hot fireball. In short, it will fry. Whether freeze or fry, the future of the cosmos is finite. Whether freeze or fry, the scientific picture does not match the biblical picture of a new creation where the 'wolf shall live with the lamb' (Isaiah 11:6) and where 'death will be no more' (Revelation 21:4).

The question leading to FINLON arises with prolepsis – that is, should one aspect of the eschatological future arrive ahead of time within our present aeon still governed by what we acknowledge as nature's laws, could we discern it? If the eschatological new creation would include the resurrection of the dead, and if a person would rise from the dead now, could we discern it? Could we understand the Easter resurrection of Jesus as the first instantiation of a new law of nature that will apply universally at the advent of the renewed creation?

In order to crack open scientific method so as to perceive and acknowledge the possibility of FINLON, Russell critically suspends two philosophical assumptions made by natural science, namely analogy and nomological universality. According to the principle of analogy, the future will be just like the past. This means that based upon analogy from observations about the natural world we make now we can project what the universe will be like sixty-five billion years from now. This needs critique. If in the near or distant future God acts to transform and redeem this world, it would be unpredictable according to the principle of analogy.

According to the principle of nomological universality, the same laws which govern the past and present will govern the future as well. This also needs critique. Again, should God the creator re-create the world so that different laws obtain – such as wolves living with lambs and the elimination of death – then existing laws would no longer apply. The law that dead people stay dead would no longer apply. What we need to say about the Easter resurrection of Jesus, according to Russell, is that the future law that dead people will rise into the new creation has occurred ahead of time. Jesus is the 'first fruits of those having fallen asleep' (1 Corinthians 15:20). On Easter, God inaugurated a new law of nature, one that we will see become universal at some point in the future.

Russell finds distinctively theological warrant for holding this view. He claims 'on *theological* grounds that the processes of nature that science describes are the result of God's ongoing action as Creator; their regularity is the result of God's faithfulness. But God is free to act in radically new ways, not only in human history but also in the ongoing history of the universe, God's creation.'[26]

At the moment when God raised Jesus from the grave on the first Easter Sunday, the law that dead people remain dead was still in effect. It remains in effect today. In this context, this divine act leaves us with an anomaly. It could appear to be a miracle, a violation of existing laws of nature. However, Russell wants us to view that original resurrection as the first instance of a general resurrection. The advent of the new creation complete with general resurrection will establish that resurrection is a universal law. Jesus' Easter resurrection was the first instance, the prolepsis. Yet, it looks like a miracle. This leads to a correlate Bobism, 'Miracle today, law tomorrow' (MTLT).

Conclusion

One could easily list many accomplishments on the part of Robert John Russell that would warrant a congratulatory handshake and an adulatory smile. He has distinguished himself as a teaching professor in his position of Professor of Theology and Science in Residence at the Graduate Theological Union. He founded and directed the Center for Theology and the Natural Sciences, a center of research and publications and public service that has exhibited unrivaled leadership in the growing field of Theology & Science. Along with colleagues in Berkeley and the Vatican Observatory in Rome he has provided planning and editorial guidance for a series of science–theology dialogues with the world's leading scientists and ecumenical theologians, resulting in a six-volume series, *Scientific Perspectives on Divine Action*. He is the Co-editor of a fine academic journal, *Theology and Science*. Each of these achievements in itself is significant.

Yet, it seems to me, the single most valuable contribution of Robert John Russell to the blossoming field of Science & Religion is his conceptual contribution. Taking advantage of his training in both physics and theology, Russell has brought to the dialogue some of the most insightful and revolutionary proposals for breakthrough into a new domain of shared understanding. Beyond warfare, beyond two languages, beyond dialogue, beyond the pursuit of consonance, Russell has advanced us to the stage of creative mutual interaction between natural science and Christian theology.

Like a pile driver ever pounding us deeper and deeper into the bedrock of scientific knowledge and limits to that knowledge, Russell has penetrated to the questions of the ultimate nature of physical reality and its contingency or dependence upon God. This God, in whom Russell pledges his faith, brings nature's world into being from nothing, provides it with the laws of regularity and sustains these laws through faithfulness, and also introduces newness and redemption to the world as an exhibition of divine love.

Notes

1 See Langdon Gilkey, *Maker of Heaven and Earth* (New York: Doubleday, Anchor, 1959, 1965) and *Religion and the Scientific Future* (New York: Harper, 1970). See also Ted Peters, 'Langdon Gilkey: *In Memoriam*', *Dialog* 44:1 (Spring 2005): 69–80.

2 Pope John Paul II, 'Message of His Holiness Pope John Paul II', in *Physics, Philosophy, and Theology: A Common Quest for Understanding*, ed. by Robert John Russell, William R. Stoeger, SJ, and George V. Coyne, SJ (Vatican City State: Vatican Observatory, 1988), M12.

3 Ian G. Barbour, *Issues in Science and Religion* (San Francisco: Harper, 1966).

4 Ian G. Barbour, *Myths, Models, and Paradigms: A Comparative Study in Science and Religion* (San Francisco: Harper, 1974); *Technology, Environment, and Human Values* (New York: Praeger, 1980); *Religion in an Age of Science: The Gifford Lectures 1989–1991 Volume 1* (San Francisco: Harper & Row, 1990) and *Ethics in an Age of Technology: The Gifford Lectures 1989–1991 Volume 2* (San Francisco: Harper Collins, 1993); and *Religion and Science: Historical and Contemporary Issues* (San Francisco: HarperSanFrancisco, 1997), a revised and expanded edition of *Religion in an Age of Science*.

5 See Ted Peters, 'Science and Religion: An Overview', in *Encyclopedia of Religion*, 2nd edn, ed. by Lindsay Jones (14 volumes, New York: Macmillan, 2005), 12: 8180–92.

6 Barbour, *Religion and Science*, 82–90.

7 Albert Einstein, 'Science and Religion', *Nature*, 146 (1940): 605–7.

8 See Peter M. J. Hess, 'God's Two Books: Special Revelation and Natural Science in the Christian West', in *Bridging Science and Religion*, ed. by Ted Peters and Gaymon Bennett (London and Minneapolis, MN: SCM and Fortress, 2002), Chapter 7.

9 Ernan McMullin, 'How Should Cosmology Relate to Theology?', in *The Sciences and Theology in the Twentieth Century*, ed. by Arthur Peacocke (Notre Dame, IN: University of Notre Dame Press, 1981), 39.

10 Ted Peters (ed.), *Science and Theology: The New Consonance* (Boulder, CO: Westview, 1998), 18.

11   Robert John Russell, 'Ian Barbour's Methodological Breakthrough: Creating the "Bridge" between Science and Theology', in *Fifty Years in Science and Religion: Ian G. Barbour and His Legacy*, ed. by Robert John Russell (Aldershot: Ashgate, 2004), 49.

12   See Robert John Russell, 'The Relevance of Tillich for the Theology and Science Dialogue', *Zygon*, 36:2 (June 2001), 296–308; 'Did God Create Our Universe? Theological Reflections on the Big Bang, Inflation, and Quantum Cosmologies', in *Annals of the New York Academy of Sciences*, vol. 950, *Cosmic Questions*, ed. by J. B. Miller (New York: New York Academy of Sciences, 2001); Robert John Russell and Kirk Wegter-McNelly, 'Science and Theology: Mutual Interaction', in *Bridging Science and Religion*, 33–4.

13   Robert John Russell, 'Bridging Theology and Science: The CTNS Logo', *Theology and Science*, 1:1 (April 2003): 1.

14   Ted Peters, 'Truth in Editing', *Theology and Science*, 1:1 (April 2003): 5.

15   Robert John Russell, 'Does the "God Who Acts" Really Act in Nature?', in *Science and Theology*, 79, Russell's italics.

16   Ibid., 83.

17   Ibid.

18   Ibid.

19   Robert John Russell, 'Introduction', in *Quantum Mechanics: Scientific Perspectives on Divine Action*, ed. by Robert John Russell, Philip Clayton, Kirk Wegter-McNelly, and John Polkinghorne (Vatican City State and Berkeley, CA: Vatican Observatory and CTNS, 2001), v. 'A variety of scientists have supported ontological indeterminism, including such contemporaries as Chris Isham, Paul Davies, and Ian Barbour. This alone, of course, is not a warrant for adopting indeterminism, only a recommendation', Russell, 'Divine Action and Quantum Mechanics: A Fresh Assessment', ibid., 297.

20   Ibid., 295, Russell's italics.

21   Ibid., 296.

22   Ibid., 295.

23   Ibid., 296.

24   Alfred North Whitehead, *Process and Reality: Corrected Edition*, ed. by David Ray Griffin and Donald W. Sherburne (New York and London: Collier Macmillan and Free Press, 1929, 1978), 7–8.

25   Robert John Russell, 'Contingency in Physics and Cosmology: A Critique of the Theology of Wolfhart Pannenberg', *Zygon*, 23:1 (March 1988): 23–43.

26   Robert John Russell, 'Bodily Resurrection, Eschatology, and Scientific Cosmology', in *Resurrection: Theological and Scientific Assessments*, ed. by Ted Peters, Robert John Russell, and Michael Welker (Grand Rapids, MI: Wm. B. Eerdmans, 2002), 19.

I

Creative Mutual Interaction Between Science and Theology

Relating the Natural Sciences to Theology: Levels of Creative Mutual Interaction

William R. Stoeger, SJ

During the last thirty-five years Robert John Russell has been pursuing a vision – the vision of an enhanced mutually creative interaction between the natural sciences and the theologies of Christianity, and of the world's other major religions. This led him to found the Center for Theology and the Natural Sciences (CTNS), and to devote his life and energy to fostering mutually enriching relationships between them – writing and researching, teaching, lecturing, sponsoring fellowships, workshops, conferences, and dialogues in the United States and in many other countries in collaboration with other institutions and foundations, tapping the ideas and expertise of many people. In gratitude for Bob's long and faithful friendship and in honor of his sixtieth birthday, I shall in this essay reflect upon this vision and goal of the mutual creative interaction between the natural sciences and theology.

In doing so, I first want to indicate its roots in the thinking of the earlier visionaries – philosophers, scientists, and theologians – and then to emphasize its pervasiveness in recent science–theology thinking and dialogue. Then I shall give a general description of the natural sciences and of theology with respect to one another in section 2, along with some discussion of the relationship between faith, theology, and religion. This will include a brief discussion of the different dimensions of theology and of the dynamism of theological development, which parallels that of scientific development. In section 3 I shall review the different ways theology interacts with the natural sciences, directly and indirectly, reflectively and unreflectively. These are important to recognize and distinguish, if we are going to harness their potential and encourage their positive creative mutual interaction, which, despite obstacles and misunderstandings, has been under way for centuries. In section 4, I shall indicate the bases or foundations for their positive mutual interaction in their differences and similarities and in their common dynamisms and operations, as well as in the careful differentiation of their application. Then I shall turn to a careful discussion of the specific avenues of creative interaction in section 5, situating Russell's schema[1] within a broader critical cognitional and self-reflective framework, which flows from fundamental commonalities of the natural sciences and theology. In section 6, I shall go on to indicate the methods and approaches which facilitate and enhance this interaction. And in section 7 I shall briefly discuss the epistemological bases for a critical realism which embraces the natural sciences, philosophy, and theology.

Though the vision of creative mutual interaction is prominent today among the protagonists of the theology–science dialogue as one of – if not *the* – controlling vision of the proper relationship between the sciences and theology, it is by no means new. It may seem revolutionary in light of the commonly held belief that religion and science are in basic conflict, and have no common ground or interests to share. But that was certainly not always the case – and certainly is not now. As is well known, even up until the time after Darwin, many were of the conviction that the natural sciences and theology should be, and essentially are, in basic harmony, if properly understood.[2] In fact, the natural sciences themselves originated as an essential part of the philosophy of nature, which was considered an important basis for Christian theological reflection. It was only gradually, after the Renaissance, that they separated from philosophy as independent disciplines with their own focus, evidential grounds, and methodology. And it was only really after the time of the French Revolution that they began to be interpreted frequently as inimical to theology and to religion.[3]

Within denominations and authoritative schools of thinking, for example within Roman Catholic and Anglican philosophical and theological circles, this conviction of the essential harmony and complementarity between theology and the natural sciences, or what eventually emerged as the natural sciences, was preserved and fostered.[4] Much more recently, of course, it has been recovered more broadly and supported more compellingly by many of the central figures in the theology–science area, including Ian Barbour, Ernan McMullin, John Polkinghorne, Arthur Peacocke, Nancey Murphy, and many, many others. In particular, there has been renewed emphasis upon theology as a legitimate source of knowledge and understanding complementary to the natural sciences and to philosophy, and sharing either the same or at least an analogous critical realist basis with them.[5] This has been strongly reinforced by well-publicized statements by religious leaders, particularly by Pope John Paul II. In a major letter on the subject of theology and the natural sciences,[6] he not only encourages but also demands the mutual creative interaction of theology and the natural sciences, arguing very compellingly from the history of both disciplines and from basic Christian theology and spirituality. At one point, Pope John Paul II asserts: 'Science can purify religion from error and superstition; religion can purify science from idolatry and false absolutes. Each can draw the other into a wider world, a world in which both can flourish.'[7]

The Natural Sciences, and Theology and Religion

Oftentimes people equate the relationship between science and theology with that between science and religion. They are indeed closely connected, but in many ways very different. In this paper I want to focus on the interactions between the sciences and theology as cognitive disciplines, leaving the much more extensive and diverse cultural aspects of the interaction between the sciences and religion on the periphery. Both the natural sciences and theology represent ways of knowing, disciplines directed toward enhanced understanding of ourselves and the world around us. As such, we want to probe their interrelationships, and the ways in which they can creatively interact. To clarify this focus, we offer a working description of the natural sciences, and of theology – along with a characterization of faith, on which it is based, and of religion, which it serves and critiques. Then we shall point out how theology develops and changes, in a way analogous to the evolution of the sciences, under the pressure of new circumstances.

How should we define the natural sciences and theology? The natural sciences are disciplines oriented toward the detailed qualitative and quantitative understanding and modeling of the regularities, processes, structures, and interrelationships ('the laws of nature') which characterize reality – relying on rigorous, repeatable analysis and experiment and/or observation. Theology, in contrast, is the discipline directed toward understanding God, and the presence, action, and self-revelation of God in our lives and in our world, and our response to that transcendent reality. One of the things to notice about these two definitions is that, whereas the objects of the natural sciences are relatively clear and well defined, the primary object of theology is not. We do not have a clear and well-defined characterization of 'God', nor of God's 'activity' and relationalities. Even more importantly, there is no procedure by which we identify an object in the world or in our experience as 'God'. The object of theology, therefore, is really not an object as such, but rather the 'horizon' or the ultimate 'ground' or 'condition of possibility', within which or upon which all depends, can be known and understood, and acquires meaning. The second thing to notice about this definition is that the evidence for God involves attention to and interpretative analysis of the transcendental and the putative revelatory experiences of our individual and communal lives. We shall return to these peculiarities later.

The bases for theology and for religion are revelation and faith. What is faith? Following Avery Dulles,[8] faith is the positive ongoing response in discernment and commitment to perceived divine revelation. A great deal can be said in elaborating this characterization of it – including its critical, its dynamic, its personal, and its practical aspects. However, here we do not have space to develop these.

What, then, is theology? As has been often repeated, according to its classical definition, theology is 'faith seeking understanding'.[9] The faithful person or community struggles to understand experience and the world that it reveals in light of his, her, their faith – in light of the perspectives and knowledge, the discernment and commitment, by which they live. Its object is 'revealed truth'. Thus, as I have already pointed out, theology expresses, however inadequately and provisionally, the cognitive content of faith. It is this which is to be related to, brought into positive interaction with, the knowledge originating from the natural sciences.

'Religion' is a much broader and more ambiguous reality than either faith or theology. Karl Peters defines it as, 'A system of ideas, actions and experiences that offers a path toward human fulfillment by relating individuals and societies to what is thought to be ultimate.'[10] As Huston Smith[11] emphasizes, religion presupposes faith and involves theology ('explanation' and understanding), but particularly denotes their expression in social institutions and behavior with authority, laws, ritual, tradition and customs, grace, and mystery as key features. It is the institutionalization of a particular communal experience of revelation, faith, and theology expressed in community organization, rituals and celebrations, regulations, beliefs, canons of interpretations, and methods of validation (discernment). This enables the proclamation, incorporation, transmission, and maintenance of belief and practice. But, at the same time, it can contribute to the imposition and the fossilization of beliefs and practices which no longer reflect the authentic faith experience of the community, and to the legitimation of ambiguous elements of other social and cultural institutions within the society.

From this we can see that the interactions of science with religion will typically involve much more than the cognitive dimensions of each, and thus will be very difficult to analyze and model in a differentiated and reliable way. This is one of the reasons why we here confine ourselves to examination of the avenues of interaction between the sciences and theology, considered as cognitive disciplines. This is also the scope of Bob Russell's analysis,[12] which we shall briefly describe later. We should be aware, however, that there is an indirect and very powerful indirect mode of interaction between the sciences and theology through the medium of the evolving cultures to which both belong. Theology can modify religion, which is a component of culture, and create a more or less positive or negative climate for scientific inquiry and pursuit. Similarly, science can help establish a cultural climate which is favorable or unfavorable toward certain types of religion, and certain types of theologies which that religion represents. We can see this in the religiously fundamentalistic and the scientistic subcultures of contemporary societies.

For future reference, we must emphasize that both the natural sciences and theology are dynamic – that is, the knowledge and understanding for which each strives develops and grows – and each finds new and different expression in different stages of development and in different contexts. There is much greater continuity and coherence within the natural sciences than in theology, but even in the sciences there are competing approaches, schools of thought, and understandings, particularly concerning hypotheses and understandings which have not yet entered the secure base of established conclusions. Furthermore, even for components of that base, there can be significant disagreement as to the philosophical interpretation of scientific findings and conclusions. The competing interpretations of quantum mechanics, or the gradualist and punctuated equilibrium views of evolutionary development, are examples. For theology, within any religion or denomination, there is a history of development of the basic normative doctrinal statements, and the accepted interpretation of them. But beyond that there are the many different approaches theologians initiate to improve our understanding and our articulation of these basic truths in light of new knowledge, expanding horizons – including those provided by the sciences – and new cultural, political, and social situations.

Connected with this development in both the natural sciences and in theology, there are different levels of scientific and theological conclusions. For the sciences, there are well-established, fundamental theories, and the 'facts' and the understandings that are associated with them. These have enjoyed long-term success and fertility. Then there are varying degrees of developing theories and understandings, and the interpretations connected with them. Finally, there are the preliminary exploratory theories and ideas which are the fruit of educated speculation and imagination being brought to bear on unresolved issues in a given science.

In theology, there are 'the mediating theologies' (which B. Lonergan refers to as *in oratione obliqua*), which are the theological articulations of the tradition coming from the ecclesial community and the authoritative theologians of the past.[13] Then there are the 'mediated theologies', which Lonergan refers to as *in oratione recta*, in which theologians, enlightened by the past, attempt to develop improved understandings of God and God's relationship with us and the world, taking into account contemporary contexts and perspectives.[14] In both cases there are often differing schools of interpretation, and therefore slightly or even markedly different theological emphases of certain common central understandings and articulations.

This can be further complicated by reference to differing philosophical models of reality and our knowledge of it. Obviously, in considering the mutual creative interaction between the natural sciences and theology in a given case, awareness both of the status, interpretation, and meaning of the scientific conclusions and perspectives and of the status, interpretation, and meaning of the theological conclusions and insights involved will be crucial. The critical methods of the relevant discipline must be brought to bear on each component before assessing the character and the promise of their interaction. For example, one of the key functions of theology is to determine the essence of what is revealed to us, and to sift that out both from the cultural and social perspectives in which it was received and from the limitations of the language and images, stories and myths through which it has been communicated and passed on from age to age. It must also articulate the philosophical presuppositions upon which a given articulation of the essential contents of revelation is based, distinguishing those from the essentials of revelation themselves. To some extent – in fact, to a great extent – theology's interaction with other disciplines, scientific and humanistic alike, enables it to carry out this crucial function.

Once the critical methods of the natural sciences and of theology have determined the status, interpretation, and meaning of both theological and scientific understanding and perspectives, and assessed the character and promise of their interaction, there remains the key challenge of relating the two within a meaningful common conceptual horizon and philosophical frame-work. We shall return to this issue in section 6.

Types of Interaction between the Sciences and Theology

In the last section, we saw how there can be – and often is – a strong indirect interaction between the natural sciences and theology via the cultural field to which both belong. This realization leads us to ask, what are the general types of mutual interaction between the two disciplines?[15]

The general case to which we have just referred in section 2 is indirect. It is also unreflective – there was no explicit intention to bring the two disciplines into interaction. It is just that the scientists carry out their research and writing within a cultural context which is either favorable or unfavorable to their pursuits, due in large part to religious influences. And it can be favorable in different ways, modifying our implicit philosophy, our language, our horizons and perspectives, our cognitive paradigms about God and nature. Similarly, theologians do their theology within a culture which has a certain positive or negative stance toward their theology, due partially to the influences of the scientific components in that culture. That affects and partially determines the theology they do.

The opposite case in general is where the interaction is direct and reflective, as when representatives of each discipline enter into dialogue, trying to understand one another's perspectives and conclusions, or discussing a common issue or problem – or when an individual struggles to integrate both areas of knowledge into his or her understandings and perspectives. Sometimes the interaction can be reflective and indirect, as when we begin to use a word or concept from one of the sciences in theological work. Finally, there can certainly be unreflective direct interactions. One example would be when a Christian scientist or community of scientists automatically finds their concept of God being altered by their scientific knowledge; they do not consciously or intentionally seek to articulate a more adequate concept of God, but the process occurs gradually under the pressure of what they know about nature and about the universe.

In light of this, it is, I believe, very relevant to consider that the natural sciences and theology, as well as other disciplines, have developed not in isolation from, but rather in interaction with, one another through their common social and cultural fields. To be sure, each has developed its own distinctiveness and identity with regard to its disciplinary focus, its evidential grounds, and its methods – in fact, as is well recognized, there has been increasing differentiation in this regard. But along with this, paradoxically, the natural sciences and theology have been interacting in mutually beneficial ways. As some have argued, the Christian religion, with its theology and its spiritualities, has provided the cultural and intellectual conditions, and the motivation, for the sciences to develop in the Western world.[16] Historically, individual scientists certainly have found inspiration, intuition, and confirmation in their religious beliefs and spiritual insights. We should mention, further, that philosophical perspectives have also had a strong influence on the development of scientific thought.

Moving in the other direction, it is also very clear that the methods and the conclusions of the sciences have had a profound influence on our implicit and on our more formal philosophical thinking, and perhaps even more on theology and spirituality themselves – on our cultural perspectives, our myths, and our stories.[17] These, in turn, strongly influence how we interpret and articulate our deepest and most important human experiences. The sciences have altered the horizons against which we search for and describe God's active presence in our lives, and the methods and criteria we use in sifting through our personal and spiritual experiences to enrich our knowledge and to improve our practical response in faith, hope, and love.

Furthermore, we can make a strong case that theology and spirituality, and their auxilliary disciplines, have been able to clarify their proper foci, and the limits of their principle interests and competencies, only by way of interaction with the natural and human sciences, and with other disciplines, including philosophy. This is also true of the sciences themselves, in their interaction with one another, and with philosophy, theology, and the humanities. All areas of knowledge and understanding have come to self-knowledge through their dialogue with one another, and through their continual interactions within their common cultural field.

Bases for the Positive Interaction of the Sciences and Theology

Before discussing the various ways in which the natural sciences and theology creatively interact, or can creatively interact, we need to look carefully at the bases or characteristics which enable them to do so. Why would we expect these two very different areas of human interest and endeavor to mutually and creatively influence and nourish one another? To answer this question, we must consider carefully both the differences and the similarities between the two disciplines. Some of these are obvious, but others are not. Laying them out explicitly will enable us to understand more clearly how they are related and how they can and do influence one another positively and negatively, and will further help us to discover what is needed in order to foster their creative interaction.

Among the differences between the natural sciences and theology are:[18] (1) their disciplinary foci or interests and their objects – they deal with very different fundamental questions and very different aspects and 'objects' of experience and reality (for instance, the sciences focus on repeatable natural phenomena and their interrelationships, whereas theology focuses on what grounds and reveals ultimate meaning and purpose); (2) their starting assumptions – for example, theology explicitly assumes the 'existence' of a horizon or ground of being (God) and the revelation of God, and the sciences do not; (3) the type of evidence that is relevant to the questions each discipline investigates; (4) their methods; (5) their procedures of validation; (6) their products and application of products; (7) the communities involved; (8) the character of their social and cultural impact; (9) their horizons of knowledge, value, and meaning. Finally, there is another difference which is not always mentioned: the natural sciences deal exclusively with what are often called categorical modes of intention and meaning, those which are determined and of limited denotation. Theology, and philosophy, often deal also with transcendental modes of intention and meaning, which are not delimited, but rather unrestricted and comprehensive in denotation. The transcendental modes, strictly speaking, are culturally invariant, even though their articulation may not be, whereas the categorical modes are dependent on cultural variations.[19] There are other differences as well, but the most important ones fall under one of these categories. A great deal could be said about each item, but the general significance of these differences is clear.

More important for our considerations than the differences are the similarities between the natural sciences and theology. It is really these, along with the realities which found or undergird them, that provide the bases for the mutual creative dynamic interaction between them. The differences, however, if not properly understood and accounted for, can fuel conflicts and mutual misunderstandings and isolation.

The fundamental feature the natural sciences and theology have in common is their orientation toward knowledge and understanding; toward truth. Though each is concerned with truth about very different issues, and has different motivations for attaining that truth, both have an absolute commitment to it – to knowledge and understanding. Additionally, there is the realist presupposition by most scientists and theologians, that the knowledge and understanding they attain in each discipline is of what in some way obtains in the world, in reality, outside the knower. In most cases this is a critical realism, sensitive to the obstructions to knowledge, but confident of the ways in which they can be overcome to attain reliable, though always limited and provisional, knowledge and understanding of nature and of its transcendent bases. We shall explore, briefly, how critical realism is possible in science and in theology in the final section of this paper.

Other similarities between the sciences and theology are: (1) both use carefully developed, though different, methods and procedures in pursuing knowledge and understanding, and definite criteria to validate their conclusions;[20] (2) both search to go beyond where they are now – the quest for knowledge and understanding continues unabated, as it is open-ended and unrestricted; (3) both are pursued and practiced in communities, in interaction with other scientists and theologians; (4) both produce knowledge and understanding which is used by interested larger communities; and (5) both, as we have already seen, share common personal and cultural fields – that is, they automatically influence and interact with one another and with components of knowledge, understanding, and behavior in individual thinkers and believers and in society at large.

Underlying these similarities are the common cognitive operations of the human person – perception, understanding, judgment, and decision – as Lonergan is continually emphasizing.[21] In the natural sciences and in theology these operations are applied to different categories of data – the data of the external world, the data of consciousness, the data of transcendental experience, the data of perceived revelation – but they are the same operations. Because of this, there is a foundation for encompassing both the natural sciences and theology, and their respective horizons, within a larger cognitive, or epistemological, horizon. It is here that they can be critically related – in terms of their respective foci, competencies and limitations, conclusions, and so on. This provides the ultimate basis for their creative mutual interaction.

Specific Avenues of Positive or Negative Interaction

Now we can present the specific avenues or levels of interaction between the natural sciences and theology. I shall first discuss the scheme I have developed, and then fit Russell's categorization within it, comparing the two. Whether a given avenue or level of interaction leads to positive or negative effects depends in large measure on whether the methods and procedures for reaching secure conclusions and the criteria for validation within each discipline were properly followed and applied, and whether the linguistic, conceptual, and intentional (categorical or transcendental) differences were properly negotiated within the common cognitive horizon embracing both. In the next section I shall discuss some of the requirements for assuring this.

The broad outline of my scheme follows the general kinds of interaction between the sciences and religion I indicated in section 3 (with reference to the cultural context example given in section 2): reflective or unreflective, direct or indirect.

Therefore, the following levels, or avenues, of interaction exist between the natural sciences and theology:

Level 1

Primarily Unreflective, or Unintentional, and Indirect – through the environment established by the religious, theological, philosophical, scientific, technological components of culture itself, for example the theological/religious climate fostering attitudes, values, images, and ideas contributing to the development of the sciences, and vice versa. There will be specific component avenues within this general category which will be more reflective, more intentional, and even more direct, which will fall under other levels. But, by and large, many of the interactions will be both unreflective and indirect.[22]

Level 2

Reflective and Indirect – through the more or less intended employment of cultural 'products' indirectly influenced by theology and/or the natural sciences in doing science or doing theology, respectively:

1 wonder, inspiration, imagination;
2 cognitive or epistemological horizons – how the kinds of knowledge and understanding characteristic of the two disciplines are conceived in relation to one another;
3 philosophical presuppositions, principles, or frameworks, including linguistic precisions and their justification;
4 concepts, such as 'matter', 'spirit', 'field';
5 constraints, disciplinary limits, and competencies;
6 methods, methodological specialties, and methodological rigor – methods can be borrowed from, or developed under the influence of, another discipline;
7 conclusions and data, for instance from archeology, medicine, biology, and influencing theology;
8 technological advances and possibilities.

Level 3

Unreflective and Direct – unintended, automatic influences having direct bearing on a theological or scientific issue, such as a scientist's concept of God, referred to in section 3, or a theological conviction undermining a purported scientific conclusion or viewpoint. We could list subcategories of these, as we did for Level 2 – some would be similar, but, since they are unreflective channels, others would be complex and difficult to specify.

Level 4

Reflective and Direct – intended, direct interactions effected between the natural sciences and theology:

1 explicit use of the conclusions of one to constrain what one says about an issue in the other – for example, in theology about God's action in creating individual species;
2 explicit consideration of the conclusions or hypotheses of one discipline in the research of the other as part of the argument in the other field, either as something which demands understanding or as something which finds consonance with the conclusions there, thus triggering the quest for understanding that consonance;
3 conclusions, hypotheses, ideas from one field providing openings, inspiration, ideas for research in the other field;
4 explicit use of conclusions, hypotheses, or criteria from either science or theology to select or rule out hypotheses or theories in the other field, or to pursue a particular line of research in that other field (this is similar to 1, but refers to theoretical and interpretative frameworks and research directions, not just to a particular issue);

5   specific use or development, of a methodology in one field, either taken
    from or inspired by a similar methodology in the other field – for example,
    the direct use of certain philosophical arguments and considerations;
6   use of metaphors, images, analogies from one field in the development and
    articulation of hypotheses, models, and conclusions in the other.

In our general scheme, I have treated the interactions between the natural
sciences and theology symmetrically, even though the character of the actual
influences of one on the other is often asymmetric, particularly in positive
reflective and direct cases. I have done this so that the scheme represents all
possible cases and indicates the mutuality of the influences, even if there are
asymmetries in particular examples. There will be innumerable specific examples,
symmetric and asymmetric, which fit into each of these levels and its sublevels. In
the next section we shall discuss some of the principal requirements for rendering
the interaction of the natural sciences and theology positive and mutually
creative. But first, we summarize Robert Russell's paths of creative mutual
interaction, and show how they relate to and fit within our scheme.

Before doing so, however, we need to point out Russell's recognition that his
classification of paths of disciplinary interaction and influence rests on two
epistemological discoveries.[23] The first is that in the hierarchy of disciplines
those on lower levels, like physics, place constraints on the ones above, like
neuroscience or psychology. At the same time the operation of new processes
and relationships at the higher levels renders them causally irreducible to the
lower-level disciplines. The second discovery is that, despite the clear
differences, there are significant methodological analogies between the natural
sciences and theology, which seem to enable a critical realistic assessment of the
cognitive content of both. In the last section of this paper, I shall briefly
examine this claim, and finally confirm it, but with some cautions.

Russell's categorization of the paths of mutual interaction tends to
emphasize the reflective interactions and to neglect those which are
unreflective.[24] He also separates the paths according to the direction of the
interaction, assigning the first five to the possible types of influence of the
natural sciences on theology, and the second three to possible types of influence
of theology on the natural sciences. All of them can be placed in one or other of
the sublevels in my scheme. He also articulates them with reference to physics,
but obviously they can be framed more generally in terms of all natural and
human sciences, which I shall do here.

The first five of Russell's paths of interaction are as follows:

Path 1   Theories in the sciences can act directly as data that place constraints
         on theology.
Path 2   Theories in the sciences can act directly as data either to be
         'explained' by theology or as the basis for a theological constructive
         argument.
Path 3   Theories in the sciences, after philosophical analysis, can act
         indirectly as data for theology.

Path 4   Theories in the sciences can also act indirectly as data for theology
          when they are incorporated into a fully articulated philosophy of
          nature (for example, the process philosophy of Whitehead).
Path 5   Theories in the sciences can function heuristically in theology by
          providing conceptual inspiration, experiential inspiration, practical/
          moral inspiration, or aesthetic inspiration.

Russell gives examples of all of these.

Comparing these with the scheme I have set up, Path 1 would correspond to
my Level 4, avenues 1 or 4. I also have Level 2.5 for indirect constraints, which
Russell does not explicitly consider. However, they might be contained in his
Paths 3 and 4. Path 2 is basically equivalent to my Level 4.2. Cases in Russell's
Path 3 would fall under Levels 2.3, 2.4, 2.6, or 2.7, depending upon the specifics
of the case. Path 4 falls under Level 2.3, and cases in Path 5 would be included
in 2.1, 2.4, 4.3, or 4.6, again depending on specifics.

It is worth pointing out that when Russell refers to 'theories of physics' or of
other sciences 'acting as data' for theology in various ways, he is using 'data' in
a very broad sense. Exactly how that 'data' is to be interpreted and used
theologically depends primarily on the theological methods being used and
secondarily on the philosophical framework which enables the proper transfer
of that 'data' from the scientific horizon of understanding and meaning to the
specific theological horizon. Thus, strictly speaking, it should be understood
that adequate philosophical analysis is essential to negotiating each of the
Paths, not just Path 3. This applies as well to Paths 6, 7, and 8, to which we
now turn.

These last three paths, which summarize Russell's synthesis of the potential
impact of theology on the natural sciences, are:[25]

Path 6   Theology can provide some of the philosophical assumptions
          underlying the natural sciences (something we have already alluded
          to in this chapter).
Path 7   Theological theories can act as sources of inspiration or motivation
          for new scientific theories.
Path 8   Theological theories can lead to 'selection rules' within the criteria for
          choosing scientific theories.

Looking at where these fit into my scheme of levels and sublevels, we see that
Path 6 really falls under Level 2.3 – the impact here is always indirect. I would
suggest expanding Path 6 to include 'justification of philosophical assumptions', as well as the source of the assumptions themselves. Path 7 would be
included in either Level 2.1 or Level 4.3, depending on whether the impact is
indirect or direct. Strictly speaking it might also fall into either Levels 1 or 3, if
it is unreflective. Path 8 will always be reflective and direct, as Russell describes
it. Thus, it falls under our Level 4.4.

Russell has enriched the epistemological dimensions of the theology–science
dialogue with his insistence upon and development of the mutual creative

interaction between theology and the natural sciences, his articulation of the paths by which it can occur, and its basis in epistemology. My aim here has been to situate those dimensions in a more comprehensive framework, which includes unreflective avenues of interaction. I also want to stimulate further reflection on how the mutual interaction between theology and the sciences can be fostered in a positive way. What are the requirements for insuring that? To answering that important question we now turn.

Insuring and Enhancing the Creative Interaction

The Paths and Levels of interaction and influence between the natural sciences and theology that Russell and I have suggested can lead to either positive or negative, creative or destructive, consequences for these disciplines and for their relationship with one another. In the history of their mutual interaction and influence, and in recent trends, we have seen both consequences occur. Can we formulate some requirements which would lead to encouraging positive, creative interaction, forestalling negative, conflictual interactions? I think we can. Some of these have already been mentioned, or alluded to, in this chapter, especially in section 4, where we discussed the differences and similarities between the natural sciences and theology as cognitive disciplines, and in the latter half of section 2, where we emphasized the importance of recognizing the dynamisms and ongoing developments of both disciplines, their different levels of theoretical reliability, and most of all the absolute need in both for increasingly more adequate and more carefully differentiated methods.

Thus, one of the first requirements is that both the natural sciences and theology continue to develop their own methods of analysis, interpretation, and validation more fully, continuing to refine them in light of their long-term success and fruitfulness. As I stressed in section 2, this methodological maturation of the disciplines is essential to assuring their mutual creative interaction. In fact, as I also pointed out there, this maturation itself only occurs as the disciplines interact with one another. This must also include the capacity to distil the central core of knowledge and understanding from the historical, cultural, and social perspectives and the linguistic limitations in which it is couched. This is true especially for theology, but is also relevant for the natural sciences. It is impossible to accomplish this in a thorough or complete manner, but there must be some conscious hermeneutic exercise in this direction.

Concomitant with this must be the growth of an adequate philosophy of science and an adequate philosophy of theology, which will enable each discipline to develop a growing 'self-awareness' or 'self-knowledge'. This must include an awareness of its relationships to other disciplines, and particularly an explicit recognition of the presuppositions upon which it proceeds. This leads both to the maturation of each discipline, and also to a realization of its limitations and competencies, its strengths and weaknesses – and those of its methods. With regard to methods again, an adequate philosophy or epistemology of each discipline will articulate the differentiated operations, modes of understanding, and discourse, as well as the horizons against which they are to be understood and employed. This is essential for relating the theories and findings of the disciplines to one another in a mutually creative way.

Associated with this self-reflective knowledge of the natural sciences and of theology – in fact, underlying it – will be a self-appropriation or appreciative recognition and understanding by scientists and by theologians of themselves as knowers,[26] and of the self-transcendence which enables and accompanies their quest. The operations by which both come to reliable knowledge and understanding – perception, insight, judgment, and decision – all require self-transcendence for their realization. This leads to the further recognition that there is a horizon of knowledge and understanding that embraces both the natural sciences and theology, within which they can be related,[27] and that the source of understanding and meaning is not in the particular methods of each, but rather in the reality we encounter and in the common operations which ground the methods and their effectiveness.[28]

The overall impact of such moves will be that all scientists, whether believers or not, will develop an appreciation of the self-transcendence that is implicit in their effective pursuit of scientific knowledge, and a growing sense of how the sciences are interactively related to other forms of knowledge and understanding, including especially philosophy and theology. At the same time, theologians – and philosophers – will grow in their openness to, and appreciation of the importance of, scientific findings and perspectives. We have already witnessed many such instances of such growth over the past fifteen or twenty years among both scientists and theologians. The fruitfulness, success, and mutual enrichment such critically engaged interaction yields is a powerful confirmation of its validity.

Critical Realism: From Science to Theology

Finally, we broach the crucial question of critical realism in the natural sciences and in theology. As we have briefly indicated above, Russell's Paths of interaction, as well as my broader schema of Levels, presupposes, or rests upon, the assumption that scientific knowledge and understanding, and theological knowledge and understanding, represent what really is the case, in some limited way. If critical realism is not warranted for either the natural sciences or for theology, then we have to go back and redirect our inquiry in a completely different way. If critical realism is valid for the natural sciences, but not for theology, then it is very difficult to see how we can support reflective, direct interactions between the natural sciences and theology.

In recent years, leading researchers in theology and science have made a case for critical realism embracing both areas, as Russell has emphasized in introducing his Paths of interaction.[29] This is based primarily on the similarities between the sciences and theology – that both carry relatable cognitive content through the models, myths, and paradigms they employ –

and on the fertility and success of the models and theories in both fields, via hypothetical-deductive inferential argument.[30]

However, Ernan McMullin has been quite critical of this approach, maintaining that it is difficult to apply critical realism to theology in any way which is similar to how it functions in the natural sciences.[31] He maintains that Barbour, Peacocke, and Polkinghorne have only provided a 'descriptive account' of their epistemological framework, and not an explanatory account of human rationality, which is what is needed; one which is 'both oriented to a scientific understanding of the world while positively open to the question of God.'[32]

What is really needed, according to McMullin and Paul Allen, is a validated account of human rationality, the recognition of the limits certain methodologies implementing human rationality encounter in the quest for understanding, the further recognition that human rationality insists on going beyond those methodological limits, prospecting for alternative evidential grounds and procedures of validation in its transcendental forays, and finally the discovery of such alternative grounds and procedures.[33]

The validated account of human rationality is found in the natural sciences in the form of C. S. Peirce's 'retroduction', a detailed extension of hypothetical–deductive inference invoked by Barbour and others, and the demonstration by McMullin that this imaginative outreach of human rationality has been and is responsible for the success and fruitfulness of the natural sciences.[34] This provides the core of an adequate philosophy of science which we have pointed out as essential for interdisciplinary engagement. The limits of the particular scientific methodology – the specific evidential grounds relevant to the sciences, and the specific ways of assessing and interpreting the evidence, formulating hypotheses, and validating them in the sciences – are encountered in cosmology and in quantum field theory. Focusing on cosmology, after it has reached certain conclusions about the dynamics, structure, history, and destiny of the universe, it raises further questions which it cannot answer, but which certainly seem legitimate.[35] These include questions about the ultimate origin and destiny of the universe, about its meaning and purpose, about the role of consciousness and mind, about the source of values. The fascination and frustration with the Anthropic Principle is one small indication of this!

Thus, it is clear that human rationality is not constrained by the limitations of scientific methods and procedures. Understanding poses further questions, informed imagination continues to operate, and retroduction continues to search for new evidential grounds, methods of interpretation and validation which are apt for the issues upon which it now focuses. This is revealed most fully as the inquirer begins to reflect on the experience of knowing itself – on the data of consciousness, as we have already mentioned briefly in sections 4 and 6 – and discovers that the operations of human rationality are self-transcending and that there is a surplus of existential meaning in reality beyond what the natural sciences can validate.[36] Rationality is both self-transcending and heuristic.

Finally, the evidential grounds and procedures relevant to philosophy and theology are discovered and found to yield long-term success and fruitfulness, at least in some cases. But here, as stressed above, is where the differentiated methods of philosophical and theological research must be carefully critiqued. How is fruitful and successful theological research to be pursued? And what are the criteria for it?

Though human rationality continues to operate fruitfully, and we can make a strong case for the legitimacy of theological knowledge, it should be apparent that critical realism as it pertains to theology is more problematic and depends on rather different conditions than the critical realism of the natural sciences. In particular, its object – God and God's relationships with what is not God – is not really articulable or definable, as we have already stressed. Furthermore, in theology the focus is on meaning, and on the events, experiences, and configurations which reveal meaning and purpose, not on phenomena and their interrelationships. Finally, in theology and philosophy, unlike the natural sciences, our imaginative hypotheses are based both on critical reflection upon our self-transcendent experiences and on our discernment of revelatory links to the divine – and the methods and criteria for validation concerning these are quite different than those in the sciences. Generally speaking, however, they do involve long-term success and fruitfulness, but in terms of the capacity for giving life and wholeness to individuals and to communities.[37]

Conclusion

In our discussions we have examined in some detail the avenues by which the natural sciences and theology can mutually interact, inspired by Russell's vision and his development of his paths of influence. In particular, we have constructed a comprehensive scheme which includes, situates, and hopefully enhances his important contributions. We have emphasized the foundations upon which relating the natural sciences and theology in a mutually creative way rests, and discussed the requirements for insuring such interaction. These include fostering the interactive growth and development of the methods of the two fields themselves, insuring the development of adequate philosophies of the science and of theology, along with that of a cognitive horizon or epistemological framework which includes both; and recognizing the self-transcending and unrestricted character of the human quest for understanding and knowledge. Finally, we discussed how the essential idea of critical realism can be legitimately transferred to theology. My hope is that these brief reflections will stimulate Russell and others to pursue the fulfillment of the vision he has shared with us.

Notes

1   Robert J. Russell, 'Eschatology and Physical Cosmology: A Preliminary Reflection', in *The Far-Future Universe: Eschatology from a Cosmic Perspective*, ed. by George Ellis (Radnor, PA: Templeton Foundation Press, 2002), 266–315 (see particularly 275–88), and references therein.

2 Arthur R. Peacocke, 'Biological Evolution and Christian Theology – Yesterday and Today', in *Darwin and Divinity*, ed. by John Durant (Oxford: Blackwell, 1985), 101–30; Arthur R. Peacocke, 'Biological Evolution – a Positive Theological Appraisal', in *Evolutionary and Molecular Biology: Scientific Perspectives on Divine Action*, ed. by Robert John Russell, William R. Stoeger, SJ, and Francisco J. Ayala (Vatican City State and Berkeley, CA: Vatican Observatory and Center for Theology and the Natural Sciences, 1998), 357–76; John H. Brooke and Geoffrey Cantor, *Reconstructing Nature: The Engagement of Science and Religion* (Edinburgh: T. & T. Clark, 1998), especially 15–72.

3 See, for instance, Michael J. Buckley, SJ, *At the Origins of Modern Atheism* (New Haven, CT: Yale University Press, 1988); Michael J. Buckley, SJ, 'The Newtonian Settlement and the Origins of Atheism', in *Physics, Philosophy, and Theology: A Common Quest for Understanding* (hereafter *PPT*), ed. by Robert J. Russell, William R. Stoeger, SJ, and George V. Coyne, SJ (Vatican City State: Vatican Observatory, 1988), 81–102.

4 See, for instance, Paul Chauchard, *Science and Religion*, trans. by S. J. Tester (New York: Hawthorne Books Publishing, 1962), 156; Ernan McMullin, 'Natural Science and Belief in a Creator', in *PPT*, 49–79, and references therein; Susan K. Wood, 'Faith and Reason', in *The HarperCollins Encyclopedia of Catholicism* (New York: HarperCollins Publishers, Inc., 1995), 509.

5 See: Ian G. Barbour, *Religion and Science: Historical and Contemporary Issues* (San Francisco: HarperSanFrancisco, 1997), 110–21; Robert John Russell, 'Ian Barbour's Methodological Breakthrough: Creating the "Bridge" between Science and Theology', in *Fifty Years in Science and Religion: Ian G. Barbour and His Legacy*, ed. by Robert John Russell (Aldershot: Ashgate, 2004), 45–59; John C. Polkinghorne, *The Faith of a Physicist: Reflections of a Bottom–Up Thinker* (Minneapolis, MN: Fortress Press, 1994); Arthur R. Peacocke, *Theology for a Scientific Age: Being and Becoming – Natural, Divine, and Human*, enlarged edition (Minneapolis, MN: Fortress Press, 1993); Nancey Murphy, *Theology in the Age of Scientific Reasoning* (Ithaca, NY: Cornell University Press, 1990); George F. R. Ellis, *Before the Beginning: Cosmology Explained* (New York: Boyars/Bowerdean, 1993).

6 'Pope John Paul II to Reverend George V. Coyne, S.J., Director of the Vatican Observatory', in *PPT*, M1–M14.

7 Ibid., M13.

8 Avery Dulles, SJ, 'The Meaning of Faith Considered in Relationship to Justice', in *The Faith That Does Justice*, ed. by John C. Haughey (New York: Paulist Press, 1977), 10–46.

9 Anselm of Canterbury, *Proslogium*, 158, 227; 158, 362.

10 Karl E. Peters, 'Storytellers and Scenario Spinners: Some Reflections on Religion and Science in Light of a Pragmatic Evolutionary Theory of Knowledge', *Zygon*, 32:4 (December 1997): 465–89 (see especially 467).

11 Huston Smith, *The Illustrated World's Religions: A Guide to Our Wisdom Traditions* (San Francisco: HarperSanFrancisco, 1994), 67.

12 See, for instance, Russell, 'Eschatology and Physical Cosmology', 275–88.

13 Gerard Walmsley, 'Applying Lonergan's Philosophy of Self-Appropriation to the Science–Religion Debate: Lonergan Meets Gell-Mann and the Mystics', in *Science and Religion in the African Context*, ed. by Augustine Schutte (forthcoming); and Bernard J. F. Lonergan, SJ, *Method in Theology* (New York: Herder and Herder, 1972), 133–6.

14 Walmsley, 'Applying Lonergan's Philosophy'; Lonergan, *Method in Theology*.

15 On this topic, see the fuller treatments in William R. Stoeger, 'Cosmologia e Teologia: Le Vie della Loro Mutua Interazione', *Giornale di Astronomia*, 1:2 (1991): 15–19; William R. Stoeger, 'Our Experience of Knowing in Science and in Spirituality', in *The Laws of Nature, the Range of Human Knowledge and Divine Action* (Tarnów, Poland: Biblos, 1996), 51–79.

16 See, for instance, Brooke and Cantor, *Reconstructing Nature*, for a critical discussion and nuanced support of these views.

17 See Stoeger, 'Our Experience of Knowing'.
18 William R. Stoeger, SJ, 'Contemporary Cosmology and its Implications for the Science–Theology Dialogue', in *PPT*, 219–47.
19 See Lonergan, *Method in Theology*, 11–12.
20 This is quite obvious in the sciences, but perhaps it is not so clear in theology. On theological method see Lonergan, *Method in Theology*, particularly his section (Chapter 5) on 'Functional Specialties', 125–45.
21 Bernard J. Lonergan, *Insight: A Study in Human Understanding* (Toronto: University of Toronto Press, 1957); Lonergan, *Method in Theology*.
22 Stoeger, 'Cosmologia e Teologia', 15–19; Stoeger, 'Our Experience of Knowing', 51–7.
23 Russell, 'Eschatology and Physical Cosmology', 275–88, and references therein.
24 Ibid., 275–88.
25 Ibid., 284–8.
26 Lonergan, *Insight*; Lonergan, *Method in Theology*, 3–25. See also Gerard Walmsley, 'Integral Self-Appropriation and the Science–Religion Encounter: Lonergan's Methodological Mediation', in *Science and Religion in the African Context*.
27 Walmsley, 'Integral Self-Appropriation and the Science–Religion Encounter'. See also Stoeger, 'Our Experience of Knowing', 51–79, where the author emphasizes that any adequate epistemology of a discipline must situate it properly within the overall manifold of types of knowledge.
28 James R. Pambrun, 'A Theological Hermeneutical Approach to Neuroscience' (paper presented at the Theology and the Natural Science Program Group at the annual convention of the Catholic Theological Society of America, Reston, Virginia, June 12, 2004), unpublished manuscript.
29 Russell, 'Eschatology and Physical Cosmology', 276, and references therein.
30 See, for instance, Barbour, *Religion and Science*, 110–21, and Russell, 'Ian Barbour's Methodological Breakthrough'.
31 Ernan McMullin, 'Realism in Theology and in Science: A Response to Peacocke', in *Religion and Intellectual Life*, 2 (1985): 39–47; Ernan McMullin, review of *Belief in God in an Age of Science* by John Polkinghorne, in *Commonweal*, 125:17 (October 9, 1998): 22–3; see also Paul Allen, 'A Philosophical Framework within the Science–Theology Dialogue: A Critical Reflection on the Work of Ernan McMullin' (PhD diss., St Paul University, Ottawa, Canada, 2001), 268–87.
32 Allen, 'A Philosophical Framework within the Science–Theology Dialogue', 74.
33 See William R. Stoeger, SJ, 'Science, Cosmology, Theology and Critical Realism', in *Modern Science, Religion and the Quest for Unity*, ASSR Series, Volume IV, ed. by Job Kozhamthadam (Pune, India: ASSR Publications, Jnana-Deepa Vidyapeeth, 2005), 39–52.
34 Ernan McMullin, *The Inference that Makes Science* (Milwaukee, WI: Marquette University Press, 1991), 112, and references therein.
35 McMullin, *The Inference*, 19; Ernan McMullin, 'Is Philosophy Relevant to Cosmology?', *American Philosophical Quarterly*, 18 (1981): 177–89 (see especially 180–81), reprinted in *Philosophical Cosmology and Philosophy*, ed. by John Leslie (New York: Macmillan, 1990), 29–50; see also Allen, 'A Philosophical Framework within the Science–Theology Dialogue', 183–4.
36 Allen, 'A Philosophical Framework within the Science–Theology Dialogue', 218–20.
37 Stoeger, 'Science, Cosmology, Theology and Critical Realism'.

CHAPTER THREE

Creative Mutual Interaction: Robert John Russell's Contribution to Theology and Science Methodology

Nancey Murphy

Few people have thought as long and hard about the intersection of theology with the natural sciences as Robert John Russell. I shall take as my task an evaluation of his contributions to understanding *methods* for relating theology and science. One of the advances in philosophy of science in the past generation was the recognition that a methodology (a theory *about* methods) is essentially both normative and descriptive. That is, one cannot stand on firm ground in pronouncing on how a discipline *should* be carried on without being able to show that the methodology also describes how the best work in the field has *actually* been done. Since Russell himself has done some of the best work on relating theology and science, a large part of evaluating his methodology is to see whether it in fact serves as a 'rational reconstruction' of his own contributions to the field.[1] Space will not permit a full examination, so I shall be able to discuss only one of his substantive achievements.

Evaluation of a theory also requires examining how it preserves what is true in earlier theories while solving problems that its predecessors could not solve. Thus, I shall also note ways in which Russell's work moves the discussion of methodology beyond earlier contributions. And, of course, I shall not be able to resist adding my own two-cents'-worth on this pet topic.

The Methodology of Creative Mutual Interaction

One characteristic of Russell's scholarship is the extent to which he credits his predecessors with most of his good ideas. Typically, then, most of what he has written on methodology begins with the work of others: Ian Barbour, Arthur Peacocke, John Haught, and Ted Peters on typologies of ways for relating science and theology; Barbour and Sallie McFague on the uses of metaphors in theology and the sciences; Barbour, Peacocke, and Ernan McMullin on critical realist accounts of science and theology. I suggest that Russell's work, while historically dependent on all of these contributions, has moved decidedly beyond them.[2]

One other earlier contribution, however, *is* central to Russell's theory: Peacocke's proposal that theology be understood as the top-most science in a non-reducible hierarchy of sciences.[3] Thus, possible legitimate relations between theology and (another) science will be the same as relations between any science and the one(s) below it. This is an asymmetrical relation. On the one hand, the characteristics of the lower-level entities and the laws governing their behavior constrain but usually do not determine higher-level phenomena. On the other hand, the higher-level phenomena tell us something about the lower level(s), namely that they must be such as to *permit* the development and behavior of the higher-level entities.

With this model in mind, Russell looks at various components of both scientific and theological research programs. All involve data; in theology this includes Scripture, religious experience, and historical events, but also, because theology is the science of God in relation to all that is, other facts about the world. In science there are theories; in theology the theories are called doctrines. Theories are both supported and constrained by data. Finally, both science and theology are imbued with philosophical assumptions such as the order of nature and the meaning of 'time'. These are possible components in epistemological relations between theology and science. Another kind of relation is heuristic: theories are not deduced or induced from data, but are human inventions requiring imagination. So another possible benefit from cross-disciplinary dialogue is the provision of new conceptual resources for theory development.

Based on the above, Russell describes eight possible 'paths' or ways of relating theology to a particular science. The first five are legitimate ways for science to inform theology. The last three are ways in which theology may inform science:[4]

1   Scientific theories may serve as data that place *constraints* on theology.
2   Scientific theories may serve as *supporting* data for theology in so far as they are explained theologically.
3   *Philosophical interpretations* of scientific theories may serve as data for theology.
4   Scientific theories may serve as data for theology when they are incorporated into a *philosophy of nature*.[5]
5   Scientific theories may function *heuristically* in theology by providing conceptual, experiential, practical/moral, or aesthetic inspiration.[6]
6   Theology may provide some of the philosophical assumptions underlying science.[7]
7   Theological theories may function heuristically in the construction of scientific theories.
8   Theological theories may lead to 'selection rules' within the criteria of theory choice; that is, for choosing among existing scientific theories that all explain the available data, or for deciding what set of data the theory should seek to explain.[8]

In summary, Russell says:

> The *asymmetry* between theology and science should now be quite apparent: Theological theories do *not* act as data for science in the same

way that scientific theories do for theology. This reflects the methodological assumption that the academic disciplines are structured in an
epistemic hierarchy of constraints and irreducibility. It also safeguards
science from any normative claims by theology. It does, though, allow for
the possibility that philosophical or theological commitments can stimulate
the search for new theories and can function as a source of 'criteria for
theory choice' among existing competing theories in the natural and social
sciences. That this has happened historically is well known; that it can and
is happening in contemporary scientific research is less generally
recognized. Together these eight paths portray science and theology in a
much more interactive, though still asymmetric, mode, which I call 'the
method of creative mutual interaction'. In particular, the theologian must
first face the challenge of science to his or her cognitive claims; yet the
scientist may find that philosophical elements pervade his or her work in
creative ways and stem, in turn, from implicit theological positions.
Neither partner in the interaction assumes a literal reading of their theories
or an unqualified authority in the mutual search for understanding; both
partners expect to gain from the interaction while pursuing their own
specialties.[9]

I hope to convey the complexity of the dynamic relations between theology and
the sciences below in an overview of some of Russell's substantive
contributions.

Progress in the Discussion

As mentioned above, one way to justify a proposed methodology is to show its
ability to incorporate what is valuable in earlier theories while solving
problems that its predecessors could not solve. In so doing, the new and better
theory makes the history of the discussion more intelligible.[10] I have mentioned
three foci of earlier discussions of science–theology methodology: metaphors,
typologies, and critical realism. Russell's current position incorporates
metaphorical relations in that drawing a concept from science to use
metaphorically in theology (or vice versa) is one fruitful heuristic device (paths
5 and 7). However, I suggest that while the construction of theology–science
typologies and the promotion of a critical realist account of both science and
theology have served an important historical role in the development of the
field, they are like ladders, in that, having climbed to our present position, we
can now kick them away.

1. Typologies

Russell's work allows us to understand what is appealing about each type, but
also shows that no one type is adequate. Consider Barbour's four types:
conflict, independence, dialogue, and integration.[11]

Conflict   One awkward thing about the extant typologies is the ambiguity as to whether a particular relation between theology and science is intended merely as an historical description or also as an account of how theology and science *ought* to relate.[12] The conflict view is clearly meant to be the former; it is hard to imagine anyone arguing that theology and science are always opposed to one another and that this is the way it *should* be!

The histories intending to show pervasive conflict between science and religion have been definitively criticized; Russell's many historical and contemporary examples of positive interactions drive more nails into their coffins. Notice, though, that Russell's methodology shows that we should in fact expect *and even celebrate* a certain degree of conflict. Science should be expected to provide both positive *and negative* data for theology (paths 2 and 1 respectively). Furthermore, both theology and science have contributed to, and in turn depend upon, metaphysical theses (paths 4 and 6) and, I shall argue, even entire worldviews. Intellectual change is uneven. An impetus for change comes from one discipline (for example, astronomy); this negatively affects a current worldview (for example, the Christian–Aristotelian synthesis along with its metaphysical underpinnings) – and this in turn requires changes in nearly every other discipline. So some conflict between science and theology is to be expected as a healthy stage in the ongoing interaction – no more lamentable than the conflict between Copernican astronomy and Aristotelian physics.

Independence   The independence thesis began as a theological proposal that *prescribed* non-interaction with science, and then shaped much of the history of modern intellectual life. The irony, if I read the history correctly, is that this redefinition of the very nature of religion and theology was, in fact, an apologetic move motivated specifically by developments *in science!* I am thinking here of Imannuel Kant's idea of non-interacting intellectual spheres, and Friedrich Schleiermacher's subsequent use of this strategy to redefine religion in terms of human subjectivity. The attempt to make theology independent of science is one of the most dramatic examples of the influence of science on theology, via philosophical interpretations (paths 3 and 4).

Yet there is something profoundly right about the liberals' protest against many conservative theologians who perceive conflict between Christianity and science. The beauty of Peacocke's and Russell's hierarchical model is that it gives due recognition to the fact that theology represents a distinct level of discourse with its own distinctive aims – but without denying all forms of significant cognitive exchange.

Dialogue   This type comes closest to Russell's account. If 'dialogue' is not further specified, all of Russell's eight paths would fall under this term. However, one valuable way of making the concept more precise is Russell's and Kirk Wegter-McNelly's emphasis on Barbour's concept of boundary questions.[13] Science raises questions that cannot be answered scientifically but call instead for theological (or metaphysical) answers – for example, if the universe had a beginning, what happened before that? Russell's methodology (as well as Peacocke's) puts this particular form of dialogue in context: any science (in a *non-reducible* hierarchy of disciplines) will raise boundary questions that can only be answered by the science(s) above it. For example, chemistry, in describing the bonding characteristics of elements and small molecules, in principle explains the possible formation of an uncountable number of macro-molecules. This raises the question of why only a tiny subset of these possibilities is found in nature. Biochemistry and biology can explain the prevalence and distribution of existing macro-molecules by explaining their function in organisms.

Integration   Total synthesis of theology with the sciences is not a possibility if theology indeed occupies its own proper level in the hierarchy of the sciences – no more a possibility than the synthesis of physics and sociology. Yet Russell's methodology countenances a limited degree of integration in its recognition that both theology and science contribute to the metaphysical theses and assumptions that underlie a worldview (paths 4 and 6).

Thus, I claim, the various typologies have been of value as a way of surveying scholars' perceptions of and attitudes toward the relations between theology and the sciences, but Russell has shown that there is no point in arguing that any one type is the true historical account or the ideal normative proposal. From this point on, the discussion needs to focus instead on Russell's eight paths. One question is whether there are possibilities which his account has omitted. The other is whether all of his eight paths are indeed legitimate. Most of the arguments are likely to concern paths 6 and 8, theology's right to contribute to or criticize science's philosophical assumptions and the legitimacy of using theological criteria in science when scientific criteria are insufficient.

2. Critical Realism

Russell ties together and designates as 'critical realism' two theses: (1) that both theology and science provide partial and revisable knowledge of reality, and (2) that science and theology employ comparable methods. These two, together, are taken to be necessary to legitimate the dialogue between theology and science; that is, the two have enough in common to learn from one another and both speak of the same world. Russell places his own methodological work within this set of views.

However, I take the two theses to be independent of one another, and only the second is needed to legitimate theology and science interaction. The term 'critical realism' in fact only applies to the first thesis regarding the descriptive–referential character of the languages of theology and science.[14]

The promotion of critical realism (in the sense of thesis 1) has been an important rhetorical move in the theology–science dialogue, in that it serves as a label for the rejection of instrumentalist, conventionalist, and constructivist accounts of science. Even more important, it stands for the rejection, on the one hand, of overly literalist accounts of theology and, on the other, of a variety of non-cognitivist accounts of theology, including aesthetic or moral interpretations, as well as 'irrealist' accounts of theological language.[15]

There has been an intense debate in philosophy of science regarding scientific realism. My own assessment is that the thesis is confused: it illegitimately attempts to use a (discredited) philosophy of language to do the work proper to epistemology.[16]

In contrast, the second thesis, regarding parallels between scientific and theological reasoning, is clear and well supported; it by itself provides adequate justification for dialogue between theology and science. Furthermore, the sophisticated accounts of scientific methodology and of religious language that are used to argue for these parallels are exactly the sorts of philosophical developments that show critical realism (in the sense of thesis 1) to be misguided.

Thus, for all the good purposes it has served, the theology–science dialogue need not mire itself in attempting to defend critical realism. Russell's methodology depends on the *denial* of non-cognitivist accounts of theology, and on the methodological parallels between theology and science, but not on critical realism.

In my judgment, then, Russell's methodology of creative mutual interaction preserves everything of value in the earlier works he cites, while solving a number of outstanding problems. Even more important is the fact that from the perspective of Russell's theory we can see *why* his predecessors' views succeeded to the extent that they did, and fell short at just the points where they failed.

Does Russell's Theology and Science fit his Methodology?

I intend in this section to pursue two goals. One is to illustrate the complex and dynamic interactions among Russell's eight paths; the other to begin to test the accuracy and sufficiency of his account by applying it to examples from his own writings. I shall have to be selective here. Russell has been quite prolific and has written on a wide range of topics.

1. Quantum Cosmology and Theology

One of the most subtle of Russell's contributions to theology and science is his assessment of the 'quantum cosmology' of Stephen Hawking and James Hartle.[17] For a variety of reasons it had been widely argued, prior to the development of Big Bang cosmology, that the universe's having a temporal beginning was irrelevant to the doctrine of creation. Interpretation of the Big Bang as representing a temporal origin was taken in a variety of ways by theologians. Some maintained the position that it is irrelevant to theology. Others took it to have significant theological implications, whether as direct evidence for creation or as needing first to be interpreted before its significance would be apparent.

Russell traces much of the controversy over the significance of the Big Bang to Langdon Gilkey's sharp dichotomization of the concepts of *ontological origination* versus *empirical/historical origination*. This dichotomization requires one to choose one or the other as the essential meaning of 'creation'. If one chooses the former, then the Big Bang theory, true or false, is irrelevant; if the latter, then the theory, if true, provides striking confirmation, but if later overturned, equally striking disconfirmation.

Russell's own position is that, properly interpreted, Big Bang cosmology provides confirmatory but inessential evidence for a doctrine of creation, itself *properly interpreted*. The controversy over what to make of Big Bang theory serves as a stimulus to ask exactly what 'ontological origination' means; in the tradition it has been closely connected to the concept of *finitude*. One of several senses in which the universe may be seen as finite is in its having a temporally finite past. Thus, if Big Bang theory shows the universe to be temporally finite this provides partial corroboration for the doctrine of creation understood in its essential meaning as ontological origination.

Next, Russell turns to quantum cosmology. In the theory proposed by Hartle and Hawking, time 'arises phenomenologically ... it is not a given, external parameter which describes the evolution of the universe'.[18] *Vastly* oversimplifying, it might be said that in the very early universe, in which quantum effects are significant, time has no 'directionality', and thus there is no point in (or of) time to which the origin of the universe can be traced. In more technical terms, in this model there is no initial singularity represented by $t = 0$. The past is finite but unbounded. Hawking's conclusion was that with no point of origin for the universe there is nothing left for God to do.[19]

Russell notes the highly speculative nature of Hartle and Hawking's theory, but shows that the *conceivability* of such a theory (apart from its truth or falsity) has implications for the doctrine of creation. In short, we have to recognize a possible second meaning of 'temporal finitude'. The assumption throughout Christian history has been that time is linear and (in the past) it either has a beginning or it does not, in which case it is eternal. The Hartle–Hawking proposal shows that there is a third possibility: that the universe is temporally finite but does not have a beginning.

This recognition solves a long-standing theological problem. Beginning with Augustine it has been recognized that it is better to think of God as creating time itself rather than creating *in* (pre-existing) time, and still 'the theological and empirical status of the beginning of time has been a continuing problem for theologians down to the present'.[20]

Russell makes use in this essay of Imre Lakatos's concept of a research program.[21] The interpretation of ontological origination as essential to the doctrine of creation serves as the 'core' theory of a theological research program. One of the 'auxiliary hypotheses' surrounding the core and bringing it closer to empirical confirmation or disconfirmation is the interpretation of ontological origination as entailing finitude. In a further-removed 'belt' of explication, 'finitude' is taken to imply temporal finitude (among other things). At this stage in the development of the research program, the $t = 0$ of Big Bang cosmology provides confirmation for the program.

Lakatos pointed out that when a potential falsifier appears, research programs are generally repaired (protected) by adding further auxiliary hypotheses. This is exactly what Russell has done when faced with the potential falsification of $t = 0$ by quantum cosmology. Using the conceptual distinctions provided by quantum cosmology itself, he has introduced an additional auxiliary hypothesis distinguishing the concept of temporal finitude from that of having a temporal origin. In order to show that this is not an *ad hoc* move (a mere linguistic trick or face-saving device, in Lakatos's terms), he has argued that it solves a long-standing problem in theology regarding God's relation to time. In particular, it gives genuine empirical content to Augustine's claim that God created time itself, even allowing us to say roughly 'when' it might have occurred!

My brief overview comes nowhere close to representing the complexity and subtlety of Russell's work. But let us see whether my summary, such as it is, has any consequences, positive or negative, for an evaluation of Russell's own methodological proposals.

2. Application

It is certainly possible to go through this single essay and find instances of all of Russell's eight paths. What I have included in my summary already exemplifies five:

1   Quantum cosmology might serve as data constraining doctrines of creation that take temporal origin of the universe to be essential.
2   Big Bang cosmology might provide data giving direct support to doctrines of creation involving temporal origin.
3   Big Bang cosmology may be taken to support creation as temporal origin only under certain philosophical interpretations.
4   Quantum cosmology suggests a radically different conception of time, an aspect of a philosophy of nature, which provides grounds for a new auxiliary hypothesis within a theological research program concerning creation (one of Russell's own contributions).
5   We could also interpret Russell's revision of the meaning of temporal finitude in theology as a heuristic use of science. (This would be a preferable interpretation if one doubts, as I do, that there is a single philosophical concept of time applicable in all domains.)

In my summary I passed over Russell's argument for the possibility of using theology to choose among existing scientific theories (path 8). Russell considered two scientific routes to quantum cosmologies. The quantum fluctuations model proposes that the material universe arises spontaneously via fluctuations in a background spacetime. The Hartle–Hawking model assumes instead 'a set of three-dimensional spaces out of which spacetime can be constructed', along with appropriate laws of physics.[22] So in the first model, time pre-exists matter; in the second, time appears along with matter. Russell notes that these theories are equally speculative and that one might choose between them on philosophical or aesthetic grounds. He then reports on the work of Chris Isham, who argues for the Hartle–Hawking model on the grounds that Augustine had already argued convincingly in the fifth century that time can only be understood as coincident with matter.[23] We can take Isham's argument as an instance of paths 6 and 8, of theology's providing a philosophical assumption underlying the selection of one scientific theory over another.

Finally, concerning both of these cosmological models, we might *speculate* that the Christian idea of God's creation of the universe out of nothing served a heuristic function in suggesting the spontaneous appearance of the universe out of a quantum vacuum (path 7).

If this latter suggestion has merit, then the convoluted history of the creative mutual interaction of theology and science, just in the case of quantum cosmology, goes something like this. The Big Bang looks very much like the Jewish idea of creation, understood as temporal origination. But for cosmologists, as for Augustine before them, there are the perplexing questions of *what* was there before, and *was* there a before? And can the universe's appearance be explained without invoking a creator? Perhaps the metaphysical dictum from the Middle Ages, '*ex nihilo nihil fit*', is not entirely true; perhaps matter can come spontaneously from a suitable sort of 'nothing'.

Meanwhile, Big Bang cosmology has provoked theologians to reconsider what they mean when they say that the universe was created by God. In order to settle disputes among the theologians about the evidential value of the Big Bang, *and* to reply to Hawking's conclusion that he had found a way to eliminate the need for a creator, Russell, following Isham and adding his own theological arguments, favors Hawking's model over those of his competitors and then uses a revised concept of time to revise the doctrine of creation itself. Creative mutual interaction indeed!

Further Reflections

I believe that I have been able to show, by examining only a single article of Russell's, that it is possible to use his methodology for describing actual work in the developing dialogue between theology and science, including both his own and others' accomplishments. I have found this a particularly stimulating exercise for my own thinking on the nature of the theology–science relationship. I particularly appreciate the way his work here illustrates the usefulness of my own application of Lakatos's scientific methodology to theology.[24] I now want to reflect on possible resources for fine-tuning Russell's work. All of my remarks will have to do in one way or another with the role of philosophy in the theology–science dialogue.

I begin with some observations that occurred to me in studying Russell's writings. First, in Russell's work on Big Bang and quantum cosmologies, the importance of science does not comprise primarily *epistemological support* for theology, but rather its value in providing resources for *reinterpretation* of theological doctrines. Second, I found it difficult to distinguish between science providing philosophical assumptions for theology and science serving a heuristic function. One could evade this problem by saying simply that science supplies *conceptual resources* for theology. This observation applies equally to influences of theology on science: theology provides conceptual resources for science.

Additionally, I was at first puzzled by Russell's concept of a *philosophy of nature*. I thought that an example might be the role of science (evolution, Big Bang cosmology) in contributing to a picture of the universe as developing in time from simplicity and disorder to complex order, in contrast to the Ancient picture of a Golden Age in the past followed by catastrophic disorder. Thus, I thought of substituting here the (rather vague) concept of a worldview, or Stephen Toulmin's concept of a *cosmopolis*, a conception of the human social order as a microcosm modeled on the cosmos. Toulmin writes persuasively about the role of Newtonian science in providing 'timbers' for a new cosmopolis after the medieval synthesis was dismantled.[25] Still another possibility would be a conceptual scheme, a useful idea in philosophy so long as it does not suggest that there is ever any single, consistent, unified scheme. Part of the job of philosophy is to attempt to discover and interpret the culture's conceptual resources and to recommend ways of putting them in better order. However, in reading further in Russell's writings I concluded that what he designates 'philosophy of nature' is much narrower than any of these: an interrelated set of concepts (time, causation, space, matter) underlying the physical sciences. This would be a small but very important part of a conceptual scheme.

All of these reflections lead me to suggest a wider account of the relations between theology and science – one that includes more specific attention to philosophy and to whatever it is we mean to get at in speaking of a world picture, or worldview, or cosmopolis. All three sorts of discipline (theology, the sciences, and philosophical subdisciplines such as metaphysics and epistemology) contribute to a (sub)culture's worldview, and also draw metaphorical, conceptual, and other sorts of resources from it. In addition, there are mutual interrelations between theology and philosophy, and between science and philosophy. Finally, there is direct interaction between theology and science.

However, after reading again through many of Russell's writings, I have come to suspect that the most sophisticated uses of science recognize their dependence on the *interpretation* (often a philosophical interpretation) of the scientific findings, and often involve the reinterpretation of theological positions. Furthermore, the conceptual resources initially provided by theology often affect science only indirectly through their influence on the development of philosophical theories. Thus, many of the interactions between theology and science are mediated in one way or another by philosophical concepts and theories.

Conclusion

I hope in this brief essay to have offered the reader a small glimpse of the ingenuity of Russell's contributions to the dialogue between theology and science, particularly to reflection on methodological issues. I have argued that his methodology both incorporates and transcends the best previous work in the field.

I have not attempted to integrate my own further reflections on these matters with Russell's theory, but hope that they might become a subject for yet another intense and fruitful conversation when again we have a chance to meet.

Notes

1   'Rational reconstruction' is a term used by Imre Lakatos. In using the history of science to evaluate a methodology one offers an account of the 'logic' of a development in science, then criticizes this 'rational reconstruction' in so far as it fails to fit the history and also criticizes the history in so far as it lacks rationality. See Imre Lakatos, 'Falsification and the Methodology of Scientific Research Programmes', in *The Methodology of Scientific Research Programmes: Philosophical Papers Volume 1*, ed. by John Worrall and Gregory Currie (Cambridge: Cambridge University Press, 1978), 8–101; 52–3.

2   One of Russell's earliest works involving an account of his own methodology is Robert John Russell, 'Entropy and Evil', *Zygon*, 19:4 (December 1984): 449–68, in which he makes particular reference to Barbour's work on metaphors. In a more recent piece, he and Kirk Wegter-McNelly give an overview of work on typologies and critical realism, along with recent developments in philosophy of science. See 'Science and Theology: Mutual Interaction', in *Bridging Science and Religion*, ed. by Ted Peters and Gaymon Bennett (London: SCM Press, 2002), 19–34.

3   There are hints of this idea in Barbour's early work, and a variety of other predecessors, but I believe that Peacocke was the first to put all of the pieces together, which he had done at least by the time he wrote *Creation and the World of Science* (Oxford: Oxford University Press, 1979). For an account of this history, see Nancey Murphy, 'Theology and Science within a Lakatosian Program', *Zygon*, 34:4 (December 1999): 629–42.

4   The most detailed development of these ideas is in Robert John Russell, 'Eschatology and Physical Cosmology: A Preliminary Reflection', in *The Far-Future Universe: Eschatology from a Cosmic Perspective*, ed. by George F. R. Ellis (Philadelphia and London: Templeton Foundation Press, 2002), 266–315. See also 'Bodily Resurrection, Eschatology, and Scientific Cosmology', in *Resurrection: Theological and Scientific Assessments*, ed. by Ted Peters, Robert John Russell, and Michael Welker (Grand Rapids, MI: Eerdmans, 2002), 3–30.

5   I believe that by 'philosophy of nature' Russell means a philosophy of space, time, matter, and causality underlying physics and cosmology. See Russell, 'Bodily Resurrection', 23; and my musings below.

6   Russell, 'Eschatology and Physical Cosmology', 278.

7   Ibid., 285.

8   Ibid., 286.

9   Ibid., 288. For a visual overview, see ibid., 277, figure 17.1.

10 This is Alasdair MacIntyre's insight. See especially 'Epistemological Crises, Dramatic Narrative, and the Philosophy of Science', *Monist*, 60 (1977): 453–72, in which he shows how this thesis resolves the stand-off between Lakatos and Paul Feyerabend on the question of whether Lakatos's methodology has any normative teeth. See Lakatos and Alan Musgrave, *Criticism and the Growth of Knowledge* (Cambridge: Cambridge University Press, 1970), 91–230.

11 See Ian G. Barbour, *Religion in an Age of Science: The Gifford Lectures 1989–1991 Volume 1* (San Francisco: Harper & Row, 1990), Chapter 1.

12 They are also often ambiguous as to whether the relations are between science and theology or science and institutional religion.

13 Russell and Wegter-McNelly, 'Science and Theology: Mutual Interaction', 21.

14 I base this judgment on the fact that 'critical realism' in theology and science is intended to incorporate the thesis of scientific realism as developed in philosophy of science, and this latter is indeed only a thesis about the referential status of scientific language. I believe many in theology and science take the methodological parallels between theology and science as justification for attributing realistic status to theological language.

15 This last I take to be fancy language for atheism.

16 See Nancey Murphy, 'Scientific Realism and Postmodern Philosophy', in *Anglo-American Postmodernity: Philosophical Perspectives on Science, Religion, and Ethics* (Boulder, CO: Westview Press, 1997), Chapter 2; and 'On the Role of Philosophy in Theology–Science Dialogue', *Theology and Science*, 1:1 (April 2003): 79–94.

17 Robert John Russell, 'Finite Creation without a Beginning', in *Quantum Cosmology and the Laws of Nature: Scientific Perspectives on Divine Action*, ed. by Russell, Nancey Murphy, and Chris J. Isham (Vatican City State and Berkeley, CA: Vatican Observatory and Center for Theology and the Natural Sciences, 1993), 293–329.

18 Ibid., 312.

19 Stephen Hawking, *A Brief History of Time* (London: Bantam Press, 1989), 136.

20 Ibid., 326.

21 See Lakatos, 'Falsification and the Methodology of Scientific Research Programmes'.

22 Russell, 'Finite Creation without a Beginning', 311.

23 Ibid., 318–19; referring to C. J. Isham, 'Creation of the Universe as a Quantum Process', in *Physics, Philosophy, and Theology: A Common Quest for Understanding*, ed. by Robert J. Russell, William R. Stoeger, SJ, and George V. Coyne, SJ (Vatican City State: Vatican Observatory, 1988), 375–408; 387.

24 See Nancey Murphy, *Theology in the Age of Scientific Reasoning* (Ithaca, NY: Cornell University Press, 1990); and 'Theology and Science within a Lakatosian Program', 629–42.

25 Stephen Toulmin, *Cosmopolis: The Hidden Agenda of Modernity* (New York: Free Press, 1990).

CHAPTER FOUR

'Creative Mutual Interaction' as Manifesto, Research Program, and Regulative Ideal

Philip Clayton

It is a privilege to honor Robert John Russell on the occasion of his sixtieth birthday and the twenty-fifth anniversary of the center that he founded, the Center for Theology and the Natural Sciences. We are creatures of history, and no one can replace the teachers who first introduced us to a field and who modeled it for us. I am a product, in part, of Bob's intellectual leadership of the CTNS/Vatican Observatory series on divine action, which still today remains the most sophisticated series yet published in the field of theology and science. Bob's conference papers and publications influenced me deeply as a fledgling in the field, and the seven years I devoted to the 'Science and the Spiritual Quest' project would never have occurred without the support that Bob and CTNS gave to this ambitious attempt to internationalize the science–religion discussion.

It is thus intriguing to analyze the current state of the theology–science discussion in terms of the motto that Bob has bequeathed to the field: *creative mutual interaction*, or CMI. I shall argue that CMI represents the most ambitious standard yet formulated for the field. Serious questions about its implementation, however, require that we construe CMI in a somewhat different sense from the sense in which it was first proposed.

CMI as Manifesto

It is standard practice to speak of 'the theology and science dialogue' or 'the science and religion dialogue'; in the present paper I focus primarily on the former. Technically, the singular is a misnomer; one should actually speak of dialogue*s*. These various conceptually distinct dialogues frequently co-exist, often without acknowledgement, in the same published collection, the same conference, and even the work of the same individual. The only way to tease them apart is to distinguish the goals that motivate a given dialogue – something, unfortunately, too rarely done.

For this reason, I urge dissatisfaction with what is probably the most commonly endorsed category in Ian Barbour's famous typology, 'Dialogue'.[1] The word 'dialogue', I fear, has become a catch-all term; even the most dismissive diatribes are dubbed contributions to the dialogue. Until diverse

51

types of dialogue are distinguished in light of the contrasting goals that motivate them, little is conveyed by the use of the label.

Consider the following six distinct goals, which I list (with no pretense to completeness) in order of the increasingly ambitious demands that they make on the scholar:

1. The 'Sermon Illustrations' Approach

In this, the loosest sense of dialogue, religious persons make allusions to scientific theories merely as illustrations of their own religious beliefs, convictions, and practices. No commitment is made to 'getting the science right', nor need it impact one's religious conclusions in any significant way. Of course, scientists also can, and do, refer to religious concepts in an equally off-hand way, which I will refer to as the *religion as whipping-boy* approach. As in both cases no commitment to understanding, or even listening to, the other is implied, one may well question whether this category of reference even deserves the name of dialogue. Nonetheless, since such usages are widespread – and, sadly, not only among non-specialists – the category must be included.

2. Negation of the Other

A (slight) step up from the first approach are those works that treat the other side with the sole purpose of 'de-clawing' it so that it will no longer be dangerous to oneself. Bertrand Russell's famous early work, *Science and Religion*, provides an excellent example. By treating religion as a mere matter of mystical or affective response, devoid of concrete truth claims, Russell sought to insure that it would not meddle with scientific inquiry in any way. This tradition was continued by R. N. Braithwaite, whose 'emotivist' theory of religious language reduced it to a mere matter of affective expression rather than propositional content. The famous 'falsification debate' spawned by Anthony Flew in the late 1950s had a similar effect: religious language that is not verifiable, he maintained, can have no meaningful cognitive content whatsoever. Arguably, E. O. Wilson's recent *Consilience* seeks in effect to debarb religion in the same way.[2]

Of course, attempts to deny the competence of science in all religious and theological matters are equally common. We might call these *Tertullian ploys*, in honor of Tertullian's famous second-century protective move, 'What has Jerusalem to do with Athens, the Church with the Academy?' Similar, and often quite sophisticated, attempts abound in the twentieth century. Karl Barth's *Church Dogmatics*, for instance, can be read as an extended attempt to define a conceptual space over which science has no hold. Theology need only achieve *Sachlichkeit*, or appropriateness to its own particular object, which for Barth is the self-revelation of God in Jesus Christ. Any impact of the natural sciences on theology, he concludes, is 'unacceptable', since theology need only pursue a 'path to knowledge that is in itself consistent' and is directed toward 'a specific object'.[3] T. F. Torrance later developed Barth's separationist strategy into a full-fledged theory of rationality with his claim that an approach is 'scientific' as long as it is 'faithful', that is, it employs methods that are appropriate to its particular object. Thus few (if any) of the methods of the natural sciences are appropriate to the theologian, whose scientificness is guaranteed by her commitment to hear and comprehend the Word of God.[4]

3. Subordinating the Other to Oneself, or Hegelian Sublation

Two goals define the type of dialogue typical of this third category: a preliminary goal of entering into the details of the theories of the other field – in what may even seem to be a highly sympathetic manner – and an ultimate goal of showing that the other, 'correctly understood', actually supports the truth of one's own perspective. I call this *Hegelian sublation*, since Hegel is famous for offering an honored place to religion, only then to subordinate it within the overarching project of his systematic philosophy. Although such Hegelian strategies come in more and less aggressive forms, all share the feature of subordinating the other to one's own project.

Two examples from the recent literature will suffice. David Sloan Wilson's *Darwin's Cathedral* appears to grant a bona fide place to religion as an autonomous realm of human belief and action.[5] In the end, however, Wilson uses the tools of recent evolutionary psychology to subsume religion within an overarching biological explanation. Since in his view religious beliefs and practices are fully explained by biological theory, religious persons' own beliefs about themselves must in the end be mistaken.[6] For examples of a similar strategy in the other direction, one might consider some recent works from the Intelligent Design movement.[7] The arguments generally begin with scientific data regarding the evolution of life, speciation, and the evolution of particular structures and organs in particular species. They then seek to show that science as we know it is unable to explain these data, and indeed could never do so. The kind of order that one finds in nature, or the patterns of development, or the 'irreducible complexity' of cells, we are told, requires the hypothesis of an Intelligent Designer who intentionally constructed the systems in question, either before creation or in an ongoing manner during evolutionary history. The result, which some advocates call 'creation science', in effect subordinates empirical science within what is in effect an expanded form of theology. Since the differences between the two have been overcome, any scientific challenge to theology is ruled out in advance.

4. Proofs of Compatibility or Coherence

Two fields can be compatible without the one being subsumed to the other. If asked to hazard a guess, I would say that the bulk of the work published in 'mainline' science and religion over the last ten to fifteen years fits into this category. The authors are often addressing an (imaginary or real) opponent who claims that no one can accept science and be a religious person at the same time. Apologists for compatibilism try to show the errors in the opponent's criticisms, sometimes offering sophisticated and involved arguments for full compatibility. Without reviewing the entire literature here, it is safe to say that the most significant advances in our field have been proofs of compatibility or coherence. Across the fields that most commonly mediate between the natural sciences and the theological disciplines – philosophy of science, history of science, sociology of science, epistemology, metaphysics, and theology – a strong case has been made for this type of compatibility.

As significant as such work is, and as respectful as I am of its accomplishments, one should not be satisfied with this type of dialogue alone. As I have elsewhere sought to show,[8] making the case for the compatibility between scientific results and *some sort of* theological response is all too easy. I first began to recognize this fact during the course of the Science and the Spiritual Quest project (1997–2003). In SSQ, scientists from almost all the world's major religious traditions sought to show that their particular religious beliefs were compatible with contemporary science. Yet clearly the religious beliefs to which they adhered were mutually contradictory, and the quest for compatibility could not reduce the tensions between them. Indeed, it was impossible not to feel a certain tug toward religious relativism as I watched this international group of scientists agree completely on the scientific conclusions while inhabiting vastly different and apparently incommensurable religious 'worlds'.

There is a logical problem here. Assume A is true (say, a scientific theory), and assume that B through Z (say, religious views) can all be shown to be compatible with A. Now if B through Z represent incompatible belief systems, such that not all of {B–Z} can be simultaneously true, then isn't it clear that the relationship of compatibility with A says nothing about the truth or falsity of B through Z? In short, establishing compatibility, though valuable, cannot be the final goal of the science–religion dialogue.

5. Unifying Science and Religion

Clearly one goes beyond mere compatibility if one is able to synthesize two different areas of knowledge into a single structure. Of course, if this unification ends up subordinating one to the other, it becomes an instance of (3) above. The unification of A and B cannot be a subset of A or B alone; it must be some third thing. For example, the scientific quest and the religious quest might be two moments of expanding human consciousness, or moments in the development of Cosmic Spirit. (Note again the ambiguity of Barbour's category 'integration': it sometimes means unification in this sense, and sometimes mere compatibility in the sense of (4) above.)

6. Creative Mutual Interaction

It might at first seem strange to construe CMI as more demanding than the previous category. But it turns out that it is actually *easier* to make both science and religion into moments of some third thing; such synthetic unifying proposals are harder to test, the criteria that govern them more obscure.

By contrast, as we shall see in the next section, CMI requires that each side make demonstrable contributions to the project of the other – contributions not just from *one's own* perpective, or from some third perspective, but *from the perspective of the other field, understood in its own terms.* This fact makes CMI clearly the most demanding of the six types of religion–science dialogue. To grant the full autonomy of two different fields of inquiry, and then to outline a research program that connects them in such a way that *each* makes tangible contributions to the success of the other – this is the highest form of dialogue that one can conceive. Perhaps we should call it dialogue on the model of the Golden Rule, since it truly does for the other what one wishes that the other would do for one's own field. This is the standard that Bob Russell has outlined for the religion–science discussion today.

CMI as Research Program

In several publications Bob Russell has presented creative mutual interaction as a research program for theology and science. The best overview of the project appears in a well-known diagram (see Figure 4.1).[9]

The diagram presents eight paths, eight ways in which the one field might influence the other. Paths 1 to 5 specify the various ways in which science may influence theology. These are the non-controversial parts of the diagram, since it's widely accepted that science can and does influence theologians in these ways. Paths 6 to 8 trace possible forms of theology–science influence. Russell describes them thus:

> [6] [T]heological theories provide some of the philosophical assumptions which underlie scientific methodology. ... [For example,] [d]o values have a partial, evolutionary grounding in nature? Would scientific theories that incorporate such ideas be more fruitful than those that do not? ... [7] Theological theories can act as sources of inspiration in the scientific context of discovery, that is, in the construction of new scientific theories. ... [8] [T]heological theories can lead to selection rules within the criteria of theory choice in physics. ... For example, if on the basis of revelation we claim that humankind bears the image of God (*imago dei*), and if the image of God includes libertarian free will and with it the possibility of enacting our choices, bodily, then we might well prefer quantum mechanics to classical mechanics, because the former is compatible with an indeterministic interpretation. (277)

Within Russell's diagram of eight paths, it's clearly this final standard that represents CMI's most ambitious, and most controversial, moment. The creative interaction is fully mutual only if fundamental theoretical decisions in physics are sometimes made *for theological reasons*, in this case 'on the basis of revelation'.

Our goal in this section is to evaluate CMI as a research program. Since Russell has often expressed his adherence to the standards for research programs spelled out by Imre Lakatos, that's a natural place to start. For Lakatos a research program includes a 'negative heuristic', that is, a hard core of beliefs that serve to define the program's essential features. In the case of

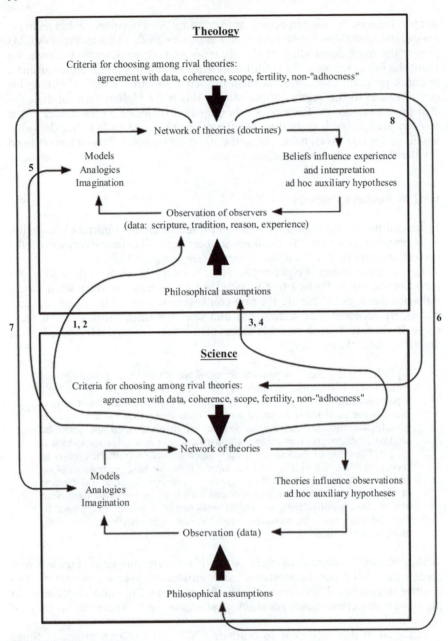

Theology

Criteria for choosing among rival theories:
agreement with data, coherence, scope, fertility, non-"adhocness"

Network of theories (doctrines)   8

Models
Analogies   5
Imagination   Beliefs influence experience
                                   and interpretation
                                   ad hoc auxiliary hypotheses

Observation of observers
(data: scripture, tradition, reason, experience)

Philosophical assumptions

7   1, 2   3, 4   6

Science

Criteria for choosing among rival theories:
agreement with data, coherence, scope, fertility, non-"adhocness"

Network of theories

Models
Analogies   Theories influence observations
Imagination   ad hoc auxiliary hypotheses

Observation (data)

Philosophical assumptions

Figure 4.1

CMI, this would presumably be the requirement that the dialogue between science and religion be bi-directional in the sense specified above. There must also be a 'positive heuristic', a long-term research policy. In our case, the positive heuristic would consist of the specific scientific subfields that the advocate of CMI examines in his attempt to establish the required bi-directional influences. Finally, Lakatos pointed out that theoretical work within some specific field of study inevitably produces a 'protective belt' of auxiliary hypotheses – specific theoretical claims, if you will – which may be falsified over time. Opponents criticize one's initial theoretical proposals, and one responds by constructing more and more complex models. As Lakatos notes, every constructive theory within a research program faces an 'ocean of anomalies'; its task is to 'turn them victoriously into examples' of the fruitfulness of one's particular research program.[10]

Lakatos disagreed with Karl Popper's claim that conclusive falsification occurs in science. There is counter-evidence, he argued, but it is recognized 'only with hindsight', for falsification always depends on the emergence of better theories that anticipate new facts.[11] Lakatos instead distinguished between 'progressive' and 'degenerating problemshifts' (for example, p. 33). A research program will be *progressive* if it produces 'novel facts', that is, if it enjoys more empirical success than its competitors, and it will be *degenerating* if it fails to produce empirical progress of this sort.

How has CMI fared as a research program? Bob Russell gave clear expression to the hard core of the program in his 1999 *Zygon* article and (at least by example) repeatedly within his various articles and introductions in the CTNS/Vatican Observatory series.[12] In the one direction the program has clearly been 'progressive', since it has been possible to show how scientific theories have deeply influenced theological formulations throughout the modern period. The more challenging task involves the other direction: the ways in which theology has impacted science. On this topic the CMI program has seen some success in Russell's reconstruction of the cosmological debates of the twentieth century. There does seem to be evidence that some of the leading astrophysicists were influenced by their religious or other metaphysical beliefs in constructing the theories that they did. Russell's treatment of Einstein's introduction of the cosmological constant, his evaluation of Alfred North Whitehead's alternative to relativity theory,[13] and in particular his treatment of the origins of Fred Hoyle's 'steady state theory' represent plausible examples of this sort of influence. Other instances of theology-to-science influence have been recorded and elaborated in the standard treatments of the history of science–religion interactions in the modern period.[14]

By contrast, I do not know of any conclusive examples of CMI in fundamental physics. In fact, to my knowledge the same null result holds for fundamental theoretical work in chemistry, molecular biology, and neurophysiology (emphatically *not* including the consciousness debate!). As it turns out, most of the sophisticated work in the CTNS/VO series falls into category (4) in my typology above, not category (6). Perhaps the most sophisticated category (4) theory in our entire field is the quantum-level theory of divine action developed by Russell, Murphy, Ellis, and Tracy (see Part III of the present book). Clearly, however, the theory's goal is to show that quantum-level divine action *is not inconsistent with* quantum theory as understood by the Copenhagen interpretation. The theory, even in its most elaborate forms, does not – and, I believe Russell would say, *should* not – influence how research in fundamental physics is carried out or what *physical* conclusions it comes to.

Likewise, Russell's work in *Evolutionary and Molecular Biology*[15] shows that God *could* influence the evolutionary process by augmenting or amplifying quantum-level divine action. Again, however, this conclusion is not meant to cause molecular biologists to do their scientific work in a different way. Finally, as far as I can tell, none of the contributions to Russell's CTNS/VO volume, *The Neuroscience of the Person*, required neuroscience to be done differently. The individual contributions either summarize existing neuroscience or offer philosophical or theological *interpretations or applications of* neuroscientific results. But such work represents only a one-way influence, not creative mutual interaction.

One must conclude, then, that the research program of CMI does not yet meet the criteria for a 'progressive problemshift' in Lakatos's sense. As the most ambitious and demanding form of science–religion dialogue that one can identify today, CMI remains an intriguing research program, and religion–science scholars may wish to attempt to establish the full bi-directional interaction that it describes. But, apart from the exceptions listed above, one cannot yet detect that the research program has been successful when applied to actual cases. Indeed, in some ways it faces an uphill battle: the practice of contemporary natural science is now more resistant to outside influences – especially religious influences – than at almost any other time in the history of science. *Interpretations* of science, *applications* of science, and the *ethics* of scientific research are deeply influenced by non-scientific factors, and rightly so. But the core methods and basic results of 'pure science' appear at present to be as insulated from the impact of religious ideas as they could possibly be.

CMI as Regulative Ideal

How, then, should we understand CMI? As the most ambitious form of theology–science dialogue, it clearly serves as a manifesto, a call to closer connections than have yet been drawn in the late twentieth and early twenty-first centuries. But just as the ideas of Karl Marx's Communist Manifesto far exceeded the actual achievements of Communism in Europe, Latin America, Russia, and China in the twentieth century, so also does the CMI manifesto exceed what CMI as an applied research program has yet been able to achieve. In more skeptical moments one might well worry that this gap between goal and practice will never be overcome. It could be, for example, that a scientist is properly guided by her religious or ethical beliefs only when their influence is limited to a *heuristic* role, that is, when they serve as a source for hypotheses, which she then tests according to the standard methods and procedures of her discipline. But this is not the same as giving religion a *constitutive* place in scientific practice, which full mutual interaction would seem to require. After all, a variety of influences can play heuristic roles for scientists: a dream (as in Kekulé's discovery of the benzene ring structure after dreaming of a snake seizing its tail[16]), or a hallucination, or for that matter a drug-induced experience. Clearly, this is not particularly noble company for religionists to keep!

Even if these more skeptical fears turn out in the end to be well grounded, they need not spell the end of CMI altogether. For, I suggest, the proposal's greatest importance may well lie in its role as a (or *the*) regulative ideal for the theology–science debate.

Recall Kant's argument in the *Critique of Pure Reason*: reason is constrained to postulate a highest ideal, the ideal of the completion of reason or, in other cases, its highest instance. We are driven to conceive this highest ideal not merely as an epistemic principle but as a single instance. Only one being would, if it existed, represent this ideal consummation of reason: the *ens realissimum*, the most real being, or God. A Creator of all reality, one that served as its ground and thereby insured the ontological unity of everything that exists – this postulation alone expresses the ultimate goal of reason in its quest for unified understanding. As Kant writes, 'while for the merely speculative employment of reason the supreme being remains a mere *ideal*, it is yet *an ideal without a flaw*, a concept which completes and crowns the whole of human knowledge. Its objective reality cannot indeed be proved, but also cannot be disproved, by merely speculative reason' (B 669).

As a transcendental ideal, the concept of God does not refer to an object given to us in experience, but rather '[raises] the use of reason in its own right to an actual object'.[17] By relativizing this concept and its function to the subject, Kant completes the long line of development in theistic metaphysics that began with Descartes's use of God as the guarantor of the veracity of human reason. God becomes 'the condition of the possibility of *the very being a subject* of the subject ... the foundation that bears the weight of the system of reason'.[18] The idea of God becomes 'the idea of something which is the ground of the highest and necessary unity of all empirical reality' (B 703). Practically speaking, God is understood as the 'ideal of the highest good' and of 'moral perfection' (B 832).

The regulative ideal has a special status among the various *regulative ideas* of reason, even while it best expresses the unity toward which reason strives. In general, regulative ideas do not meet the standards for constitutive knowledge; hence they are things we cannot actually believe to be true. The idea of God, for example, arises from the need of reason to view the world in such a way '*as if* all such connection had its source in one single all-embracing being, as the supreme and all-sufficient cause' (B 714). But nor are such ideas arbitrary fictions, for they accurately identify principles that regulate the pursuit of reason. Only if we clearly formulate for ourselves how reason works – what it presupposes and what it inherently strives for – only then, Kant realizes, can we engage in the quest for knowledge in a coherent manner.

What does all this have to do with CMI? In the first section of this chapter we saw that the CMI approach represents the most ambitious goal in the science–religion dialogue. The second section showed that, as a research program, CMI has not yet achieved the sorts of results that would make it progressive in Lakatos's sense, and there are reasons to think that such successes may continue to elude its supporters, given natural science as we know it today. Thus my thesis: just as the idea of God serves as the regulative ideal for reason according to Kant, *CMI expresses the regulative ideal for the theology–science debate.*

What does this imply? Creative mutual interaction becomes the ideal in light of which the other five categories of religion–science dialogue in the typology are interpreted. Each of the others represents a particular subgoal for a particular segment of the dialogue or for a particular period of its history, but none expresses the final *telos* of the dialogue. Relating science and theology comprises more than reducing the one to the other, or merely showing their compatibility, or constructing some third, higher perspective that transforms both into aspects of a single project. Instead, the goal that retroactively defines the entire dialogue is the goal of creative mutual interaction: relating theology and science such that each can make contributions to the project of the other. Anything less than this fails to establish a full complementary relationship between these two fundamental human activities. Hence, anything short of CMI means that the discussion has failed to achieve the highest goal that one can conceive for it – even if that failure is unavoidable.

Obviously, this exalted position should come as good news for advocates of CMI. It comes at a cost, however. A regulative ideal in the sense described may make a great manifesto, but it is not in itself a progressive research program. Recall again the parallel with Kant: it may be that the idea (or ideal) of God is fundamental for expressing what it is that reason seeks, yet that does not in itself show that constitutive knowledge of God is possible. So too the theology–science debate finds itself confronted with CMI as a regulative ideal that helps to define the very idea of the endeavor – even if one must admit that we will inevitably fall short of this goal.

It is interesting to apply this conclusion to two of the ideas that are most fundamental to Christian theology: the ideas of the resurrection and the eschaton. CMI suggests that the science-and-Christian-theology debate will only have achieved its goal when belief in the actual resurrection of Jesus from death is not only shown to be *compatible* with scientific conclusions but also, conversely, when it begins to serve as an impetus for *actual research and positive empirical results* in the natural sciences. Although I cannot make the case here, I believe that even the first of these two goals remains problematic. Historical–critical work requires some level of analogy between alleged past events and the events of present experience; yet our overwhelming present experience is that dead persons do not rise from the dead. Be that as it may, it is even more clear that the second requirement is not fulfilled: physicists, biologists, and empirical historians do not, and in my view *should* not, do their actual scientific work differently as a result of the resurrection claim (though they may well *live differently* because of it). Where such religion-to-science applications have been attempted in these fields, they have not resulted in acknowledged 'progressive problemshifts' within the relevant fields themselves.

What is true of the resurrection topic is even more true of eschatology. Physics offers no way to conceive that the physical universe would be brought to an end by an act of God and transformed into 'a new heaven and a new earth'. Even less has this idea given rise to progressive problemshifts in fundamental physics that have yielded increased empirical content. Indeed, I doubt whether eschatological ideas *should* have this function. Their theological significance is, as Augustine well realized, to express the limits on this entire natural, finite, created order and to herald the coming of a new order, which will be directly established by God. If Augustine was right in claiming this to be the authentic content of the eschatological proclamation, then eschatology *could* never engage in full mutual interaction with 'normal science'.

Conclusion

Sometimes the best way to understand the true nature of a dialogue is to understand its limits. We best understand the effort to integrate science and religion if we understand those inherent differences between them which place limits on their full integration. Of all the formulations currently on the market, CMI does the best job of spelling out the regulative ideal for the field. As a result, it reveals the boundaries of the discourse more clearly than any other proposal.

It is important in closing to distinguish the Kantian argument of this chapter from the *via negativa* as it is found in, for example, the mystical and apophatic traditions. I am *not* claiming that we know in advance that all talk of God is merely symbolic or apophatic, and hence that any integration of religious metaphysics and scientific research is impossible. Nor have I sought to pre-specify any precise boundaries for the theology–science dialogue. In the case of a regulative ideal, there are good reasons to think that we will never achieve the goal; but how far toward it actual work in the field may progress remains an open question.

Let us then put our best efforts into advancing the theology–science dialogue toward CMI, its ultimate goal. Let us, in particular, not be satisfied with the partial results that subdiscussions achieve along the way. In the end, it is probably more important to describe the theology–science dialogue in terms of the ideal that ultimately defines it, rather than in terms of particular subgoals achieved by particular players at particular times. Only by focusing on the big picture in this way will we be able to advance as far as possible toward the ultimate, if ultimately unreachable, goal. The fact that we will not finally remove the epistemic gaps between the scientific study of the natural world and theological reflection on its ultimate origins is no reason not to explore their interconnections as fully as possible.

Notes

1   Ian Barbour, *Religion and Science: Historical and Contemporary Issues* (San Francisco: HarperSanFrancisco, 1997).

2   E. O. Wilson, *Consilience: The Unity of Knowledge* (New York: Knopf, 1998).

3   Karl Barth, *Church Dogmatics*, ed. by G. W. Bromiley and T. F. Torrance (Edinburgh: T. & T. Clark, 1956–75), I/1, 7.

4   See T. F. Torrance, *Theological Science* (London: Oxford University Press, 1969).

5   David Sloan Wilson, *Darwin's Cathedral: Evolution, Religion, and the Nature of Society* (Chicago: University of Chicago Press, 2002).

6   See also Philip Clayton and Jeffrey Schloss (eds), *Evolution and Ethics: Human Morality in Biological and Religious Perspective* (Grand Rapids, MI: Eerdmans, 2004).

7   William Dembski, *The Design Inference: Eliminating Chance Though Small Probabilities* (New York: Cambridge University Press, 1998); *Intelligent Design: The Bridge Between Science and Theology* (Downers Grove, IL: InterVarsity Press, 1999); *No Free Lunch: Why Specified Complexity Cannot be Purchased without Intelligence* (Lanham, MD: Rowman and Littlefield, 2002); and Dembski (ed.), *Signs of Intelligence: Understanding Intelligent Design* (Grand Rapids, MI: Brazos Press, 2001). For a related argument, see Michael Behe, *Darwin's Black Box: The Biochemical Challenge to Evolution* (New York: Free Press, 1996).

8   See Clayton, 'Wildman's Kantian Skepticism: A Rubicon for Divine Action', *Theology and Science*, 2:2 (October 2004): 186–90; Clayton, 'Gaining an Overview of the Divine Action Debate: A Ten-Year Retrospective', in the Capstone Volume to the CTNS/VO series, ed. by Robert Russell, Nancey Murphy, and William Stoeger.

9   See Robert J. Russell, 'The Relevance of Tillich for the Theology and Science Dialogue', *Zygon*, 36:2 (June 2001): 269–308. The diagram appears on page 275.

10 See Imre Lakatos, 'Falsification and the Methodology of Scientific Research Programmes', in *Criticism and the Growth of Knowledge*, ed. by Lakatos and Alan Musgrave (Cambridge: Cambridge University Press, 1970), 50 and 111.

11 Ibid., 34–6.

12 See, in addition to the various volume introductions, Robert J. Russell, 'Finite Creation without a Beginning: The Doctrine of Creation in Relation to Big Bang and Quantum Cosmologies', in *Quantum Cosmology and the Laws of Nature*, ed. by Russell, Nancey C. Murphy, and Chris J. Isham (Vatican City State and Berkeley, CA: Vatican Observatory and Center for Theology and the Natural Sciences, 1993), 293–329; Wesley J. Wildman and Russell, 'Chaos: A Mathematical Introduction with Philosophical Reflections', in *Chaos and Complexity*, ed. by Russell, Nancey C. Murphy, and Arthur R. Peacocke (Vatican City State and Berkeley, CA: Vatican Observatory and Center for Theology and the Natural Sciences, 1995), 49–90; Russell, 'Special Providence and Genetic Mutation: A New Defense of Theistic Evolution', in *Evolution and Molecular Biology*, ed. by Russell, William R. Stoeger, SJ, and Francisco J. Ayala (Vatican City State and Berkeley, CA: Vatican Observatory and Center for Theology and the Natural Sciences 1998), 191–223; and Russell, 'Divine Action and Quantum Mechanics: A Fresh Assessment', in *Quantum Mechanics*, ed. by Russell, Philip Clayton, Kirk Wegter-McNelly, and John Polkinghorne (Vatican City State and Berkeley, CA: Vatican Observatory and Center for Theology and the Natural Sciences, 2002), 293–328. See also note 9 above.

13 Robert J. Russell, 'Whitehead, Einstein and the Newtonian Legacy', in *Newton and the New Direction in Science*, ed. by George V. Coyne, SJ, Michael Heller, and Jozef Zycinski (Citta Del Vaticano: Specola Vaticana, 1988), 175–92.

14 David C. Lindberg and Ronald L. Numbers (eds), *God and Nature: Historical Essays on the Encounter between Christianity and Science* (Berkeley, CA: University of California Press, 1986); Lindberg and Numbers (eds), *When Science and Christianity Meet* (Chicago, IL:

University of Chicago Press, 2003); John Hedley Brooke, *Science and Religion: Some Historical Perspectives* (Cambridge: Cambridge University Press, 1991); John Hedley Brooke and Geoffrey Cantor, *Reconstructing Nature: The Engagement of Science and Religion* (New York: Oxford University Press, 2000); John Hedley Brooke, *Of Scientists and their Gods* (Oxford: Oxford University Press, 2001).

15 See Russell, 'Special Providence and Genetic Mutation'.

16 See Friedrich August Kekulé, 'Origin of the Benzene and Stuctural Theory', in Arthur Zucker, *Introduction to the Philosophy of Science* (Upper Saddle River, NJ: Prentice Hall, 1996), 34–5.

17 Costantino Esposito, 'Kants philosophische Religionslehre zwischen reiner und praktischer Vernunft', in *Akte des 7. Internationalen Kant-Kongresses*, ed. by G. Funke (Bonn, 1991), vol. II/2, 244.

18 Christian Link, *Subjektivität und Wahrheit: Die Grundlegung der neuzeitlichen Metaphysik durch Descartes* (Stuttgart: Klett-Cotta, 1978), 193; cf. Immanuel Kant, *The Critique of Pure Reason*, B 595ff., *The Critique of Practical Reason*, A 226.

CHAPTER FIVE

'Creative Mutual Interaction' as an Epistemic Tool for Interdisciplinary Dialogue

J. Wentzel van Huyssteen

Robert John Russell's dedication to the 'theology and science' dialogue is well known and well documented, but his cutting-edge contributions to this conversation are especially appreciated and greatly respected by all of us who live and work in this interdisciplinary field. For more than twenty years Russell has taken the lead in carefully articulating the possibilities and limitations of interdisciplinary dialogue, focusing specifically on theology and the natural sciences. His own methodological contribution to the nature of this kind of interdisciplinarity can best be described as 'creative mutual interaction.'[1] I feel very honored by the invitation to reflect on the nature and scope of this methodology, and to try to probe deeper the philosophical meaning and implications of this important proposal for a multileveled research strategy for theology and the sciences.

Russell's methodology is, I believe, best illustrated in a recent and ambitious interdisciplinary case study which explores possible interdisciplinary links between the 'bodily resurrection' of Christ, Christian eschatology, and scientific cosmology.[2] Russell starts out by identifying the resurrection of Jesus (the defining *kerugma* of the Christian faith, but curiously neglected in interdisciplinary discourse) as a challenging shared research trajectory for Christian theology and science. On Russell's view, the bodily resurrection of Jesus represents a test case of the highest order for those in the field of theology and science who are developing models for a constructive interaction between these very diverse reasoning strategies.[3] In this specific case study Russell explicitly presupposes two 'mainstream' theological themes: the 'bodily resurrection' of Jesus of Nazareth and the implied eschatological transformation of the universe into a new creation. In doing so he wants to show that this powerful 'test case' not only serves to help us to avoid conflict between theology and the sciences, but also reveals methodologically a plausible relationship of creative mutual interaction between these very diverse domains of thought.

In developing the notion of 'creative mutual interaction', Russell also wants to highlight two crucial epistemic issues that have been raised and established by the generally accepted, broader methodological framework of our time, and that have enabled 'theology and science' to grow so richly as an interactive field of research over the past four decades, namely *epistemic hierarchy* and *analogous methodologies*.[4] 'Epistemic hierarchy' refers to the claim that the sciences and the humanities, including theology, can be placed on a series of hierarchical epistemic levels that reflects the increasing complexity of the phenomena they study. On this view, 'epistemic hierarchy' implies that lower levels place *constraints* on upper levels, but upper levels cannot be reduced entirely to lower levels. Thus, physics would place constraints on biology and neurophysiology, while at the same time the processes, properties, and laws of these upper-level sciences cannot be reduced to those of the lower level.

I believe this statement can be fine-tuned to express better Russell's deepest epistemological intentions: this hierarchy, if a truly epistemic hierarchy, is a *descriptive* hierarchy in so far as it tells us something about how a broad spectrum of disciplines reflects the increasing complexity of the structures of our world, and thus the related disciplinary levels on which we have come to know this world. I would be wary if disciplines themselves are locked into a hierarchical pattern, even if the increasing complexity of structures in our world descriptively suggests this kind of hierarchy. Therefore, the complex spectrum of disciplines should not aim to reflect the kind of epistemic priority that would privilege one reasoning strategy as epistemically more basic, foundational, or 'true' than others 'higher up' on the hierarchy. Russell argues correctly, therefore, that 'epistemic hierarchy' should protect our interdisciplinary dialogues not only against the kind of epistemic reductionism that reduces upper level entirely to lower levels,[5] but also against the kind of epistemic privileging that would see the quality of one 'level' of knowledge as more foundational than that of another level. For precisely this reason, I have introduced in my own work, for the theology and science dialogue, a notion of interdisciplinarity that is not rigidly tied in to hierarchical levels (epistemic or otherwise), but which rather explores transversally the porous boundaries between a broad spectrum of disciplines, and also the resultant interactive connection between even very diverse disciplines in an ongoing multileveled discourse.[6]

A second crucial issue raised by the current methodology in 'theology and science', which has far-reaching implications for interdisciplinary dialogue, Russell labels *analogous methodologies*. For different disciplines in interdisciplinary dialogue, this implies that within the epistemic 'hierarchy', as discussed above, each level involves similar methods of theory construction and testing. Like scientific theories, theological doctrines also are to be seen as working hypotheses that we hold fallibly, constructed through metaphors and models, and tested in the light of the 'data' of theology which now include the results of science.[7] The natural question that arises here is whether it might not be problematical to transfer concepts across disciplinary borders, in this case from natural science to theology, to then talk about 'theological data' and 'testing', as this may reveal exactly the kind of epistemic disciplinary privileging that I have warned against before. However, Russell correctly reminds us that there are indeed important differences between the methods of theology and those of the natural sciences,[8] which should naturally prevent an epistemic privileging of the methodology of the natural sciences, especially physics, *vis-à-vis* theology. For this reason, and to solidify this important proposal, I personally would prefer to speak of the *epistemic resources* of theology (instead of 'data') and of *problem-solving* (instead of 'testing') as a more fruitful methodological link between disciplines as radically diverse as theology and the sciences.

What is especially interesting about the claim that theological methodology is analogous to scientific methodology is that for Russell it denotes both a *description* of the way many theologians actually work and a *prescription* for progress in theological research. Again, theological doctrines are to be seen as working hypotheses held fallibly, constructed through metaphors and models, and tested in the light of the data of theology *now including the results of the sciences*.[9] I totally agree that there are epistemological similarities in the way theologians construct hypotheses in their own distinct process of theory-forming. I would want to be more careful, however, to want to 'test' these hypotheses in the light of presuppositions and worldviews that are now called the 'data' of theology and that may actually include the results of science. When in the field of theology and science we reach the exciting point where transdisciplinary conversation actually leads to interdisciplinary results, how can the new theological hypotheses that emerge, now affected by or even transformed by the results of science, be seen as the 'data' of theology when in fact these are the (often provocative) new hypotheses that should indeed be justified by interdisciplinary standards for conceptual problem-solving? This is precisely the reason why I have argued for the strengths *and* weaknesses, the possibilities *and* limitations of interdisciplinary dialogue, and why we should be so wary of epistemic reductionism when we negotiate disciplinary borders. For this conversation, it raises the legitimate question: should we even be talking of 'data' and 'testing' within the domain of a reasoning strategy like Christian theology, especially when the most defining presuppositions of this particular discussion ('bodily resurrection' and 'eschatological transformation') can never be 'tested' in any scientific sense of the word? This is not to say, of course, that scientific argument cannot bring a certain plausibility and credibility to ancient religious doctrines as we try to bridge the daunting hermeneutical and epistemological distances between these asymmetrical reasoning strategies. Moreover, the radically pluralist nature of theological traditions; the epistemological challenge of asking about the credibility of claiming any form of 'authority' for ancient biblical texts; philosophical shifts in what we mean today by 'rationality' or 'reason'; and the hermeneutical realities of our multi-interpreted (also: religious) experiences, all give us reason to pause before pointing to Scripture, tradition, reason, and experience as the 'data' of theology.[10]

I very much agree with Russell that we have to 'expand' our methodologies to allow for creative interaction between theology and the sciences. Certainly accepted, justified theories in physics, in paleoanthropology, or in any of the sciences for that matter can indeed place important constraints on theology (directly or indirectly). However, because of overly empiricist connotations, I would hesitate to call such theories 'data' for theology. Russell is certainly correct in developing the theme that scientific facts/results can lead to serious worldview changes in theology, and to the necessary fine-tuning of theological doctrines. For example, in the same way that scientific cosmology places constraints on what theology can claim eschatologically, paleoanthropology and evolutionary biology place constraints on what theological anthropology can claim about the origins and nature of *homo sapiens*. At the same time, theology should challenge the sciences to take seriously the philosophical presuppositions it works with. The most challenging aspect of an interdisciplinary dialogue between theology and the natural sciences, however, may be for theology to lift up the specific limitations of this conversation. This implies a quite specific appeal from theology to the sciences: an appeal for a sensitivity to that which is particular to the broader, non-empirical or philosophical dimensions of theological discourse. This respect for disciplinary integrity means that Christian theology has an obligation to explore conceptual problems that may not be empirically accessible, but that can indeed creatively interact with the data from science because they may complement and enrich the worldviews in which science is embedded. In lifting up this creative mutual interaction between asymmetrical reasoning strategies, Russell's argument dovetails neatly with my own: an argument for interdisciplinarity that is precisely about the fact that Christian theology is answerable to canons of inquiry defensible within the various intersecting domains of our common discourse.[11]

Russell has very helpfully enhanced his model of 'mutual interaction' by claiming *five ways* that science can influence theology, and then also *three ways* that theology can influence science (or more specifically, the philosophical assumptions that underlie science). Russell narrows this down to the interdisciplinary dialogue between physics and theology, and states that the five paths that can lead from physics to theology are the following:[12]

1   theories in physics can act *directly* as data that place constraints on theology (for example, a theological theory about divine action should not violate special relativity);

2   theories can act *directly* as data either to be 'explained' by theology, or as a basis for a constructive theological argument (for example, $t = 0$ in standard Big Bang cosmology can be explained theologically via creation *ex nihilo*);

3   theories, after philosophical analysis, can act *indirectly* as 'data' for theology (for example, an indeterministic interpretation of quantum mechanics can function within theological anthropology by providing a physical precondition for the bodily enactment of free will);

4   theories in physics can also act *indirectly* as the 'data' for theology when they are incorporated into a fully articulated philosophy of nature (cf. A. F. Whitehead and process theology);

5   theories in physics can function *heuristically* in the theological 'context of discovery' by providing conceptual or aesthetic inspiration (for example, biological evolution may inspire a fresh interpretation of God's immanence in nature).

To illustrate what he means by 'creative mutual interaction', Russell also reverses the direction of influence by adding three new paths that represent possible influences of theology on the philosophical assumptions that underlie science:[13]

1 historically theological ideas provided some of the philosophical assumptions that underlie scientific methodology. For example, the doctrine of the *creatio ex nihilo* played an important role in the rise of modern science by combining the Greek assumption of the rationality of the world with the theological assumption that the world is contingent – both of these helped give birth to the empirical method and the use of mathematics to represent natural processes;[14]

2 theological theories can act as sources of inspiration in the construction of new scientific theories;

3 theological theories can lead to, or be suggestive of, election rules within the criteria of theory choice in science. For example, if one considers a theological theory to be true, then one can delineate what conditions must obtain within physics for the possibility of its being true; these conditions in turn can serve as motivations for an individual research scientist or group of colleagues to pursue a particular scientific theory.[15]

For Russell, these different mutually interactive 'paths' that connect theology and physics now clearly reveal the asymmetry between theology and the sciences: theological theories do *not* act as data for science, placing constraints on which theories can be constructed in the way that scientific theories constrain theology. Theology can, however, have an influence on science: it can play a constructive and heuristic role within the implicit worldview and philosophy of nature that undergird science. Together these eight 'paths' portray interdisciplinarity between the natural sciences and theology in a much more interactive mode. And it is this dynamic interaction that Russell has called *the method of creative mutual interaction*.[16] Russell wisely notes that we would have a sign of real interdisciplinary progress in 'theology and science' if both sides find the interaction fruitful within their own disciplinary standards of progress.[17] This indeed might lead not only to a rethinking of theological concepts and doctrines in the light of science, but also to theology challenging the philosophical assumptions of the sciences.

For all these reasons I have found Robert John Russell's methodological proposal for the 'theology and science' dialogue, in spite of our mainly conceptual differences, to be remarkably consonant with my own proposal for understanding interdisciplinary discourse. In my own recent work I have argued that a multidimensional understanding of interdisciplinary dialogue, rightly conceived, should enable us to move away from abstract, over-generalized models and blueprints for 'doing' interdisciplinary work, and specifically for 'doing' theology and science, and instead focus on developing, first contextually and then transversally, the merits of each concrete interdisciplinary problem in terms of the very specific science and the very specific theology involved.[18] Happily, I would argue, we have lost all chance of developing some kind of universal natural theology that would claim to rival the empirical excellence of the natural sciences. But what does all of this mean for the interdisciplinary dialogue between theology and the sciences? Pluralism in both theology and the sciences, along with a rising awareness that science and religion are really vastly different cognitive domains, has of course intensified this problem. Some of the most important factors determining the complexity of the theology and science dialogue today can, therefore, be summarized as follows:

- profound differences as to the nature and identity of these very different reasoning strategies;
- differences in how we form and hold on to beliefs in these very different systems of thought;
- differences in how we justify holding our beliefs in disciplines as radically different as theology and the sciences; and
- the fact that contemporary postfoundationalist epistemology has convincingly shown us that it has actually become impossible, and certainly implausible, even to talk about 'theology and science' in such a generic, abstract sense.[19]

Our increasing awareness of the radical social and historical contextuality of all our disciplinary reflections has now made it abundantly clear that in interdisciplinary dialogue the rather vague term 'theology and science' should be replaced by focusing on specific theologians, doing very specific kinds of theologies, attempting to enter into interdisciplinary dialogue with very specific scientists, working within specified sciences on clearly identified and very specific (shared) problems. Robert John Russell's case study on bodily resurrection, eschatology, and cosmology has indeed been an excellent example of this approach.[20]

Furthermore, I believe that in such an integrative and interdisciplinary praxis for 'theology and the sciences' terms such as *transversality* and *contextuality* should take center stage, revealing the value of identifying shared concerns and points of agreement and, maybe more importantly, exposing areas of disagreement and putting into perspective specific divisive issues that need to be discussed. We also need to keep in mind that in any interdisciplinary conversation the different discourses often represent radically diverse perspectives, reflecting different and distinct methods of investigation, which means they cannot be reduced to each other or derived from each other.[21] The challenge, however, is to show that it is often at the boundaries between disciplines that new and exciting discoveries may take place. But a timely warning should be issued here: an interdisciplinary approach is likely to be fruitful only as long as one is scrupulously attentive to the contextual meaning of words and the proper use of concepts.[22] Even if identical concepts are used as we cross disciplinary borders in theology and the sciences, they might not, even remotely, mean the same thing. But these diverse and asymmetrical uses of the same concepts or phrases may, at the same time, alert us to promising liminalities between the disciplines. Indeed, discourse might begin at this very point of intersection and tension. Thanks to the multiplicity, abundance, and completeness of human experience, our different discourses do continually intersect with one another at many points. Interdisciplinary dialogue, then, is an attempt to bring together disciplines or reasoning strategies that may have widely different points of reference, different epistemological foci, and different experiential resources. This 'fitting together', however, is a complex, multi-leveled transversal process that does not take place within any given discipline,[23] but within the transversal spaces between disciplines.

Against this background I have argued for a *postfoundationalist notion of rationality* that creates an epistemological space for the interdisciplinary dialogue between theology and the sciences.[24] Leaving behind modernist notions of universal rationality, and accepting the challenge of fragmentation and pluralism in theology and the various sciences, I have argued for distinct and important differences between reasoning strategies used by theologians and scientists. At the same time, however, I have argued that shared rational resources may actually be identified for the different cognitive domains of our lives. This implies, as Russell has correctly indicated, that there must be special epistemic links or connections between different and asymmetrical modes of human knowledge. Thus an interdisciplinary rationality is revealed that supports the claims, by at least some in our epistemic community, for a public voice for theology in our complex contemporary culture. On this view theologians, and also scientists of various stripes, should be empowered to protect the rational integrity of their own disciplines, while at the same time identifying overlapping issues, shared problems, and even parallel research trajectories as we cross disciplinary lines in multidisciplinary research. On a more philosophical level, this should be a challenging answer to one of modernity's most powerful demands, namely that theological reflection, as well as the many forms of contemporary scientific reflection, ultimately require universal epistemological guarantees to qualify as 'real science'.

A postfoundationalist approach to interdisciplinary dialogue reveals the way we live and reflect on our lives as deeply embedded in historical, cultural, and conceptual contexts, but also shows, at the same time, that we are free to employ our rather unique modes of rationality across contextual, cultural, and disciplinary barriers. For this reason it would be in interdisciplinary dialogue, correctly conceived, that we rediscover the public voice of religion and theology. Here theology is neither transformed, modernistically, into natural science, nor rejected as non-science. It does emerge, however, as a reasoning strategy on a par with the intellectual integrity and legitimacy of the natural and social sciences, even as it defines its own powerful domain of thought that in so many ways is also distinct from, and asymmetrical to, that of the sciences. On this view, for instance, the theologian may join forces with the scientist in drawing clear boundaries *vis-à-vis* the reductionist views of scientism, but also has a moral obligation to resist all forms of theological imperialism that may impinge on science: two ideologies that both have the power to destroy interdisciplinary dialogue.

I believe that a notion of creative mutual interaction between theology and the sciences is enhanced philosophically by a notion of postfoundationalist rationality. In *The Shaping of Rationality* (1999), I argued *against* theology's epistemic isolation in a pluralist, postmodern world, and *for* a postfoundationalist notion of rationality that reveals precisely this interdisciplinary, public nature of all theological reflection. In an earlier work, *Duet or Duel? Theology and Science in a Postmodern World* (1998), I also argued that evolutionary epistemology may facilitate the kind of postfoundationalist notion of rationality that could actually take us beyond the confines of traditional disciplinary boundaries and modernist cultural domains. This interdisciplinary notion of rationality allows us to revise human rationality along the following lines.

First, it acknowledges contextuality and the embeddedness of all our reflection in human culture (and therefore, in specific scientific or confessional traditions), and thus acknowledges the fact that our theological presuppositions are already influenced by the scientific culture of our times.

Second, it takes seriously both the epistemically crucial role of interpreted experience or experiential understanding and the way that tradition shapes both the epistemic and non-epistemic values that inform our reflection, our thoughts about God, and (what some of us believe to be) God's presence in the world.

Third, it allows us to explore freely and critically the experiential and interpretative roots of our beliefs from within our deep commitments, and to discover patterns in our lives and thoughts that might be consonant with what we regard as the canon(s) of our respective theological or scientific traditions.[25] The persuasiveness of these patterns should be taken up in critical interdisciplinary reflection, where their problem-solving ability should then be evaluated and judged in an interpersonal and cross-contextual conversation.

Fourth, rationality itself can now be seen as a skill that enables us to gather and bind together the patterns of our interpreted experience through rhetoric, articulation, and discernment. It is on this point that the important postfoundationalist notion of *transversality* replaces modernist, static notions of universality in a distinct move to see human reason as dynamic and practical in the way we use it to converse with one another through critique, interpretation, narration, and rhetoric. In *The Shaping of Rationality* I argued for the 'transversal performance' of rationality precisely when referring to this dynamic and multileveled interdisciplinary interaction of our discourses with one another.[26] The notion of transversality is hugely helpful to highlight the kind of human dynamics of consciousness that enables us to move between domains of intelligence with a high degree of cognitive fluidity,[27] and as such it is at the heart of my notion of interdisciplinary reflection.

In the dialogue between theology and other disciplines, transversal reasoning facilitates different, but equally legitimate, ways of viewing or interpreting issues, problems, traditions, or disciplines. On this view interdisciplinary dialogue can, therefore, be seen as multidimensional and thus on convergent paths moving toward an imagined vanishing-point: a transversal space where different voices are not in contradiction, nor in danger of assimilating one another, but are dynamically interactive with one another.[28] In this multidisciplinary use of the concept of transversality there emerge distinct characteristics: the interweaving of many voices, the dynamics of conscious-ness, the interplay of social practices are all expressed in *a metaphor* that points to a sense of transition, a lying-across, extending over, intersecting, meeting, and conveying without becoming identical. Transversality thus provides a philosophical window to the wider world of communication through thought and action. It also represents a strong reaction against both rationalist/ modernist impulses to *unify* all faculties of knowledge into a seamless unity and the positivistic impulse to claim science as a superior form of knowing. It clearly also represents a protest against the imperialism of all kinds of ideological thought. In this sense it is a vibrant and constructive postmodernist move to integrate all our ways of knowing, without again totalizing them in any modernist sense.

Philosophically, transversality implies the distinct move away from the unity and domination of reason, to the pluralization of human rationality.[29] But on this view the plural nature of human reason does not imply that different rationalities now exist independent of one another as incommensurable intellectual domains. In fact, different domains of human rationality, and therefore also different disciplines, while having their own integrity and specific identities are in many ways connected and intertwined.[30] This plurality is non-hierarchical and irreducible, and highlights important differences between various disciplines, even as it opens up the exploration of transversal spaces that allow for the connection of different domains of rationality. And very important for the 'theology and science' dialogue, this also allows for the emergence of paradigmatic interdisciplinary networks, which, although different disciplines in dialogue are never fully integrated, does open up the possibility to learn from one another and, in fact, to actually benefit by taking over insights that are presented in interdisciplinary dialogue.

On this view, transversal rationality facilitates a multiperspectival approach to dialogue, where rationality actually exists in the intersecting connections and transitions between disciplines. In interdisciplinary dialogue, it is precisely these shared domains of rationality, these intersecting, overlapping concerns, that have to be carefully identified. This interwovenness of many different voices opens up spaces for the performance of human cognitive fluidity at work, revealing the interdisciplinary conversation as transitional and interrelational, and the performance of human rationality as transversal. Wolfgang Welsch puts a related idea quite succinctly: transversal rationality is rationality in movement; it is an ability, a skill, and as such is dynamically realized in these interactive processes.[31] As such, transversal rationality exists in what Bakhtin has called the chronotopical moment, the here and now where time and space are intrinsically connected.[32] In this interdisciplinary sense, then, rationality *happens*! And hence this way of thinking is, first of all, always concrete, local, and contextual, but then becomes a medium that points beyond local context to transdisciplinary conversation. Its initial perspectives are highly contextual, but its performances transcend the local and the concrete and facilitate interdisciplinarity.

In revisioning interdisciplinary activity as a form of *transversal reasoning*, then, human rationality is no longer seen as an isolated and austere form of reasoning, but as a practical skill that enables us to gather and bind together the patterns of all our daily experiences, and then make sense of them through communal, interactive dialogue.[33] Moreover, the notion of transversality enables us to honor precisely the non-hierarchical asymmetry between theology and the sciences, and to see human reason as dynamic and practical as we use it to converse with one another through critical interpretation, dialogue, and rhetoric. The notion of transversality thus moves interdisciplinary dialogue to a new and cutting-edge position and identifies the creative mutual interaction of the multileveled dialogue between theology and the sciences as different but equally legitimate ways of looking at the world.

True, interdisciplinary reflection in theology and science will therefore be achieved when the conversation proceeds not in terms of imposed 'universal' rules, nor in terms of purely *ad hoc* rules, but in terms of the intersubjective agreements we reach through persuasive rhetoric and responsible judgments, and where both the strong personal convictions so typical of Christian commitment and the public voice of theology are acknowledged in cross-disciplinary conversation. On this view, Christian theology should be able to claim a 'democratic presence' in interdisciplinary conversation. On this view, theology will share in interdisciplinary standards of rationality, which, although always contextually and socially shaped, will not be hopelessly culture- and context-bound. On this view, too, theology could become an equal partner in a democratic, interdisciplinary conversation with the sciences, where an authentic Christian voice might actually be heard in a very pluralist situation. This kind of theology will share in interdisciplinary standards of rationality, even as we respect our widely divergent personal, religious, or disciplinary viewpoints, and the integrity of our widely diverse disciplines.

In my own most recent work, then, I have argued for a revisioning of theology's public voice as a necessary epistemological requirement for successful interdisciplinary dialogue; for the clearing of an interdisciplinary space where not only very diverse and pluralist forms of theological reflection, but also science and other disciplines might explore shared concerns and discover possible overlapping epistemological patterns in an ongoing interdisciplinary conversation. A postfoundationalist notion of rationality thus enables us to communicate across boundaries and to move transversally from context to context, from one tradition to another, from one discipline to another. The tentative and mutual interdisciplinary understanding that we achieve through this I have named, following various other scholars, a *wide reflective equilibrium*.[34] This 'wide reflective equilibrium' points to the optimal problem-solving, the fragile communal understanding, we are capable of in any given moment in time. It never implies complete consensus, but it does exemplify the fragile accomplishments of our interpersonal and interdisciplinary communication, a sense of mutual agreement and of 'not being puzzled anymore'.[35] As such, it also establishes the necessity of a multiplicity of voices and perspectives in our ongoing processes of mutual assessment.

In the 'wide reflective equilibrium' of communal agreement, scientists and theologians who are deeply committed to the 'theology and science' dialogue may finally find the safe but fragile public space we have been searching for, a space for shuttling back and forth between deep personal convictions and the scientific and theological criteria that finally result from responsible interpersonal dialogue. Francis Schüssler Fiorenza has eloquently captured this postfoundationalist strategy by stating that, through a back and forth movement, the communicative strategy of reflective equilibrium seeks to bring into balance or equilibrium the principles reconstructed from practice with the ongoing practice itself.[36] On this view, also in theology and science, our already agreed-upon principles, criteria, and background theories provide a critical, independent constraint that prevents these principles from being mere generalizations of our contextual judgments and practices, while at the same time these principles can be critically questioned as well. Aiming for a wide reflective equilibrium as an epistemic goal of interdisciplinary dialogue is, finally, truly postfoundationalist and non-hierarchical because no one disciplinary voice, and no one set of judgments, practices, or principles, will be able to claim absolute priority over, or to be foundational for, any other. On the contrary, on this view interdisciplinarity is achieved when different disciplinary voices successfully manage to identify mutual concerns in shared transversal spaces and use these moments of intersection between theology and other disciplines as the key to interdisciplinary conversation.

The most challenging aspect of an interdisciplinary dialogue between theology and the sciences, however, may be for theology to lift up the specific limitations of this conversation. This implies a quite specific appeal from theology to the sciences: an appeal for a sensitivity to that which is particular to the broader, non-empirical or philosophical dimensions of theological discourse. This kind of disciplinary integrity means that Christian theology has an obligation to explore conceptual problems that are not empirically accessible. As we saw, my argument for interdisciplinarity has been precisely about the fact that Christian theology is answerable to canons of inquiry defensible within the various domains of our common discourse. And in this open, interdisciplinary dialogue we can learn that criteria for conceptual problem-solving, whether in theology or the sciences, should never be the sole possession of a single perspective or discipline. Because of the transversal rationality of interdisciplinary discourse, not only shared problems and common concerns, but also criteria from other reasoning strategies can indeed be appropriated between disciplines as diverse as theology and the sciences. It is precisely to this kind of creative mutual interaction that Robert John Russell's work now powerfully points us.

Notes

1 Robert John Russell, 'Bodily Resurrection, Eschatology, and Scientific Cosmology: The Mutual Interaction of Christian Theology and Science', in *Resurrection: Theological and Scientific Assessments*, ed. by Ted Peters, Robert John Russell, and Michael Welker (Grand Rapids, MI: Wm. B. Eerdmans, 2002), 3–30.

2 Ibid.

3 Ibid., 4.

4   Ibid., 10.

5   Ibid., 4.

6   See J. Wentzel van Huyssteen, *The Shaping of Rationality: Toward Interdisciplinarity in Theology and Science* (Grand Rapids, MI: Wm. Eerdmans Publishing Company, 1999), and van Huyssteen, *Alone in the World? Science and Theology on Human Uniqueness*, The Gifford Lectures (Grand Rapids, MI: Wm. B. Eerdmans, 2006).

7   Russell, 'Bodily Resurrection, Eschatology, and Scientific Cosmology', 4.

8   Ibid., 11.

9   Ibid.

10 Ibid., 12.

11 See also Delwin Brown, *Boundaries of Our Habitations: Tradition and Theological Construction* (New York: SUNY Press, 1994), 4ff.

12 Russell, 'Bodily Resurrection, Eschatology, and Scientific Cosmology', 13.

13 Ibid., 16.

14 Ibid.

15 Ibid., 17.

16 Ibid.

17 Ibid.

18 Van Huyssteen, *The Shaping of Rationality*, and van Huyssteen, *Alone in the World?*

19 Van Huyssteen, *Alone in the World?*

20 Russell, 'Bodily Resurrection, Eschatology, and Scientific Cosmology'.

21 See van Huyssteen, *The Shaping of Rationality*, 235ff., and Jean-Pierre Changeux and Paul Ricoeur, *What Makes Us Think? A Neuroscientist and Philosopher Argue About Ethics, Human Nature, and the Brain* (Princeton, NJ: Princeton University Press, 2000), 4.

22 Changeux and Ricoeur, *What Makes Us Think?*, 25.

23 Ibid., 87.

24 Van Huyssteen, *The Shaping of Rationality*.

25 Brown, *Boundaries of Our Habitations*, 55ff.

26 Van Huyssteen, *The Shaping of Rationality*, 135–9; 247–50.

27 Steven Mithen, *The Prehistory of the Mind: The Cognitive Origins of Art, Religion and Science* (London: Thames & Hudson, 1996) 70ff., 136ff.

28 Donald Capps, 'The Lesson of Art Theory for Pastoral Theology', *Pastoral Psychology*, 47 (May 1999): 332ff.

29 Wolfgang Welsch, *Vernunft: Die Zeitgenössige Vernunftkritik und das Konzept der transversalen Vernunft* (Frankfurt am Main: Suhrkamp Taschenbuch, 1996), 432ff., 603f.

30 Ivica Novakovic, 'Theology: Speculative or Combinatorial?' (PhD diss., Princeton Theological Seminary, 2004), 159ff.

31 Welsch, *Vernunft*, 764.

32 M. M. Bakhtin, *The Dialogic Imagination: Four Essays* (Austin, TX: University of Texas Press, 1981), 84; see also Calvin Schrag, *The Resources of Rationality* (Bloomington & Indianapolis, IN: Indiana University Press, 1992), 83ff.

33 Schrag, *The Resources of Rationality*, 148ff.

34 See van Huyssteen, *The Shaping of Rationality*, 277ff.; see also Eberhard Herrmann, 'Rationality, Warrant and Reflective Equilibrium', in *Reflective Equilibrium: Essays in Honour of Robert Heeger*, ed. by Wilbren Van den Burg and Theo van Willigenburg (Kluwer: Dordrecht, 1998), 103–14.

35 Herrmann, 'Rationality, Warrant and Reflective Equilibrium', 104.

36 Francis Schüssler Fiorenza, *Foundational Theology: Jesus and the Church* (New York: Crossroad, 1984), 301f.

CHAPTER SIX

The Sciences and the Religions: Some Preliminary East Asian Reflections on Christian Theology of Nature

Heup Young Kim

> The rise of science in the nineteenth century induced a revision in Christian theology – what has sometimes been called the second Reformation. Some may think that Canon Warren exaggerates, but at least he calls attention to the seriousness of the new challenge, when he says that the impact of agnostic science will turn out to have been as child's play compared to the challenge to Christian theology of the faith of other men.[1]

This well-known passage of Wilfred Cantwell Smith, a forerunner of global or 'world theology', though exaggerated as he admitted, contains an undeniable truth about the value of non-Christian religions in relation to science that Christian theology should take seriously.[2] Nonetheless, Christian theologians participating in contemporary dialogue between science and *religion* do not seem to listen to this prophetic warning of a wise person of the West as carefully as it deserves. Rather, most of them still seem to stick to the 'child's play', ignoring the irreversible reality of a 'religiously plural world'. Science and religion dialogue remains a Western phenomenon.

In what follows, I would like to file a criticism of the agenda set by the Center for Theology and the Natural Sciences. What CTNS sees as a gulf to be bridged between science and religion is but a narrow stream compared to the wide ocean that separates the myopia of Christian theology from the broad vision of a global theology which acknowledges plurality of the world's religions. For *Science and Religion* to deal with the reality of pluralism among cultures and religions, we need to advance to a dialogue between *The Sciences and The Religions*.

Instead of addressing Robert John Russell directly, in this chapter I shall engage his teacher, Ian G. Barbour. Even though Barbour identifies his own work in terms of an engagement between science and religion, his domain, in fact, is only science and Christian theology. I will offer a critique of this unnecessarily narrow position. Then I will propose a constructive alternative oriented around understanding nature through East Asian eyes, from the vantage point of the *Tao*.

The Myth of the Bridge

The child's play of the science–theology dialogue is vividly manifested in a popular metaphor of 'building bridges between religion and science'.[3] This dramatic but romantic metaphor is not so much convincing as it is awkward and mystifying to Koreans and East Asian people. For it was in fact *science* that attracted these people when Western missionaries came to East Asia to plant their churches in this strange world with complex histories of multiple East Asian religions. In this non-Christian world, Christianity was first welcomed because of the formidable power and impressive advantages of modern science that Euro-American missionaries brought with them. Because of this, East Asians are accustomed to viewing science as an inseparable part of Christianity. A number of missionaries explicitly utilized science as the means to indicate the superiority of Christian faith and Western civilization and accordingly the need for Christian conversion for true salvation and superior civilization, the intention of which was not innocent of Western imperialism. The most famous example was Matteo Ricci (1552–1610), who introduced 'the emerging physical sciences' as 'the foundation for the Christian faith and the revelation of Jesus Christ'.[4] His translations of science classics such as Euclid's *Elements of Geometry* were intended as a tool for his Catholic mission in China.

To a people with this historical experience, it is not so much a description of reality as a quixotic myth that science and Christian theology are the two great worlds divided by a big ocean, desperately requiring a bridge to connect them. On the contrary, they see them as two phenomena of the same world. In fact, they recognize the existence of a really great ocean separating their world (the East) and the Christian world (the West, more precisely the Occident). They do not perceive the same great ocean between science and Christian theology, as some Western scholars romantically fantasize, but only some rivers.

Furthermore, they notice the pre-existence of bridges across those rivers between the two children Jerusalem and Athens. Hence, to their eyes, it would be not so much a matter of 'creating' or 'building' original bridges as of 'rehabilitating' damaged bridges, 'repairing' broken bridges, 'renovating' old bridges, or 'adding' fancy new bridges. From this vantage point, 'creating bridges' is a misleading metaphor that does not fit the reality of global religious history and the contemporary geography of world religions. The bridge metaphor would be far more convincing and appropriate *when sciences meet non-Christian or, more broadly, non-monotheistic religions.* That is to say, *where sciences really meet religions!*

Ian G. Barbour is without doubt a great leader ('the doyen', '*the* pioneer', or 'the dean') in the dialogue between religion and science, a most important theological movement in this century.[5] Many scholars in this movement praise him as a (or the most) significant 'creator' or builder of bridges between science and theology, as evidenced in the CTNS *Festschrift* celebrating his fifty years in this field.[6] Although Barbour was born and spent his childhood in Beijing, to my East Asian mind his thought, a prototype of science and religion discourse, still preserves some remnants of the myth of bridges. In this chapter, as I admire his contributions greatly, I will juxtapose some important themes from an East Asian perspective that Western studies in religion and science, represented by Barbour's theology of nature, have missed, neglected, and dealt with insufficiently.

Christian Theology versus the World's Religions

Barbour's works are valuable first and foremost as a seminal interdisciplinary study between natural sciences and *Christian theology*. His 'classic' typology, 'four views of science and religion', is an analysis of the relationship between science and theology exclusively in the Christian context, as its central arguments are in defense of traditional Christian theism and in the division between natural theology and the theology of nature.[7] Hence, the title of his celebrated book *When Science Meets Religion* is something of a misnomer (likewise, his work *Religion and Science*). The book should have been titled *When Science Meets Christian Theology* or *When Science Meets Theology* (likewise, *Theology and Science*). This unfortunate misnomer is *religiously* offensive and 'politically incorrect' from the vantage point of the geography of world religions as well as of the political economy of language in the twenty-first century. With this phraseology, Barbour could not avoid the criticism that he views science and religion dialogue as a Western, Christian project.

   Conflict is the first model and a major underlying theme of Barbour's typology, which shows that his thought is culturally influenced. Whereas the history of the religiously homogeneous West (Occident) is filled with bloody religious wars and conflicts, such a religious warfare is ironically uncommon in the history of religiously plural East Asia. In this world of *harmony*, exemplified by the *yin–yang* relationship, neither was there serious conflict between science and religion.[8] In fact, *conflict* is a more Western concept based on Greek *dialectical* dualism.[9] In this world of *jen* (or *ren*, being-in-togetherness), the habit of the negative golden rule 'not to do to others what you would not want them to do to you' is more appreciated, as 'epistemological modesty' and 'ethical *humility*' are crucial virtues; to treat others as 'guests' or 'friends' to bring harmony in the world. The habit of the positive golden rule 'to love others *in your own ways*', as preferred in the Christian West, is carefully avoided because it could cause the opposite attitudes of 'epistemological immodesty' and 'ethical *hubris*', the tendency to treat others as 'strangers' or 'enemies' in a conflict complex (*Enemies, Strangers, or Partners*).[10] These erroneous attitudes had been a root cause for the modern failure of the arrogant Western Christian mission in the East. Theologians in science and religion dialogue, including Barbour, seem not to be fully liberated from these habits of epistemological immodesty and ethical hubris.

   As both religion and science are culturally dependent, 'the relationship between science and religion is profoundly culture-dependent'. Hence, Yong Sik Kim is right to continue, 'Understanding the science–religion relationship in China cannot be achieved by checking the presence or absence of those religious concepts, practices, groups, and links that were relevant in the Western scientific development (*as if the relation that developed in the West could be the only kind of relation that religion can have with science*). Study of the relationship in China should examine different kinds of relationship that were meaningful in the context of Chinese science, religion and society.'[11] Although China was his birthplace, Barbour does not seem to have discerned these 'different kinds of relationship' and the contemporary reality of religious pluralism in the post-Christian world beyond his 'Western bias'.[12] His 'methodological breakthrough' also has greater plausibility in the context of Christian theology.[13]

Suspicion, not Consonance

Methodological 'consonance' between science and religion is nothing new to the people in East Asia. So, striving for consonance looks like a genetic consequence for the two children of the same parents, the Christian father and the Greek mother (or vice versa).[14] Metaphorically, they are family members in *the same forest*. Scholars in the science and religion dialogue seem to be reluctant to leave their old home in the forest to see the outer world with new vistas and challenges of 'other religions'. Remaining in the forest and claiming theirs as *the* dialogue of science and religion is a suspicious attitude, vulnerable to a disguised, high-tech, missiological, and political plot for evangelism and cultural imperialism for the perpetuation of the Christian and Western hegemony.[15]

In this regard, it is appropriate and necessary to employ a 'hermeneutics of critique and suspicion', a theological method for contemporary Christian theology, in contemporary science and religion dialogue in order to overcome the 'social optimism' and politico-cultural naïvety that it seems to hold (for example, the bridge metaphor).[16]

An immediate and profound issue for carrying out a genuine science and *religion* dialogue is how to include the wisdom of the other world religions in the discussion, as suggested by some participants in the dialogue.[17] However, the question is whether there really is any space open for non-Christian religions or Christian theologies beyond the Western walls to be part of the dialogue, still conceived as domestic affairs within the same Western forest (the doyen is still doing that!).[18] For example, the yet-to-be prevailing debates on theism such as the existence of God, divine design, and natural theology are important but are *only* theological issues. In the interreligious or religiously plural context, it is unwise and presumptuous to continue those stereotypical issues of the missionary era as the governing themes of the dialogue between science and *religion*.

In 'the third epoch' of World Christianity, Asian and African Christians now know that God has many names beyond traditionally Westernized Christian categories, concepts, narratives, metaphors, and symbols.[19] While criticizing the material or physical reductionism of science, ironically Barbour also seems to commit to a religious reductionism, a shrinking of the grand magnitude of global Christian theology for the third millennium into the scale of traditional theism in the modern West. He writes, 'Theism, in short, is not inherently in conflict with science, but it does conflict with a metaphysics of materialism.'[20] But this is not so much a helpfully perceptive statement from the perspective of interreligious dialogue and global Christian theology. For materialism and theism refer to axiomatic presuppositions ('belief systems') for the natural sciences and Christian theology, as Barbour himself agrees.[21]

Diversity within Christian Theology

To me, an East Asian constructive theologian, Barbour's theology looks conservative with no hint of proper hermeneutics of suspicion; it is politically naïve and problematically old-fashioned. What is lacking in his thought, first of all, is the complex issue of 'knowledge and power'; borrowing his favorite idiom, 'a critical realism' of *power*.[22] David Tracy stated well, 'There is no innocent interpretation, no unambiguous tradition, no history-less, subject-less interpreter, no abstract, general situation, no method to guarantee certainty.'[23] Through Barbour, however, the old dogma seems to have returned again as a central player in the game of religion and science dialogue.

His theology consists of an intriguing synthesis of two contradictory traditions, Barthian neo-Orthodoxy and Whiteheadian process philosophy. The former seems to constitute the theological side (faith) of his thought, while the latter the metaphysical side (science). The point of departure for his theology is his faith commitment in line with neo-Orthodox doctrines: 'As I see it, neo-orthodoxy rightly stresses the centrality of Christ and the prominence of Scripture in the Christian tradition.'[24] But Barbour usually concludes his thought in line with process theology, as he finds it 'helpful' in his 'attempt to integrate scientific and religious concepts'.[25] These two sides are always in tension in his thought and reveal a self-contradictory aspect of his theology.

An example of what I mean is found in his distinction between natural theology and the theology of nature. For a process theologian would not need such a distinction of a *metaphysical* natural theology and a *constructive* theology of nature. His theology of nature seems to begin in accordance with the classic definition of theology, *fides quaerens intellectum* (faith seeking understanding). However, tensions occur when he reduces the *intellectum* to process metaphysics. At this juncture, the pendulum of his thought swings to the opposite direction, the process side. A neo-Orthodox theologian whose aim is to overcome the neo-Calvinist's fallacy of propositional reductionism with respect to the Word-event of God would dislike metaphysics. Moreover, it is noteworthy that a more profound dimension of *intellectum* in the contemporary development of Christian theology is not so much in the field of metaphysics (a theory) as in hermeneutics (an interpretation).

Further, Barbour engages in an apologetics in defense of traditional theism, an attitude also seemingly self-contradictory to the neo-Orthodox propensity in his theology of nature (not a metaphysical theism, but a faith proclamation!).[26] As already noted by Paul Tillich, the argument for the doctrine of a 'personal

God' is not so helpful and effective in this age of ecological crisis when the anthropomorphic and anthropocentric nature of Christianity is under serious attack from many sides.[27] Barbour classifies Ralph Burhoe's evolutionary naturalism as a conflict model, because he thinks 'Burhoe's view of the impersonal system of nature seems to conflict with the Christian understanding of a loving, personal God who transcends nature.'[28] This somewhat odd statement clearly shows Barbour's conservative Christian prejudices toward the personal God and the natural–supernatural dualism. If his process theism of nature (a theological integration of science) is a model of integration (methodologically), why cannot Burhoe's evolutionary naturalism of religion (a scientific integration of theology) also be so, yet should be regarded as a conflict model? In this classification, Barbour's typology does not seem to be so much a descriptive analysis as a dogmatic judgment of his theological position.

His tireless endeavors in finding things in science 'not incompatible with some forms of theism' are neither fertile nor so encouraging.[29] In danger of the categorical superimposition and the 'fallacy of displaced concreteness', this sort of apologetic attitude hinders a genuine dialogue.[30] Moreover, theology does not need to defend its theistic faith against science or to beg science for an endorsement. God does not need to earn the proofs of his existence from the natural sciences!

Furthermore, postmodern, feminist, ecological, third-world, Latin-American liberation, Asian, and African theologies have fervently criticized the patriarchal, modern, rational, white, male, first-world privatization and reductionism of Christian theology. With Christian theology moving into the third millennium, a macro 'paradigm change' is in progress.[31] The aged dogmatics such as neo-Orthodoxy and the first-world systematic theologies are under suspicion and revision, while the 'winds of the Spirit' are in favor of 'constructive theology'.[32] Moreover, no contemporary and future Christian theologies can ignore Asian and African theologies with 'the rise of new Christianity' where 'the myth of Western Christianity' is completely wrecked and Euro-American Christianity no longer occupies the center but becomes only a *minority* of global Christianity.[33]

Interreligious Dialogue as a Central Theme of Global Christian Theology

Most significantly, Barbour does not pay proper attention to the interreligious dimension of contemporary Christian theology, though he perpetuates the use of the term 'religion' in the place of Christianity or theology.[34] Religious pluralism has been spreading even more speedily, broadly, and seriously than Smith had predicted. Interreligious encounter is not only a global phenomenon, but has also become a local affair in the heart of Western Christianity. In major Western cities such as London, Paris, Amsterdam, New York, Los Angeles, Chicago, and San Francisco, any person can witness Buddhist Zen centers and people practicing T'ai-chi (Taiji), Taoism, and Confucianism (for example, Boston Confucianism).[35] In this religiously plural situation, whatever name it has, whether interreligious dialogue, interfaith dialogue, comparative theology, or the theology of religion, it is a significant feature of contemporary Christian theology that one cannot ignore. Tracy was correct to recognize that 'dialogue among religions is no longer a luxury but a theological necessity.'[36] More directly, 'It is dialogue or die.'[37]

In fact, religion and science dialogue can learn much from the experiences of interreligious dialogue and the wisdom of East Asian religions. As I have suggested elsewhere, a successful dialogue for theologians can constitute two methodological stages, namely 'a descriptive–comparative stage' (interreligious dialogue) and 'a normative–constructive stage' (theology of religion).[38] In the light of Barbour's typology, these two stages can be called simply 'dialogue' and 'integration'. Unlike an opaque distinction in the typology, however, dialogue and integration here refer to two different hermeneutical moments. In this first stage, one should take 'an attitude of *reverence*' in order to respect views and presuppositions that the other partners hold (that is, an epistemological modesty).[39] One should be careful of one's innate proclivity to superimpose one's categorical schema on others – be descriptive, not prescriptive!. Otherwise, one cannot promote genuine dialogue but falls into a 'fallacy of misplaced concreteness'. A fruitful dialogue may compel one to have the courage to make an *epoche*, 'faithful agnosticism', or a bracketing-off of one's own a priori axioms.[40]

In this stage of dialogue, such an apologetics for theistic persuasion as Barbour employs is not so much an effective strategy as a risk, because it can lead to the suspicion that the purpose of the dialogue is *de facto* an extended version of Christian exclusivism or a crafty plot for mission and cultural imperialism. In this descriptive moment, a theologian should be self-critical and self-suspicious so as to overcome the missiological habits of epistemological immodesty and ethical hubris. In deep humility and even with courage to bracket off one's own theological agenda, as in the dialogue with the other religions, should one open one's heart to listen to the narratives that new discoveries of natural sciences expose about the mystery of God, humanity, and the cosmos as closely as possible.

In the second stage, however, theologians have the complete freedom to do a constructive theology for themselves and their own Christian communities. In this theological moment, Barbour's proposal for the 'theology of nature' is appropriate, but only with the understanding that no theology is *creatio ex nihilo* and without limits. A theology is inevitably constructed on the basis of a theologian's limited religio-cultural experiences in their particular social location, so that a theology so conceived carries over inexorably the prejudices and limitations of the theologian who constructs it.

Where do Sciences really meet Religions?

A comparison of two different traditions in terms of concepts, methodology, or metaphysics is beneficial for certain comparative studies, but also suspicious. For often it does not progress beyond an armchair scholar's mind game to search for a phenomenological parallel or proof texts of one's dogma and agenda in (or one's cultural strength or hegemony over) the other tradition (or culture). Particularly, the historical consequences of the latter by the Christian West have been devastating, as Orientalism and post-colonial criticisms have exposed.[41] Therefore, I am proposing to seek a more concrete locus for the dialogue between the partners from different religious traditions and scholarly paradigms elsewhere than in such a metaphysical conceptuality.

In this twenty-first century, the era of science, theologians ought to accept the natural sciences as grand narratives for humanity that are as valuable as religious traditions. They need to regard an encounter between science and religion as a 'fusion of hermeneutical horizons'.[42] In this encounter, theologians should make the utmost effort, with 'an attitude of *respect* and epistemological modesty', to listen attentively to the voices and stories that contemporary sciences are revealing about the mystery of life, humanity, and the cosmos. In this moment of listening, scientific proofs for the existence of God, the divine design, or the purpose and the *telos* of the life system are not primary subject matters. After all, the goal of scientific narratives lies also in the quest for the way of life to attain full humanity in a new techno-scientific situation. The real meeting-point between science and religion, therefore, is not so much in an abstract metaphysics or a methodology of parallelism, but in a hermeneutics (not just an epistemology) of the human person, the way of life, or more concretely the ortho-praxis of humanization, that is, how to be fully human.

Here is the Confucian wisdom – not a speculative postulation for unverifiable supernatural knowledge, but a pragmatic embodiment of practical wisdom for common humanity. In this regard, Hans Küng made a helpful correction. With the rejection of the generally accepted dipolar view (Middle Eastern and Indian religions), he argued for a tripolar view of world religions. The East Asian religions of Confucianism and Taoism should be regarded as 'a third independent religious river system' of sapiential character, 'equal in value' and in contrast to 'the first great river system, of Semitic origin and prophetic character' (Judaism, Christianity, and Islam) and 'the second great river system, of Indian origin and mystical character' (Hinduism, Buddhism, and others).[43]

Hence, Confucianism as a wisdom tradition does not situate its primary focus in a theoretical speculation, though that is constitutive, too, but on learning the *Tao* (*Dao*, the way in the unity of theory and praxis) of wisdom to attain full humanity.[44] The principal aim of Confucian investigation resides not so much in the formulation of metaphysics or speculative theory, but in the enlightenment of the *Tao* toward the embodiment of the ortho-praxis of human life (right living). Confucianism argues that one can achieve the embodiment of the *Tao* through one's individually and collectively rigorous practice of self-cultivation in the 'concrete-universal' network of relationships under the direction of the *Tao* of wisdom.[45]

Sanctification is a doctrine of Christian theology homologically equivalent to this Confucian teaching of self-cultivation. Hence, I have argued that an ideal locus for the dialogue between Confucianism and Christianity is not metaphysics, psychology, or the philosophy of religion, though these are important, but a faith in radical humanization (more related to the ortho-praxis or spirituality), namely self-cultivation and sanctification.[46] In a similar manner, I am proposing that an ideal locus for the dialogue between science and religion lies not so much in a metaphysical theory, a phenomenological parallelism, or technical knowledge, but in the common human quest for the *Tao* to cultivate and sanctify our scientific and religious knowledge to form a *practical* wisdom through mutual self-criticism and self-transformation.[47] Then, the issue of how to transform new scientific knowledge and technologies (data) into practical wisdom for the *Tao* of life in the 'socio-cosmic' network of relationships in the unity of social and ecological concerns becomes a *koan* (an evocative point of departure) for science and religion dialogue.[48] That is to say, the *koan* for science and religion dialogue is how to transform new discoveries in the natural sciences into useful wisdom for humanity toward a *new cosmic humanity* in order to embody the *Tao* of life fully into the socio-cosmic web of the universe, transcending the uncontrollable greed of commercialism and unlimited selfish desires for convenience. Without doubt, this *koan* refers to spirituality.

Some Preliminary Reflections from an East Asian Perspective

The possibility of mutual self-transformation, self-cultivation, and sanctification contains a constructive suggestion that East Asian interreligious dialogue can make the advancement of dialogue between the sciences and the religions. By learning and adding the insights of interreligious dialogue and East Asian religions, science and religion dialogue could progress beyond its current confinement in the isolated Christian temporality (*when* science meets religion) toward the real, religiously plural globe (*where* science*s* really meet religion*s*). Hence, it is imperative for science and religion dialogue to include dimensions and insights of interreligious dialogue in the discussion in order to make *genuine sciences and religions dialogues* in a real global sense (and so formulate a global Christian theology of nature or science). Here (*where* science*s* *really* meet religion*s*) are some of my preliminary reflections for future studies:

1 The primary locus for dialogue between the sciences and the religions should not be about theoretical metaphysics (knowledge), but about the *Tao* (way) of life (*wisdom*) in the common quest for a new cosmic humanity through mutual self-transformation; that is, through self-cultivation and sanctification. I have elaborated on this theme above.

2 The distinction between *inter*-religious dialogue and *intra*-religious dialogue is helpful for science and religion dialogue.[49] The prime purpose for dialogue is neither to formulate apologetics for one's hypothesis, theory, or system of thought, nor to proselytize dialogue partners, but for mutual learning and growth through self-criticism, cross-examination, and self-transformation.

3 The East Asian notions of *nothingness, vacuity,* and *emptiness* are worth serious consideration for the dialogue, as the reality of Non-Being becomes

plausible in both the new physics and Christian theology.[50] The conception of God as the 'Absolute Nothingness' might be a theological strategy better and more profound than the notion of *kenosis*, an inevitable logical consequence of the conservative doctrines of a personal God and divine omnipotence to solve the problem of theodicy (that is, from Non-Being to Being versus from Being to Non-Being). When criticizing scientific materialism, theologians in the dialogue do not seem to be free from the deep-seated habits of essentialism and substantialism, a plausible cause of materialism. Process theology's theme of 'becoming' seems not to be a good option either because its basis is unavoidably associated with a metaphysical dualism ('the dipolar God') of being ('entity'). A contemplation of nothingness would yield a better alternative to overcome this fundamental dilemma of the modern, Western mode of theological thinking (cf. the apophatic tradition of Christian spirituality and the negative theology of *via negativa*).[51]

4   The traditional Christian notion of linear time and the supremacy of time, still operative in the theology and science dialogue (that is, *when* science meets religion), should be scrutinized in the light of new physics and East Asian religious thoughts that underscore *the significance of space*. The logic of causality in Western thought, still prevailing in the dialogue, should be re-evaluated by the possibility of '*synchronicity*', a conceptual foundation of East Asian thought, *I-Ching*.[52]

5   The traditional Christian (or Greek) understanding of 'nature', customary in the dialogue, is problematic, because it cannot avoid the pejorative connotation inherited by the hierarchical dualism between the supernatural and the natural. The notion of *kenosis* (self-empting to be natural) is a helpful but insufficient alternative, because it still holds the vestiges of dualism and definitional ambiguity. Hence, it is worth taking into consideration the profound Taoist insights of nature and *wu-wei* (cf. 'let it be itself').[53] In Chinese characters, nature means '*self-so*', 'spontaneity', or 'naturalness'; that is, 'the effective modality of the system that informs the actions of the agents that compose it'.[54] In other words, *nature* in East Asian thought is the primary 'self-so' (natural) manifestation of the *Tao*. Natural science in Chinese denotes 'self-so' science, at least in the lexicography, so that it does not refer to mere knowledge but to wisdom. In the Bible, nature as God's creation is 'good', and the denial of its goodness as 'self-so' was in fact a fallacy of Gnosticism. With an enhanced clarification of the ambiguous English term 'nature', Barbour's project for the 'theology of *nature*' would make more sense.

Notes

1   Wilfred Cantwell Smith, 'The Christian in a Religiously Plural World', in *Christianity and Other Religions*, ed. by John Hick and Brian Hebblethwaite (Philadelphia, PA: Fortress Press, 1980), 91.

2   See Wilfred Cantwell Smith, *Towards a World Theology: Faith and the Comparative History of Religion* (Maryknoll: Orbis, 1981).

3   W. Mark Richardson and Wesley J. Wildman, 'General Introduction', in *Religion and Science: History, Method, Dialogue*, ed. by Richardson and Wildman (New York and London: Routledge, 1996), xi–xiii.

4   Scott W. Sunquist (ed.), *A Dictionary of Asian Christianity* (Grand Rapids, MI: William B. Eerdmans Publishing Co., 2001), 703, 703–5. See also Jacques Gernet, *China and the Christian Impact: A Conflict of Culture*, trans. by Janet Lloyd (Cambridge: Cambridge University Press, 1985), 20–22, 57–63.

5   John Polkinghorne and Robert J. Russell, 'Acclaims', in *When Science Meets Religion: Enemies, Strangers, or Partners?*, by Ian G. Barbour (San Francisco: HarperSanFrancisco, 2000); Ian G. Barbour, *Nature, Human Nature, and God* (Minneapolis, MN: Fortress Press, 2002), back cover.

6   Robert John Russell (ed.), *Fifty Years in Science and Religion: Ian G. Barbour and His Legacy* (Aldershot: Ashgate, 2004); see Robert John Russell, 'Ian Barbour's Methodological Breakthrough: Creating the "Bridge" between Science and Theology', in *Fifty Years in Science and Religion*, 45–59.

7   For a summary of the typology, see Ian G. Barbour, *Religion and Science: Historical and Contemporary Issues* (San Francisco: HarperSanFrancisco, 1997), 7–38; also Barbour, *When Science Meets Religion*, 1–38. 'Conflict', the basis of his typology, virtually denotes 'incompatibility' 'with any form of theism' (*When Science Meets Religion*, 2). For the division between natural theology and the theology of nature, see *Religion and Science*, 98–105; *When Science Meets Religion*, 27–38.

8   See Yong Sik Kim, 'Some Reflections on Science and Religion in Traditional China', *Journal of the Korean History of Science Society*, 7:1 (December 1985): 40–49.

9   Cf. Shu-hsien Liu and Robert E. Allinson, *Harmony and Strife: Contemporary Perspectives, East & West* (Hong Kong: The Chinese University Press, 1988).

10   See Robert E. Allinson, 'The Ethics of Confucianism & Christianity: the Delicate Balance', *Ching Feng*, 33:3 (1990): 158–75.

11   Y. Kim, 'Some Reflections', 44. Italics are mine.

12   Barbour, *When Science Meets Religion*, 5–6. Cf. Christopher Southgate et al., *God, Humanity and the Cosmos* (Edinburgh: T. & T. Clark, 1999), 10–12.

13   Russell, 'Ian Barbour's Methodological Breakthrough', 47.

14   Cf. Southgate et al., *God, Humanity and the Cosmos*, 24–7.

15   See Samuel P. Huntington, *The Clash of Civilizations: Remaking of World Order* (New York: Touchstone, 1997).

16   For the hermeneutics of suspicion, see David Tracy, 'Theological Method', in *Christian Theology: An Introduction to Its Traditions and Tasks*, ed. by Peter C. Hodgson and Robert H. King (Minneapolis, MN: Fortress Press, 1994), 36; also David Tracy, *Blessed Rage for Order: The New Pluralism in Theology* (Minneapolis, MN: Seabury Press, 1975), 104, 147, 210. For Barbour's social optimism, see Southgate et al., *God, Humanity and the Cosmos*, 347–8.

17   See Southgate et al., *God, Humanity and the Cosmos*, 13, 226–43, 394.

18   I am concerned here with 'the inherent dominative mode' or 'an exercise of cultural strength'. See Edward W. Said, *Orientalism* (New York: Vintage Books, 1979), 28, 40.

19   See *Proceedings of the Congress of Asian Theologians (CATS), 25 May–1 June 1997, Suwon, Korea*, ed. by Dhyanchand Carr and Philip Wickeri (Hong Kong: Continuation Committee of the Congress of Asian Theologians, 1997–98).

20   Barbour, *Religion and Science*, 82.

21   Barbour seems to agree with this point (see *Nature, Human Nature, and God*, 5).

22   In fact, John Bowker argued, 'the really persistent issue between religion [theology] and science is not so much about different kinds of knowledge claims, but rather one of power'

(in J. Wentzel van Huysteen, 'Foreword', in *God, Humanity, and the Cosmos*, xxii); see John Bowker, *Is God A Virus? Genes, Culture and Religion* (London: SPCK, 1995), 116–17. For the problem of knowledge and power, see Said, *Orientalism*, 15, 24, and 36.

23   Tracy, 'Theological Method', 36.

24   Barbour, *When Science Meets Religion*, 22, also 101 and 160; *Nature, Human Nature, and God*, 3.

25   Barbour, *Nature, Human Nature, and God*, 6, also 101–18. See also *Religion and Science*, 303–32, 293–304; *When Science Meets Religion*, 174–80.

26   As much as he criticizes design arguments as deistic (perhaps from a neo-Orthodox perspective), Barbour needs to explain why his process theology is not so much deistic (or metaphysical) from a similarly coherent perspective. See *When Science Meets Religion*, 114.

27   Barbour, *Religion and Science*, 81.

28   Barbour, *When Science Meets Religion*, 158; see also 157–9.

29   Barbour, *Religion and Science*, 80.

30   Alfred N. Whitehead, *Science and the Modern World* (New York: Macmillan, 1967), especially Chapter III.

31   For example, see Hans Küng, *Theology for the Third Millennium: An Ecumenical View*, trans. by Peter Heinegg (New York: Doubleday, 1988); Hans Küng and David Tracy, *Paradigm Change in Theology: A Symposium for the Future*, trans. by Margaret Köhl (New York: Crossroad, 1989).

32   For example, see Peter C. Hodgson, *Winds of the Spirit: A Constructive Christian Theology* (Louisville, KY: Westminster John Knox Press, 1994).

33   Philip Jenkins, *The Next Christendom: The Coming of Global Christianity* (Oxford: Oxford University Press, 2002), especially 79–105.

34   In numerous places in his writings he also identifies 'theological' or 'Christian' as 'religious' (for example, 'religious experience', 'religious community', 'traditional religious doctrines', in *When Science Meets Religion*, 114, 113). This is offensive to readers outside of Christian and Western traditions.

35   See Robert Cummings Neville, *Boston Confucianism: Portable Tradition in the Late-Modern World* (Albany, NY: State University of New York Press, 2000); Diana L. Eck, *A New Religious America: How a 'Christian Country' Has Become the World's Most Religiously Diverse Nation* (San Francisco: HarperSanFrancisco, 2001).

36   David Tracy, *Dialogue With The Other: The Inter-religious Dialogue*, Louvain Theological & Pastoral Monographs, No. 1 (Louvain: Peeters Press, 1990), 95; also, David Tracy, 'Introduction', 58.

37   Diana L. Eck, *Encountering God: A Spiritual Journey from Bozeman to Banaras* (Boston: Beacon Press, 1993), x.

38   Heup Young Kim, *Wang Yang-ming and Karl Barth: A Confucian–Christian Dialogue* (Lanham, MD: University Press of America, 1996), especially 139–41.

39   The attitude of reverence or respect, important for ecological concern, is a spiritual basis for Confucian (and Neo-Confucian) learning (especially in the Korean Confucianism of Yi T'oe-gye, 1501–70). See Heup Young Kim, *Christ & the Tao* (Hong Kong: Christian Conference of Asia, 2003), 111–16.

40   See David Lochhead, *The Dialogical Imperative: A Christian Reflection on Interfaith Encounter* (Maryknoll: Orbis, 1988), especially 40–45.

41   See Said, *Orientalism*; Bill Ashcroft, Gareth Griffiths, and Helen Tiffin (eds), *The Post-colonial Studies Reader* (London and New York: Routledge, 1995).

42   See Hans-Georg Gadamer, *Truth and Method*, 2nd edn, trans. by Joel Weinsheimer and Donald G. Marshall (New York: Crossroad, 1989).

43   Hans Küng and Julia Ching, *Christianity and Chinese Religions*, trans. by Peter Beyer (New York: Doubleday, 1989), xii–xiii.

44 As a widely used root metaphor of all East Asian religions such as Confucianism, Taoism, and Buddhism, *tao* is a very inclusive term with various connotations. For an example of Confucian definition: 'Tao is a Way, a path, a road, and by common metaphorical extension it becomes in ancient China the right Way of life, the Way of governing, the ideal Way of human existence, the Way of the Cosmos, the generative–normative Way (Pattern, path, course) of existence as such', Herbert Fingarette, *Confucius – The Secular as Sacred* (New York: Harper & Row, 1972), 19.

45 See H. Kim, *Wang Yang-ming and Karl Barth*, 33–6, 171–4.

46 See ibid., 139.

47 The neo-Confucian teaching of *chi-hsing ho-i*, an attribute of the *Tao*, refutes the dualism of knowledge and practice, insisting on their ontological unity (see ibid., 29–32). Cf. Daniel Hardy, 'The God who is with the world', in *Science Meets Faith*, ed. by Fraser Watts (London: SPCK, 1998), 136–7.

48 H. Kim, *Christ & the Tao*, 142–8. I proposed the *Tao* paradigm of theology (*theo-tao*) and Christology (*Christo-tao*) in order to overcome the dualism in contemporary Christian theology between the *logos* model (*theo-logos*; in the context of religion and science dialogue, a metaphysical theology) and the praxis model (*theo-praxis*; in this context, an ecological ethics); see the chapters on *theotao* and *Christotao* in ibid., 135–54, 155–82.

49 See Raimon Panikkar, *The Intrareligious Dialogue* (New York and Ramsey: Paulist Press, 1978).

50 Though simplistic, Fritjof Capra is helpful in this regard. See his *The Tao of Physics: An Exploration of the Parallels Between Modern Physics and Eastern Mysticism*, 2nd edn (Boulder, CO: Shambhala, 1983), especially 208–23.

51 See Heup Young Kim, 'The Word Made Flesh: A Korean Perspective on Ryu Young-mo's Christotao', in *One Gospel – Many Cultures: Case Studies and Reflection on Cross-Cultural Theology*, ed. by Mercy Amba Oduyoye and Hendrik M. Vroom (Amsterdam: Rodopi, 2003), 129–48, especially 143–4; also, H. Kim, *Christ & the Tao*, 155–82, especially 167–72. Cf. Southgate et al., *God, Humanity and the Cosmos*, 43.

52 'Synchronicity takes the coincidence of events in space and time as meaning something more than mere chance, namely, a peculiar interdependence of objective events among themselves as well as the subjective (psychic) states of the observer or observers', C. G. Jung, 'Foreword', in *The I Ching or Book of Changes*, trans. by Richard Wilhelm, 3rd edn (Princeton, NJ: Princeton University Press, 1967), xxiv; see also xxi–xxix.

53 Barbour, *When Science Meets Religion*, 113. Cf. Southgate et al., *God, Humanity, and the Cosmos*, 233–5; Jürgen Moltmann, *God in Creation*, trans. by Margaret Kohl (London: SCM Press, 1985), 87–8; see also Jürgen Moltmann, *Science and Wisdom*, trans. by Margaret Kohl (London: SCM, 2003), Chapter XII. Unfortunately, Moltmann also misunderstood the *Tao* because of his seemingly excessive positivism of 'hope', certainly based on the Western bias of linear time (see ibid., 189).

54 Michael C. Kalton, 'Asian Religious Tradition and Natural Science: Potentials, Present and Future', presentation to the CTNS Korea Religion & Science Workshop, Seoul, Korea, January 18–22, 2002.

II

Quantum Physics and Divine Action

Atoms May Be Small, But They're Everywhere: Robert Russell's Theological Engagement with the Quantum Revolution[1]

Kirk Wegter-McNelly

Among scholars who in recent decades have contributed to the constructive reformulation of theological doctrine in light of contemporary developments in the natural sciences, Robert Russell stands out for his creative efforts to engage the quantum revolution of the twentieth century. Russell is best known for his bold attempt to leverage the standard indeterministic interpretation of quantum theory for a non-interventionist account of objectively special divine action. However, his numerous writings on quantum physics have also probed the theological significance of other aspects of its interpretation, such as complementarity and non-locality. In this essay I review the scope of Russell's long-standing interest in quantum physics and highlight some of the key developments and changes in his thought.

I begin by surveying the first decade of Russell's writings on quantum physics, starting with an essay that appeared in 1984. Next I treat Russell's writings from 1995 to the present, in which he has developed and defended his quantum approach to special divine action. I pay particular attention to his argument for the ubiquity (more recently, 'pervasiveness') of quantum events in the physical order of the world. The notion of a quantum event and the question of its ubiquity are of crucial importance to Russell's argument because they specify his more general claim that quantum indeterminism provides room in the world for God to act specially as frequently or infrequently as God desires without needing to violate its divinely given economy in the process (all the while, of course, acting generally to sustain the world in existence).

One important objection that has been raised against Russell's argument for the possibility of God acting through quantum events is that his proposal fails to convince for lack of a clear account of what he means by a 'quantum event'.[2] This objection is motivated by the fact that the meaning of this seemingly straightforward notion has, in fact, been hotly debated by physicists and philosophers of physics, owing to its close conceptual proximity to one of the most vexing and unresolved issues in the study of the foundations of quantum theory, the 'measurement problem'. Russell's efforts to respond to this objection have, in my opinion, not been entirely successful. To remedy this situation, or at least to point out where I think the remedy lies, I conclude by reviewing several recent attempts in the physics literature to solve the measurement problem and clarify the meaning of a quantum event. These proposals show the general direction Russell's research program must take if it is to overcome the charges leveled against it and garner broader support in the future.

Russell's Early Interest in Quantum Physics

Russell's first published thoughts on the theological significance of quantum physics appeared in 1984, shortly after he arrived in Berkeley, California to establish the Center for Theology and the Natural Sciences (CTNS), now an affiliated center of the Graduate Theological Union. In an essay co-authored with Jesuit physicist Andrew Dufner written in response to the environmental crisis of the early 1980s, Russell probed several aspects of contemporary physics – including special and general relativity, quantum physics, conservation laws, energy, and thermodynamics – for resources to help to revitalize the Christian creation tradition.[3]

At the center of Dufner and Russell's discussion of quantum physics lay Niels Bohr's principle of 'complementarity'. Bohr famously argued that in the quantum realm, unlike in the macroscopic realm, descriptions of physical processes in terms of trajectories in space and time and descriptions of those same processes in terms of determinable causes cannot be unified into a single perspective but instead are complementary to one another; in situations where one kind of description applies, the other does not.[4] Dufner and Russell suggested that the limit imposed on causal descriptions of quantum processes by this principle might be not merely an epistemological limit but an ontological one as well. Such a limit, they cautiously claimed, would reflect a 'measure of freedom' in the world that would allow divine and human actors previously unrecognized access to physical processes. In this first of Russell's engagements with quantum physics one can already see the basic strategy of leveraging quantum openness toward a richer account of divine action.

It is interesting to note, however, that Dufner and Russell couched the idea of openness in the language not of indeterminism but of complementarity (that is, in terms of the limit imposed by complementarity on causal descriptions of quantum processes). The concept of causal indeterminism, in the sense of physical processes underdetermining the outcome of individual quantum events, did not enter explicitly into their discussion. It seems possible that they had something like the idea of underdetermination in mind when they commented somewhat obliquely that causality 'does not smoothly effect its results, but only in packets of cause for packets of effects'.[5] But whether they meant by this that one can speak intelligibly of quantum causation only at the statistical and not at the individual level is unclear. In any case, Dufner and Russell tied the idea of quantum openness to the issue of complementarity in a way that Russell would eventually abandon, perhaps in recognition of the argument's rhetorical limitations. Even more sophisticated popular discussions of quantum theory tend to present the idea of complementarity not as Bohr originally did in terms of causal and spacetime descriptions, but in terms of related dual conceptualities such as wave/particle, position/momentum, and time/energy.[6]

Dufner and Russell also found quantum physics theologically and ecologically relevant for what they judged to be its 'thoroughly "organic"' description of physical reality. They felt that such a biologically oriented characterization of composite quantum objects was legitimate because of the strikingly holistic quality of these objects, which manifest properties that are not reducible to the properties of their parts. Careful attention to these objects, they suggested, would lead to a view of the world in which 'the delicacy and dignity of the whole transcends final or exhaustive analysis.'[7] They were hopeful that this view could deepen religious communities' awareness of the connection between humanity and the rest of creation.

In 1985 Russell published an essay on the theological relevance of David Bohm's alternative formulation of quantum theory in an issue of the journal *Zygon* dedicated to Bohm's work.[8] While not uncritical of Bohm's project, Russell offered a sympathetic account of his views. He saw in Bohm a critical realist who wished to affirm the ontological significance of quantum physics against Bohr's allegedly more instrumentalist perspective. Here Russell moved away from the more generous perspective of his previous essay, where no such discomfort with Bohr's views had been voiced.

Russell also chose not to mention the idea of organicism in this essay, but he was clearly taken with the holism of Bohm's formulation. He suggested that the non-local structure of the 'quantum potential' in Bohm's early work and the interconnectedness of the 'implicate order' in his later, more philosophical writings could provide a foundation upon which to construct a theological view of the world as the 'single, whole and yet ongoing creation of God.'[9] Wanting to connect Bohm's work in physics and philosophy to his own theological interests, Russell characterized Bohm's larger project as friendly, at least implicitly, to the notion of God. He interpreted Bohm's argument for the infinitely layered character of the physical world as pointing to a panentheistic and impersonal God enfolded within nature. Although this perspective did not lend itself to supporting Russell's own personal theism, he felt that it might nonetheless be adapted to allow for a God who acts purposively within the uncertainties of quantum processes. He also noted, here for the first time, that already in 1958 Anglican priest and physicist William Pollard had pursued the idea of God acting through quantum openness without violating the laws of nature. But rather than embrace Pollard's 'bottom–up' approach to a physics-friendly account of providence, Russell appeared to favor constructing a view more amenable to Bohm's infinitely layered world in which indeterministic and deterministic levels might well alternate without end.[10] If Bohm were correct, then God's activity should not be thought of as percolating up from the bottom indeterministic rung of nature, so to speak, but as enfolded within each level of nature, whether deterministic or indeterministic.[11]

Two points are worth noting here. First, although the term 'non-interventionism' had not yet entered into Russell's vocabulary, he was obviously impressed by Pollard's development of the idea, notwithstanding his other concerns with Pollard's approach. Second, Russell eventually abandoned Bohm's account of the world's infinitely many layers and instead embraced Pollard's bottom–up approach. Why? I suspect that Russell's initial enthusiasm for Bohm's work was curbed by the steady resistence to Bohm's ideas among his (Russell's) colleagues and the failure of Bohm's alternative formulation to generate a distinctive research agenda, as well as the specter of divine determinism in Bohm's approach.

Following his review of Bohm's work, Russell shifted his focus back to quantum physics more generally in an essay published in the *CTNS Bulletin* that dealt with the implications of quantum theory and relativity theory for a 'theology of nature', a term which Russell borrowed from Ian Barbour.[12] What is most striking about Russell's discussion of quantum physics in this essay is his retreat from the earlier claim (made jointly with Dufner) that Bohr's notion of complementarity could be interpreted ontologically as well as epistemologically. Here, Russell argued that the term reflected the direction of Bohr's larger interpretive program. Because this program confined itself to epistemological matters, it was therefore 'incommensurable' with Werner Heisenberg's more metaphysically minded view of quantum indeterminism as the actualization of potentialities.[13] Russell even counseled the inevitability of having to choose between Bohr's epistemological strictures and Heisenberg's metaphysical pursuits, arguing that when concepts such as these emerge from conflicting interpretative agendas they should not both be employed in the service of a single theological agenda. On the one hand, embracing Bohr's views, could promote theological reflection on the relation of conflicting models in religious traditions and on the participatory character of all knowledge, including theological knowledge, but, on the other hand, it could also block exploration of the potentially exciting theological implications of Heisenberg's more metaphysical interpretation. Despite arguing for their incommensurability, Russell made no judgment at the time regarding which option was preferrable.

In 1988 Russell expanded and systematized his earlier reflections in an essay he wrote for the first CTNS/Vatican Observatory volume, *Physics, Philosophy, and Theology*.[14] His aim in this essay was twofold: to mine quantum physics for theological metaphors and to establish its constructive role in systematic theology. His remarks began in a somewhat defensive tone, probably because his views on these matters were becoming more widely known and being critiqued. He objected strenuously to the argument that quantum theory could be dismissed as insignificant for theological reflection on the grounds that it applies only to the microscopic realm. Quantum physics, he contended, is deeply relevant to our understanding of the macroscopic world because quantum processes produce the world we know. One can see this quite vividly, he claimed, in the two types of statistics that play a role in quantum theory: Fermi–Dirac statistics and Bose–Einstein statistics. These lead, on the one hand, to the impenetrability of matter (Fermi–Dirac statistics) and, on the other, to the interpenetrating, cohesive character of fields of interaction (Bose–Einstein statistics). Russell also identified several points at which quantum physics is relevant to a general theological discussion of the character of the world: the fact that quantum randomness is a fundamental feature of nature not reducible to human ignorance; the fact that quantum particles in their absolute indistinguishability from one another produce the remarkable variety of different types of matter known to science; and finally, the fact that the world exhibits a holistic (that is, non-local) character at the quantum level.

Russell then proposed two connections between quantum theory and his own theological vision of the unfolding of creation in response to Sallie McFague's call for the development of relevant and life-giving theological metaphors (*Metaphorical Theology* had appeared in 1982 and *Models of God* in 1987). First, he interpreted quantum indeterminacy as revealing an element of 'surprise' within nature, which he argued resembles God's surprising, redemptive work of bringing about the Kingdom. He saw in quantum indeterminism the kind of objective transformation, and felt in his response to this indeterminism the kind of subjective astonishment, that can only result from something truly new occurring in the world. He also saw in quantum indeterminism a hidden dimension of the world, again like the Kingdom of God, 'invisible yet most real of all', producing and transforming the mundane world we know.[15] Russell then interpreted quantum non-locality as a manifestation of nature's 'gossamer' quality, which he thought of as the harmony of creation manifesting itself at each moment globally rather than locally. Russell found the fragile, web-like character of quantum correlations suggestive of both the unitive character of the Body of Christ and the unitive goal of interreligious dialogue.[16]

Not willing to rest content with metaphorical connections, Russell turned next to quantum theory's potential for playing a constructive role in systematic theology, updating much of what he had previously written on the subject. Although he affirmed his most recent judgment that Bohr's principle of complementarity points to an essentially epistemological limitation, he also returned to his earlier view, arguing that complementarity could have at least an indirect ontological implication in so far as it prevents a complete specification of the 'key influences that determine reality'.[17] Though intrigued by comparisons between instances of complementarity in physics and various instances of similar-sounding traditional formulations in Christian theology (for example, the union of divine and human, justification and sanctification, freedom and destiny), Russell warned of the danger of equivocating when transferring concepts from science to theology. As a result, he was reluctant to let the formal similarity between the concept of complementarity in quantum physics and traditional theological concepts serve as a warrant for their normative role in contemporary theological construction.

Russell also took up the issue of quantum indeterminism, which he argued demonstrates the theological significance of quantum theory in several ways. Before reviewing his comments on this topic, however, it is worth pausing to note that in moving from a discussion of complementarity to a discussion of indeterminism Russell chose not to repeat his previous argument that the two perspectives are incommensurable. Here he concluded only that while Bohr's view leads to epistemological insights, Heisenberg's view carries ontological lessons. It seems safe to say that Russell's desire to foster a wider conversation among his colleagues triumphed over his desire to defend a particular point of view.[18]

Russell began his comments on indeterminism by agreeing with Arthur Peacocke that a God who creates a world governed by quantum processes should be understood as a God of law *and* chance, a God for whom 'even the random character of elementary processes contributes something essential to the greater panorama out of which emerge the conditions for genuine alternatives, and eventually the reality of free will and authentic relationship characterized by love.'[19] But he also felt that the shift from law-versus-chance to law-and-chance was not enough.[20] Because quantum statistics underlie both the impenetrability of matter and the interpenetrability and cohesive character of field interactions, Russell claimed that one should not say that God creates in the midst of, or in response to, chance, but rather that God works directly through the remarkable properties of quantum chance to create an ordered world. He also once again approvingly cited Pollard, though still without discussing Pollard's views in detail. What coalesced in this essay was not yet a detailed account of quantum divine action but a rather Whiteheadian image of God acting providentially in quantum chance by 'a constant persuasive re-directing of our choices through the creative divine immanence in all processes and events.'[21] This image reflects Russell's long-standing sympathies with Alfred North Whitehead's thought, despite his general desire to avoid affixing the label 'process' to his own theological perspective.

Finally, Russell turned to the concept of non-locality (now more commonly referred to as 'entanglement'). He connected this remarkable quantum phenomenon to the notion of divine immanence, arguing that physically separated events which are nonetheless co-present to one another could, from a theological perspective, be understood as co-present and coherent to God so that, theologically speaking, 'differences need not be contradictions, distinctions need not be isolations'.[22] Borrowing language from Paul Tillich, Russell characterized quantum non-locality as manifesting creation's essential coherence within its existential ambiguity.

Russell's early creative efforts to bring theology into conversation with quantum theory focused on a variety of provocative issues emerging from this comparatively new branch of physics: complementarity, the organicism/holism of quantum objects, Bohm's alternative formulation, quantum statistics, non-locality, and indeterminism. From the outset Russell was keenly interested in the openness of physical processes implied by quantum theory, but he struggled to find the best way to articulate and develop his account of this openness. Starting with Bohr's notion of complementarity and then moving to Bohm's account of the infinite layers of reality, he settled finally on Heisenberg's indeterminism. Russell also struggled to characterize the relationship between Bohr's and Heisenberg's views, both of which he found theologically stimulating. He has opted in most of his writings to avoid judging the debate and instead to highlight the implications of both perspectives. Finally, he found quantum holism useful for articulating creation's wholeness before God, a theme which he developed in his discussions both of Bohm and of non-locality, but which he eventually chose to set aside in favor of exploring more fully the relationship between indeterminism and divine action. I turn now to a detailed examination of this last theme, which Russell has developed extensively in his more recent writings.[23]

Quantum Divine Action

The first version of Russell's argument for the possibility of non-interventionist objectively special divine action (NIODA) on the basis of quantum indeterminism appeared in an essay he published in the *CTNS Bulletin* in 1995.[24] The impetus for this argument apparently came from two different directions, both research projects with which Russell had been involved during the early 1990s: the CTNS/Vatican Observatory series of conferences, especially the 1993 conference that led to the publication of *Chaos and Complexity* (*CC*), and CTNS's federally funded effort in the mid-1990s, led by Ted Peters, to examine the ethical and theological implications of the Human Genome Project.[25] Although Russell did not contribute an essay to *CC*, his synthetic and constructive introduction to the volume clearly spelled out the NIODA agenda.[26] The aim of this agenda, according to Russell, was to show that God could act specially, that is, in particular events, without either violating the laws of nature or being explainable solely in terms of a humanly subjective experience of the religious importance of the event (*à la* Schleiermacher). The aim of NIODA, then, was to provide a *non-interventionist* account of the possibility of *objectively special* divine action.

In his 1995 *CTNS Bulletin* essay, Russell took his first step toward providing such an account by linking quantum indeterminism and genetic mutation. He took his cue, first of all, from other scholars at the *CC* conference, including Nancey Murphy, Thomas Tracy, and George Ellis, who had argued that the randomness in quantum theory, unlike in chaos theory, should be construed ontologically rather than epistemologically and therefore could be helpful in pursuing the NIODA agenda.[27] He also reviewed for the first time the details of Pollard's earlier argument, namely that gene mutations can produce macroscopic effects (that is, individual alterations in the genotype can lead to biologically significant changes in the phenotype). Russell argued that if quantum indeterminism could be shown to play a role in genetic mutation, divine action would be conceivable precisely where it had allegedly been most seriously undermined – in the processes of biological evolution. As he has written more recently, 'the presence of "chance" in nature does not imply an absent God and a "pointless" world but an ever-present God acting with purpose in the world.'[28]

The lynchpin in Russell's argument was his contention that quantum chance enters necessarily into an explanation of why DNA point-mutations occur. He acknowledged that a host of classical (that is, non-quantum) factors might also play a significant role in evolutionary change, but he argued convincingly that genetic mutation, the source of variation upon which classical factors operate, is ultimately traceable to events that occur at the quantum level (for example, the making and breaking of hydrogen bonds). He characterized this argument as a kind of a 'bottom–up' approach to divine action, abandoning his earlier preference for Bohm's infinitely layered world of alternating deterministic and indeterministic levels. 'Quantum statistics is all we have,' he wrote in no uncertain terms, 'for *there is no underlying and fully determinate natural process.*'[29] Russell has remained committed to this trajectory of thought in his more recent writings, though he has softened the language so that quantum indeterminism now registers as a hypothesis worth exploring.[30]

Russell's initial presentation of his argument for quantum divine action was clear and straightforward, but it was also relatively brief and undeveloped. Significantly, it did not deal with the question of whether random quantum events happen with sufficient frequency to provide God with, so to speak, a suitably open and flexible canvas. What came across in this initial presentation was that Russell saw no problem with the idea of quantum events simply happening ubiquitously. The difficulty with this idea, as he himself later saw, is that the basic formalism of quantum theory contains no reference at all to any actual events. It contains only the continuous, deterministic, and joint evolution of 'possible' events (that is, 'superpositions') as represented by the changing shape of the multivalued wavefunction (typically notated as 'Ψ') under the guidance of the Schrödinger equation. Those who crafted the mathematical formalism of quantum theory in the 1920s recognized this problem but could not arrive at a generally agreed-upon solution. Max Born's famous interpretation of Ψ as a guide to the relative probability of an object taking on different possible values worked spectacularly well in the laboratory, but it did not solve the deeper question of how or why Ψ ever ceases to evolve continuously by 'collapsing' randomly and discontinuously onto a particular value. Because something apparently quite like Ψ-collapse happens paradigmatically in laboratory measurements, this conundrum has come to be called the 'measurement problem'. Russell simply assumed that quantum events occur ubiquitously, but he failed to defend this assumption with reference either to the notion of Ψ-collapse or to the measurement problem.

Did Russell mean to imply that God causes Ψ-collapses to occur? This question points to a second and related ambiguity in his initial account. To uncover this ambiguity, it is necessary to introduce a distinction that bears on the meaning of the term 'quantum event'. (I will assume for the sake of engaging Russell's argument that quantum events, in the sense of Ψ-collapse, occur ubiquitously in the world.) The definition of a quantum event as a Ψ-collapse combines two distinct ideas. First, it includes the collapse itself, that is, Ψ changing from a multivalued superposition to a single value. I will call this the 'process' of a quantum event. In addition to this process, however, there is the additional fact that Ψ collapses onto one particular value from among all the possibilities present. I will call this the 'outcome' of an event. The ambiguity of Russell's initial presentation, which has led to some confusion, lies in the fact that it was unclear whether Russell meant to say that God acts by causing the process of quantum events, the outcome of these events, or both.

I think Russell must, at the very least, have intended to say that God determines the outcome of quantum events. It is not difficult to see why. The outcome is obviously the point at which quantum underdetermination and

randomness directly come into play. Unfortunately, Russell's early characterization of this issue blurred the distinction between process and outcome, and
at times gave the impression that the process of events rather than its outcome
was the central point of the argument. Consider the following passage:
'[N]ature provides a set of necessary causes, but this set is not sufficient to bring
about the actual event. If that is true, we can argue that the addition of divine
causality completes the set of sufficient causes. In short, quantum events occur
in part because of the direct action of God.'[31] Here process language prevails as
Russell's God helps to 'bring about' quantum events by causing them to
'occur'. What Russell failed to communicate in this passage is that, above all
else, a God of quantum chance must determine the specific outcome of
quantum events.

In fact, I think Russell would have wanted to avoid claiming that God causes
the process of quantum event. As someone committed to non-interventionism,
he has always eschewed locating God in gaps that can be seen to reflect human
ignorance of natural causes. But suppose that sufficient evidence were
eventually to compel physicists to accept some physical account of the
'process' of quantum events (for example, one current speculative proposal
links Ψ-collapse to the amount of mass present in any interaction[32]). A divine
action argument focused on the underdetermination of the process of quantum
events would then come to be seen in retrospect as a kind of God-of-the-gaps
argument.

Russell's initial lack of clarity around this issue, coupled with his avoidance
of the measurement problem, made his proposal seem interventionist, despite
his intentions to the contrary. Because he did not address the possibility of
physical solutions to the measurement problem (in terms of the 'process' of
events), God appeared to be made responsible for the ubiquity of quantum
events: that which otherwise would not have occurred at all, God brought
about by innumerous special acts. What Russell intended to convey, I believe,
is instead that the underdetermination associated with the *outcome* of quantum
events could be seen as allowing God to bring about what otherwise would not
have occurred *in exactly the way that it did in fact occur*. This awkward way of
putting the point nevertheless shows the value of distinguishing between the
process and outcome of quantum events.

After publishing his initial account of the quantum divine action argument,
Russell refined and expanded it in three separate essays that appeared at
roughly the same time. I limit my discussion here to the fullest of these
accounts found in the essay he contributed to the CTNS/VO volume
Evolutionary and Molecular Biology.[33] In this essay Russell noted that he
was interested in quantum randomness specifically in the sense of the
underdetermined *outcome* of quantum events. But he also argued that
Heisenberg's account of the *process* of actualization by which a quantum
system goes from a superposition of 'coexistent potentialities' to one actual
state cannot be attributed 'to interaction with other processes'.[34] It is unclear
whether Russell understood this kind of interaction to be impossible in
principle or whether he was merely noting the lack of any widely agreed-upon
account of such interaction at the time (the latter certainly continues to be

true). In any case, this formulation appears to incorporate both the outcome
and the process of quantum events into the scope of their underdetermination.
That Russell still thought God needed to be involved in the process as well as
the outcome of quantum events seems clear from his claim that, if Heisenberg
were correct, one could view nature from a theological perspective as
'genuinely open to God's participation in the bringing to actuality of each
state of nature in time.'[35]

When Russell finally turned his attention to the measurement problem,
however, the argument he presented clearly prioritized God's activity in the
outcome rather than the process of quantum events. He defended the ubiquity
of quantum events on the grounds that quantum processes occur in the
universe whenever elementary particles interact irreversibly with larger
objects.[36] Such events should not, he felt, be limited to laboratory
measurement.[37] The significance of this argument is that the concept of
'irreversibility' functions as a scientific term here rather than as a theological
term. It is not God, then, but the physical phenomenon of irreversibility that
causes the process of quantum events to occur. What role is left for God to
play? 'Before God acts, the quantum system is in a superposition of potential
states. But when God *acts*, the effect of that action, together with that specific
superposition, decides *which quantum outcome becomes actual*.'[38] Heisenberg's
language of actualization is still present, but now it is the specific outcome that
counts.

One further piece of evidence supporting my view that Russell's argument
really ought to be understood in terms of outcomes rather than processes can
be found in his discussion of Thomas Tracy's and Nancey Murphy's
contributions to *CC*. Russell wrote that Tracy's view of God acting in only
some quantum events, a view which he personally *rejected*, nonetheless
powerfully evoked the *specialness* of special divine action because it made
'God's direct acts in key quantum events ... special not only because their
indirect outcome is special, but also because God normally does not act in
other quantum events beyond creating them and sustaining them in being.'[39]
More recently Russell wrote that although Murphy had God acting in some
particular event 'as in all events ... still in this occasion, with two states
superposed before the event, God will choose one state in particular and not
the other ..., thus conveying God's intentionality in this particular event.'[40]
One way of stating Russell's view would be to say that if God is to be identified
as the cause of the process of quantum events, then one must appeal to God's
general rather than special providence. Recall that Russell has always worked
from the presumption that while general providence is compatible with
physical determinism, special providence is not. When God acts specially,
according to Russell, there needs to be 'room' in the structure of natural
processes for God to act. This is why quantum indeterminism is crucial to his
argument. But to make the process of a quantum event the result of special
providence is to turn God into a physical cause and to put a theological
explanation in direct competition with some future scientific account of how
this process might occur, once again raising the possibility of a God-of-the-
gaps objection. In retrospect, then, it seems right to conclude that Russell

intended all along to characterize God's special action in quantum events in terms of the *specific outcomes* that obtain rather than in terms of the fact *that* specific outcomes obtain.

Russell's most recent essay advancing his argument for quantum divine action appeared in the CTNS/Vatican Observatory volume *Quantum Mechanics*.[41] His primary aim in this essay was to strengthen the argument by responding to concerns that had been raised by critics in the intervening years.[42] He began once again by taking up the question of what it means to be a 'quantum event'. He argued that he had not meant to imply that God alters the wavefunction between measurements, makes measurements on a given system, or alters the probabilities of obtaining a particular result, but meant instead to say that 'God acts with nature to bring about the outcomes of particular measurements consistent with the probabilities given before the event occurs.'[43] One sees Russell's dismissal of the motion that God makes measurements on a system, a growing appreciation for the need to avoid having God compete with natural causes by controlling the process of quantum events, while retaining for God the role of choosing some particular outcome. For to measure a system is only to cause the process of Ψ-collapse, not to cause one particular outcome to result (quantum randomness prohibits the latter).

Turning to the problem of ubiquity, Russell expanded his argument that quantum events should be thought of not in terms of what happens in the laboratory but in terms of 'irreversible interactions'.[44] He suggested that we adopt the term 'measurement' for any irreversible interaction, regardless of the levels involved, and identified three types of interaction: micro–macro, micro–meso, and micro–micro. The first of these types was discussed by early figures such as Bohr, who maintained a sharp distinction between quantum objects and classical measuring devices; in fact, Bohr took this distinction to be the key to understanding the nature of a quantum event. Russell, however, rightly recognized the problem with maintaining two separate and unrelated ontologies, one for quantum objects and another for classical objects.[45] He argued that irreversibility can be used to characterize not only interactions of this type but others as well. For example, in the case of micro–meso interactions, meso-scale (microscopic and perhaps also sub-microscopic) objects with enough degrees of freedom would render an interaction with a quantum object irreversible, 'at least in practice'.[46] Russell's qualifier here is important. For the argument to work, irreversibility must be shown to be a reliable indicator of Ψ-collapse; without Ψ-collapse there is no physically underdetermined outcome to be divinely specified, only Ψ's deterministic evolution according to the Schrödinger equation. If a convincing case cannot be made for in-principle irreversibility, then Russell does not have Ψ-collapse and his argument collapses instead. This is why a resolution of the measurement problem involving a naturalistic explanation of Ψ-collapse is so crucial to Russell's argument. Unfortunately, Russell confused the issue when he suggested that, from the point of view of the Copenhagen family of interpretations, the 'measurement problem' is not really a 'problem' at all but a synonym for processes not governed by the Schrödinger equation.[47] The measurement problem *is* a problem for the Copenhagen approach, not in the sense of how to explain why a particular outcome occurs but in the sense of how to explain why definite outcomes occur at all.

In a footnote Russell acknowledged that using the concept of irreversibility in the quantum context was highly problematic because it emerges not from quantum considerations but from an entirely different (and non-fundamental) domain of physics, namely the field of thermodynamics. Although he employed the term as though its meaning were self-evident, he admitted that this was 'overtly not the case'.[48] As John Polkinghorne has noted in his contribution to *Quantum Mechanics*, to say that a quantum event occurs in the irreversible registration of a quantum object's properties is to extend what appears to happen in the laboratory far beyond what we have any warrant for claiming.[49] As a result, it is best to understand Russell's argument for the irreversibility of quantum events as an analogy: in quantum events there is some process that occurs which is similar to what happens in thermodynamic irreversible systems. The problem with analogies is that they lack argumentative force. So far, Russell has not presented a convincing argument for the application of the concept of irreversibility to quantum theory and thus has failed to make his case for the ubiquity of quantum events. His willingness to replace the term 'ubiquitous' with 'pervasive' in recognition of the fact that the development of Ψ under the guidance of the Schrödinger equation does not constitute a quantum event fails to put to rest, as he had hoped, concerns about quantum events as the means by which the physical world providentially unfolds.[50]

Clarifying the Meaning of 'Event' within Quantum Theory

The general direction of my analysis of Russell's argument for quantum divine action suggests that he ought not wed himself to the double claim that both the outcome and the process of quantum events must be under-determined for special divine action to occur. For the argument to function as he intends, it ought to be linked solely to the underdetermination associated with random outcomes. This would free Russell to press physicists for a fuller account of the process of events (that is, the narrow sense of the 'measurement problem', how it is that Ψ-collapse happens at all), which would help him defend his claim that quantum events are pervasive (formerly, ubiquitous) in the natural order.

Fortunately for Russell, a number of solutions to the measurement problem have been proposed since the advent of quantum theory and are readily available for investigation. Although none has yet emerged as the clear empirical frontrunner, by the light of Russell's own methodology this should not keep us from entering into the dispute to investigate where the stakes lie for the theological discussion or, even better, to see where the theological arguments might push the scientific research agenda forward. This would be 'creative mutual interaction' at its best. To start the conversation, I have elected to discuss three recent attempts by physicists to clarify the meaning of the term 'event' within quantum theory. I make no claim to have chosen the most theologically promising proposals, but each commends itself by providing a clear account of quantum events and answering the question. How often do quantum events occur? My comments in this final section are necessarily impressionistic. Much more would need to be said about each proposal to establish its relation to the relevant theological issues. I offer these brief comments in hopes of encouraging further investigation into the theological implications of such proposals.

Decoherence

The concept of 'decoherence', first proposed in the 1970s, has been touted by some as providing a solution to the measurement problem.[51] According to this concept, quantum effects occur because of the coherence of the (phase) relationships among a wavefunction's different components. To make this concept more concrete, consider the example of a single electron interfering with itself as it passes through a two-slit experiment. Interference occurs because of the coherent relationship between the two components of Ψ_e, the electron's wavefunction, corresponding to passage through each of the two slits (in a highly simplified version of Paul Dirac's way of notating wavefunctions, $\Psi_e = <\text{left slit}| + <\text{right slit}|$). If a detector is placed at one of the slits, the joint wavefunction of the electron and the detector, Ψ_{e+d}, becomes entangled. And because the detector is large by quantum standards, having many degrees of freedom, the result of this entanglement is that the coherence between the two components of Ψ_e is very quickly destroyed – they 'decohere' – and the superposition previously present in Ψ_e effectively collapses onto a single state (Ψ_e becomes $<\text{left slit}|$ or $<\text{right slit}|$).[52] This process is not rare, its supporters argue, but is in fact exceedingly common. Quantum objects become entangled in complex environments all the time, causing superpositions effectively to disappear and bringing about our familiar macroscopic world of definite outcomes.

Although some physicists initially claimed that decoherence solved the measurement problem, it was subsequently pointed out that the idea of decoherence actually misses the mark, if only slightly. The problem is that the entanglement of wavefunctions does not, strictly speaking, destroy their coherence or superpositions. It merely relocates these aspects of the individual wavefunctions into the combined wavefunction of the system. Although Ψ_e 'effectively' collapses into a definite state, Ψ_{e+d} now contains the original superposition. What is remarkable about decoherence is that this transition happens without there ever being a break in the Schrödinger evolution of any of the systems. In decoherence, unlike in the standard Copenhagen approach, the Schrödinger equation always applies everywhere. There is never a moment at which Ψ_e collapses; there is only the so-called 'unitary' (translation: deterministic) evolution of Ψ_{e+d}, before and after entanglement, and always under the guidance of the Schrödinger equation. Surprisingly, this unitary evolution of Ψ_{e+d} is what typically leads to the non-unitary evolution of Ψ_e.

Although the decoherence program does have room for a certain kind of quantum event, namely the interaction of quantum objects and the entanglement of their respective wavefunctions, there is no genuine Ψ-collapse. The implication for Russell's program is clear. Decoherence cannot be the entire story if Russell's argument is to succeed.[53] What Russell needs is a solution to the measurement problem that involves true Ψ-collapse, not just the effective collapse of entanglement/decoherence. He has a serious stake in physicists finding a solution to the measurement problem that goes beyond decoherence. Interestingly, Polkinghorne commented in his contribution to *Quantum Mechanics* that the very short timescales associated with decoherence might provide a way of circumventing the charge that quantum divine action would be episodic.[54] However, he missed the central point that there is no Ψ-collapse in decoherence, and thus no quantum events at all in the sense that is relevant to Russell's argument.

The Transactional Interpretation

Over the past several decades John Cramer has developed an interpretation of quantum theory that he calls the 'transactional interpretation'.[55] Based on initial insights by John Wheeler and Richard Feynman, Cramer's basic move is to treat Ψ as a real physical object that can travel either forward or backward in time. When a Ψ-wave traveling forward in time meets one traveling backward in time, they perform a kind of handshake that (randomly) determines the outcome of their associated event. In Cramer's view, all of the strange features of the world predicted by quantum theory (for example, entanglement, tunneling) are really just artifacts of the straightforward(!) process of wavefunctions traveling forward and backward in time. Cramer does not alter the standard formalism in any way, but he radically reinterprets the dynamics of wavefunction propagation.

How often do quantum events occur in Cramer's interpretation? According to Cramer, this is to ask the wrong question. In fact, there is no 'when' to quantum events because the handshake between wavefunctions happens supratemporally in spacetime along the entire world-lines of the entities involved in the transaction. A transaction can thus be envisioned as a standing wave that exists across spacetime between the temporally originating and temporally concluding events of the interaction in question. There is a collapse in this interpretation, but it is no longer time-localized. Though the notion of a supratemporal 'quantum event' might at first seem jarring and ungainly, it might also lead to interesting new ways of articulating the idea that God acts in quantum events.

Event-Enhanced Quantum Theory

In contrast to the method employed in the former two approaches of reinterpreting the standard formalism of quantum theory, some physicists have attempted to solve the measurement problem by actually modifying the Schrödinger equation, often by adding a term to drive the process of Ψ-collapse (for example, in response to the presence of more mass, more degrees of freedom, or some other physical consideration). Here I focus on one such proposal, labeled 'event-enhanced quantum theory' (EEQT) by its authors, Philippe Blanchard and Arkadiusz Jadczyk.[56] EEQT stays close to the standard formalism, modifying it only minimally by introducing a means of identifying and including 'classical' subsystems within the wavefunction as well as a clear method for coupling them to quantum subsystems.[57] EEQT is built upon the notion of irreversibility tied to macroscopic interactions with classical subsystems, and thus fits well with Russell's intuitions regarding irreversibility. Within the framework of EEQT, one still has random Ψ-collapses, but in this case the collapse makes an explicit appearance in the formalism and has two different aspects, the timing of collapse and the outcome of collapse, each of which is generated by a random mechanism within the formalism.

One interesting question to ask of EEQT is whether controlling the timing of events is equivalent to what I have referred to as causing their 'process'. If so, could one then think of God as causing the timing of events? Applying my argument from the previous section here would lead us to raise a God-of-the-gaps objection. But there is a new facet to this situation that changes things, namely that the timing mechanism in the formalism of EEQT is random. This randomness exposes the previously unnoticed assumption in my argument against making God the cause of Ψ-collapse. The assumption is that however Ψ-collapse occurs in detail, it must occur deterministically in general. In EEQT, however, the mechanism that causes Ψ-collapse is as random as the mechanism that produces the specific outcome of Ψ-collapse. So in this case, one could legitimately argue that God causes both the process and the outcome of quantum events, which would allow God an even more subtle means of controlling the development of quantum events. Significantly, the authors of this proposal claim that it may have testable consequences.[58] Be that as it may, this and the other proposals I have discussed provide good examples of scientific research programs that have the potential to foster further reflection on the notion of quantum divine action.

Russell's sustained efforts to sort out the theological implications of quantum theory over the past two decades are especially valuable for the ideas they have generated, but they are equally valuable for the standards they have set for interdisciplinary scholarship in theology and science. His ongoing research program in quantum divine action provides a powerful example of how one ought to go about building constructive but critical connections between scientific and theological claims. His interest in quantum theory more generally has produced numerous helpful investigations into important issues in the philosophy of physics. I am sure that I am not alone in my hope that he will continue to explore these issues with the same rigor and creative spirit in the years to come.

Notes

1 The title recalls one of Russell's early witticisms aimed at those who felt that quantum considerations would not apply to the macroscopic realm; see Robert J. Russell, 'Quantum Physics in Philosophical and Theological Perspective', in *Physics, Philosophy, and Theology: A Common Quest for Understanding*, ed. by Robert J. Russell, William R. Stoeger, SJ, and George V. Coyne, SJ (Vatican City State: Vatican Observatory Publications, 1988), 369, footnote 2.

2 John Polkinghorne has been Russell's chief critic over the years regarding his argument for quantum divine action. Polkinghorne raised this particular issue in his contribution to the CTNS/Vatican Observatory volume *Quantum Mechanics*; see John C. Polkinghorne, 'Physical Process, Quantum Events, and Divine Agency', in *Quantum Mechanics: Scientific Perspectives on Divine Action*, ed. by Robert J. Russell, Philip Clayton, Kirk Wegter-McNelly, and Polkinghorne (Vatican City State and Berkeley, CA: Vatican Observatory and Center for Theology and the Natural Sciences, 2001), 187. A distinct but equally important concern regarding Russell's proposal is whether he is right to presume that God can act specially in the world only if its processes are underdetermined at the physical level. I have labeled this presumption 'theo-physical incompatibilism' and have questioned its legitimacy in my essay 'Does God Need Room to Act? Theo-Physical In/Compatibilism in Noninterventionist Theories of Objectively Special Divine Action', in *Capstone Conference Proceedings: Scientific Perspectives on Divine Action*, ed. by Robert J. Russell, William R. Stoeger, and Nancey Murphy (Vatican City State and Berkeley, CA: Vatican Observatory and Center for Theology and the Natural Sciences, forthcoming).

3 Andrew J. Dufner, SJ, and Robert J. Russell, 'Foundations in Physics for Revising the Creation Tradition', in *Cry of the Environment: Rebuilding the Christian Creation Tradition*, ed. by Philip N. Joranson and Ken Butigan (Santa Fe, NM: Bear & Co., 1984), 163–80.

4 See, for example, Niels Bohr, 'Causality and Complementarity', in *Philosophical Writings*, ed. by Jan Faye and Henry J. Folse, vol. 4, *Causality and Complementarity: Supplementary Papers* (Woodbridge, CT: Ox Bow Press, 1998 [1934]), 83–91. One helpful illustration of Bohr's notion of complementarity can be found in so-called 'which path' experiments. The cumulative interference pattern produced by photons in a Mach–Zehnder interferometer can be said to be caused by the fact that each photon travels an undeterminable path through the interferometer. One can alter the experimental setup so that a determination of which path each photon has taken is possible, but then the interference pattern disappears. The original setup precludes a spacetime account of the photons' behavior, and the altered setup precludes a causal account of why a particular photon took one path or the other. The causal and spacetime descriptions, being linked to distinct and mutually exclusive experimental arrangements, are thus 'complementary' to one another. For further discussion of such experiments, see George Greenstein and Arthur G. Zajonc, *The Quantum Challenge: Modern Research on the Foundations of Quantum Mechanics*, The Challenge Series (Boston: Jones and Bartlett, 1997).

5 Dufner and Russell, 'Foundations in Physics', 178. The term 'indeterminacy' appears near the end of the essay (180), but without elaboration.

6 See, for example, John C. Polkinghorne, *Quantum Theory: A Very Short Introduction* (Oxford: Oxford University Press, 2002), 36–7.

7 Dufner and Russell, 'Foundations in Physics', 177–8.

8 Robert John Russell, 'The Physics of David Bohm and its Relevance to Philosophy and Theology', *Zygon*, 20:2 (June 1985): 135–58.

9 Ibid., 152.

10 William G. Pollard, *Chance and Providence: God's Action in a World Governed by Scientific Law* (London: Faber and Faber, 1958), 94–7, 106–7. For Bohm's perspective, see, for example,

David Bohm, *Causality and Chance in Modern Physics* (Philadelphia, PA: University of Pennsylvania Press, 1957). Prior to Pollard's work, discussions of divine action in light of quantum indeterminism had appeared in the writings of theologians Karl Heim and E. L. Mascall. Heim argued that quantum indeterminism had destroyed the 'iron law of causality' and thus opened the possibility for a renewed appreciation of God, the true absolute; Karl Heim, *The Transformation of the Scientific World View*, trans. by W. A. Whitehouse (New York: Harper & Brothers, 1953), 161. Mascall argued that the degree of autonomy given by God to creation was enough to secure the probability of an event's occurrence, but not its actual happening. According to Mascall, God appears to have 'reserved to himself the final decision as to whether a specified event occurs or not'; Eric L. Mascall, *Christian Theology and Natural Science: Some Questions in Their Relations*, Bampton Lecture Series (New York: Longmans, Green & Co., 1956), 201. Russell reviews these historical precursors to his argument in Robert J. Russell, 'Special Providence and Genetic Mutation: A New Defense of Theistic Evolution', in *Evolutionary and Molecular Biology: Scientific Perspectives on Divine Action*, ed. by Robert J. Russell, William R. Stoeger, SJ, and Francisco J. Ayala (Vatican City State and Berkeley, CA: Vatican Observatory and Center for Theology and the Natural Sciences, 1998), 208ff.

11   Russell, 'The Physics of David Bohm', 154–5.

12   Robert J. Russell, 'How Does Scientific Cosmology Shape a Theology of Nature?', *CTNS Bulletin*, 6:1 (Winter 1986): 1–12. To my knowledge, Barbour first introduced this term in Ian G. Barbour, *Issues in Science and Religion* (New York: Harper & Row, 1971), 452.

13   Russell, 'How Does Scientific Cosmology Shape a Theology of Nature?', 5.

14   Russell, 'Quantum Physics in Philosophical and Theological Perspective'.

15   Ibid., 356.

16   I have extended Russell's early exploration of the theological significance of quantum non-local correlations in Kirk Wegter-McNelly, 'The World, Entanglement, and God: Quantum Theory and the Christian Doctrine of Creation' (Ph.D. dissertation, Graduate Theological Union, 2003), *64/03* (2003).

17   Russell, 'Quantum Physics in Philosophical and Theological Perspective', 360.

18   Despite aggressively promoting his argument for quantum divine action in more recent publications, Russell has always wrestled with the tension between promoting his own point of view and muting it in order to make room for others to enter the conversation.

19   Russell, 'Quantum Physics in Philosophical and Theological Perspective', 362.

20   Peacocke first presented his views of God as embracing both law and chance in Arthur Peacocke, *Creation and the World of Science* (Oxford: Oxford University Press, 1979).

21   Russell, 'Quantum Physics in Philosophical and Theological Perspective', 362.

22   Ibid., 365.

23   In 1993 Russell published an essay on the topic of 'quantum cosmology' and its theological implications. Because the issues relevant to my discussion of quantum theory enter negligibly into this topic I will not review this and related writings in Russell's corpus. See Robert J. Russell, 'Finite Creation Without a Beginning: The Doctrine of Creation in Relation to Big Bang and Quantum Cosmologies', in *Quantum Cosmology and the Laws of Nature: Scientific Perspectives on Divine Action*, ed. by Robert J. Russell, Nancey C. Murphy, and Chris J. Isham, 2nd edn (Vatican City State and Berkeley, CA: Vatican Observatory and Center for Theology and the Natural Sciences, 1996), 291–326.

24   Robert J. Russell, 'Theistic Evolution: Does God Really Act in Nature?', *CTNS Bulletin*, 15:1 (Winter 1995): 19–32.

25   For the results of the latter research project, see Ted Peters (ed.), *Genetics: Issues of Social Justice* (Cleveland, OH: Pilgrim Press, 1998).

26   See Russell's introduction for a helpful table that locates NIODA among the various other options; Robert J. Russell, 'Introduction', in *Chaos and Complexity: Scientific Perspectives on*

Divine Action, ed. by Russell, Nancey C. Murphy, and Arthur R. Peacocke (Vatican City State and Berkeley, CA: Vatican Observatory and Center for Theology and the Natural Sciences, 1995), 9–13.

27 Nancey C. Murphy, 'Divine Action in the Natural Order: Buridan's Ass and Schrödinger's Cat', 325–58, Thomas F. Tracy, 'Particular Providence and the God of the Gaps', 289–324, and George F. R. Ellis, 'Ordinary and Extraordinary Divine Action: The Nexus of Interaction', 359–96 – all in *Chaos and Complexity*; Pollard, *Chance and Providence*, 56.

28 Robert J. Russell, 'Divine Action and Quantum Mechanics: A Fresh Assessment', in *Quantum Mechanics*, 296.

29 Russell, 'Theistic Evolution', 23, italics original. This point of view is reiterated in Russell, 'Divine Action and Quantum Mechanics', 295.

30 Russell, 'Divine Action and Quantum Mechanics', 303–5.

31 Russell, 'Theistic Evolution', 23.

32 See Roger Penrose, *The Emperor's New Mind: Concerning Computers, Minds, and the Laws of Physics* (Oxford: Oxford University Press, 2002), 475ff.

33 Russell, 'Special Providence and Genetic Mutation'. The other publications are Robert J. Russell, 'Does the "God Who *Acts*" Really *Act*? New Approaches to Divine Action in Light of Science', *Theology Today*, 54:1 (April 1997): 43–65; Robert J. Russell, 'Does the "God Who Acts" Really Act in Nature?', in *Science and Theology: The New Consonance*, ed. by Ted Peters (Boulder, CO: Westview Press, 1998), 77–102.

34 Russell, 'Special Providence and Genetic Mutation', 203.

35 Ibid.

36 Ibid., 214.

37 Ibid., 204, footnote 39.

38 Ibid., 210, italics mine.

39 Ibid., 215.

40 Russell, 'Divine Action and Quantum Mechanics', 316.

41 Ibid., 293–328.

42 Earlier John Polkinghorne had rejected Pollard's (and by extension Russell's) attempt to link divine action and quantum indeterminism, calling it 'a rather hole-and-corner sort of providence'; John C. Polkinghorne, 'The Quantum World', in *Physics, Philosophy, and Theology*, 340. To Polkinghorne, God acting clandestinely in the indeterminism of quantum events seemed more a denial than an affirmation of God's presence. Although this criticism is misguided, Polkinghorne rightly saw that such an approach was doomed to fail without a clearer understanding of the measurement problem. In his contribution to *CC*, he raised the issue of ubiquity. To base one's account of divine action on the notion of quantum measurements would, he felt, be to provide an 'episodic account of providential agency'. John C. Polkinghorne, 'The Metaphysics of Divine Action', in *Chaos and Complexity*, 152.

43 Russell, 'Divine Action and Quantum Mechanics', 296, footnote 11. The list of possibilities Russell rejected was delineated in Nicholas T. Saunders, 'Does God Cheat at Dice? Divine Action and Quantum Possibilities', *Zygon*, 35:3 (September 2001): 517–44.

44 Russell, 'Divine Action and Quantum Mechanics', 294.

45 Ibid., 307, footnote 48.

46 Ibid., 306.

47 Ibid., 307.

48 Ibid., 307, footnote 47.

49 Polkinghorne, 'Physical Process, Quantum Events, and Divine Agency', 187–8.

50 Russell, 'Divine Action and Quantum Mechanics', 310.

51 For an introduction to the scientific and philosophical issues, see H. Dieter Zeh, 'Basic Concepts and Their Interpretation', in *Decoherence and the Appearance of the Classical World in Quantum Theory*, ed. by Erich Joos et al., 2nd edn (Berlin: Springer, 2004), 7–40.

52 Counter-intuitively, this happens regardless of whether or not the detector registers the electron. The lack of registration of the electron after sufficient time also implies the collapse of Ψ_e but on the slit without the detector. Collapses induced by a negative-result like this one are referred to as Renninger-style null measurements, after Mauritius Renninger who first noticed the phenomenon. Within the framework of decoherence, Renninger measurements draw attention to the fact that objects do not have to 'bump into one another' for their wavefunctions to become entangled.

53 I have argued, however, that decoherence's near miss in solving the measurement problem has other theological advantages, such as describing a world in which vast distances and sharp distinctions do not detract from the fact that the universe remains a united, entangled whole. See Wegter-McNelly, 'The World, Entanglement, and God', section 6.2. In order to develop a non-interventionist account of special divine action on the basis of decoherence and entanglement, where there is no Ψ-collapse and thus no quantum indeterminism, I would need to develop and defend the legitimacy of a theo-physical compatibilist perspective.

54 Polkinghorne, 'Physical Process, Quantum Events, and Divine Agency', 189.

55 Cramer has published a number of different accounts of his interpretation since it first appeared in 1986. See, for example, John G. Cramer, 'The Transactional Interpretation of Quantum Mechanics', Computing Anticipatory Systems – CASYS 2000 – Fourth International Conference, vol. AIP Conference Proceedings, vol. 573 (American Institute of Physics, 2001), 132–8. A much more extensive and detailed version of the argument can be accessed online at http://mist.npl.washington.edu/npl/int_rep/tiqm/TI_toc.html.

56 See, for example, Philippe Blanchard and Arkadiusz Jadczyk, 'Events and Piecewise Deterministic Dynamics in Event-Enhanced Quantum Theory', *Physics Letters A*, 203 (31 July 1995): 260–66.

57 This approach calls for the development of an ontology more sophisticated than Bohr's to support the distinction between classical and quantum subsystems.

58 Blanchard and Jadczyk, 'Events and Piecewise Deterministic Dynamics', 260–61.

CHAPTER EIGHT

Indeterminacy, Holism and God's Action

Ian G. Barbour

Robert John Russell has said that my *Issues in Science and Religion*, published in 1965, was influential in starting him on a lifelong exploration of the relationship between these fields of inquiry.[1] My own indebtedness to him began in 1977, when he came to Carleton College to teach physics and we taught a seminar on science and religion together. He moved to Berkeley and in 1981 founded the Center for Theology and the Natural Sciences, which under his direction has been in the last quarter-century a source of inspiration to me and to many others. The series of working groups and publications sponsored by CTNS and the Vatican Observatory was a model of detailed interdisciplinary research on significant topics. The science/religion course program, the CTNS publications and conferences, and the graduate courses taught through the Graduate Theological Union have been major factors in the growing interest in these questions in the English-speaking world – and more recently in other cultures. I was deeply moved by the thought and time he put into organizing a celebration of my eightieth birthday in 2003 and editing the papers presented there.[2] I am enduringly grateful for both the intellectual companionship and the personal friendship we have shared over the years.

However, the purpose of the present volume is not simply to express gratitude to Bob Russell but rather to pursue further some of the questions he has been asking. Since we both started our careers as physicists, it would be appropriate to consider the relevance of quantum physics to a theological understanding of divine action. I will note the many points on which we agree and try to clarify what I see as points of disagreement.

Newtonian physics, which provided the model for all the natural sciences until the early twentieth century, was *deterministic* and *reductionistic*. It appeared that, at least in principle, the future of all systems could be predicted from accurate knowledge of the present state of all their constituent parts. Quantum physics challenged determinism by portraying a fundamental *indeterminacy* in the atomic and subatomic world. It also challenged reductionism by portraying a *holism* in which the behavior of larger systems cannot be represented as the sum of the activities of their component parts. The holism already evident at the quantum level is even more significant in the emergence of new kinds of behavior at higher levels in complex organisms, giving rise to what has been called *top–down causality* from higher to lower levels in addition to bottom–up causality originating at lower levels.

In considering God's action in the world, Russell has emphasized *quantum indeterminacy*. I have emphasized *holism* at all levels and the role of *top–down causality*. I will argue that the process thought of Alfred North Whitehead and his followers combines indeterminacy, holism, and a role for divine action in integrated events at all levels. In successive sections I shall explore first, indeterminacy and God's action at the quantum level; second, holism in quantum physics; third, holism and God's action at higher levels; fourth, interiority in process thought; and finally, God's action in process thought.

Indeterminacy and God's Action at the Quantum Level

Both Russell and I have defended critical realism as a middle ground between classical realism and instrumentalism in the philosophy of science. We have maintained that the uncertainty in our knowledge of the quantum world does not arise from the inadequacy of current quantum theories (as Albert Einstein and David Bohm held), but reflects a fundamental indeterminacy in nature itself (as Werner Heisenberg and some of Niels Bohr's later writings suggest). We hold that quantum indeterminacy is ontological and not simply an epistemological limitation. We claim that quantum systems have multiple potentialities until a measurement is made. In technical terms, before a measurement is made a quantum system changes deterministically and continuously as a superposition of states described by the Schrödinger Equation. It only collapses discontinuously to an unpredictable value within a range of probabilities when a measurement is made.[3] Both Russell and I take the *measurement* of a quantum system to refer to any irreversible interaction with other systems, not just to the action of an observer in a laboratory. In the spontaneous decay of a radioactive atom or the emission of a photon, for example, there is no action by an observer disturbing the system. Russell calls the collapse of the wavefunction in all such interactions a *quantum event*.[4]

On the theological side, Russell and I agree that we are not pursuing a *natural theology* that seeks evidence for the existence of God in the findings of science. We are attempting a *theology of nature* that asks how belief in God based on religious experience and an historical tradition can be related to the scientific understanding of nature today. Specifically, we ask how divine action in nature might be possible *without supernatural intervention* in violation of the laws of nature. We agree that if God realizes one among the range of potentialities in an existing quantum system, this would not be an intervention in the sense of altering what would otherwise be determined by physical laws, for the outcome is not determined by such laws. No input of energy is needed since the energy of the alternative potentialities is identical. Quantum (micro) events in a larger number of identical initial systems would usually be distributed across the range of probabilities and would average out statistically in their effects on large-scale (macro) phenomena. But in some cases an amplification of quantum events occurs. One photon can register on the retina of the eye. One neuron firing can initiate system-wide changes in patterns of brain activity, and the disruption of one bond in a DNA strand could be a genetic mutation that alters evolutionary history.

Russell maintains that in addition to establishing the initial conditions and physical order of the cosmos, God acted in *every* quantum event before the advent of life to realize a particular outcome. After the advent of life, he says, God acted only in *some* quantum events in order to allow for creativity and human freedom. 'God acts in all quantum events in the universe until the rise of life and consciousness anywhere. God then increasingly refrains from determining the outcome, leaving room for top–down causality in conscious, and preeminently in self-conscious, creatures.'[5] In a recent article, Russell concludes that

> for those somatic events in which 'mind' in a sentient organism acts on neurophysiology to carry out agency, God does not act to determine the specific outcome. In all other cases, what we take as quantum indeterminism is merely hidden divine action; there is no genuine novelty in subatomic nature, though there is genuine novelty at the level of sentience.[6]

Nicholas Saunders has raised a number of objections to Russell's proposal, but I do not find any of them compelling. He claims that in the view Russell advocates, 'God ignores the probabilities predicted by orthodox quantum mechanics and simply controls the outcome of particular measurements.'[7] But in his writing, Russell has maintained that God's quantum activity is always consistent with the probabilities before the event. Saunders criticizes Russell's dependence on a particular (realist) interpretation of quantum theory rather than remaining on solid scientific ground.[8] But Russell has repeatedly acknowledged that any interpretation of quantum theory that goes beyond its mathematical formalism reflects philosophical assumptions that are not derived from science alone. Saunders also says that Russell's proposal makes God's action too episodic and too interventionist and yet too limited in its power to effect major changes except over immense periods of time. These objections have all been considered in the writings of Russell and others.[9]

Saunders has given a valuable and wide-ranging analysis of various theories of divine action at the quantum level and their philosophical assumptions. He points out, for example, that in defending non-interventionist divine action (in which there is said to be no violation of the laws of nature) we need to indicate whether we think laws are *descriptive* (describing observed regularities) or *prescriptive* (specifying necessity and determinism). I also appreciated Saunders's clarity in summarizing both sides of the debate as to whether *human freedom* is compatible or incompatible with determinism in nature, which parallels the debate on *divine freedom* and determinism in nature. But I am more dubious about his claim to be the first person to give careful scientific scrutiny to proposals for divine action at the quantum level. 'Notably lacking from almost all of the accounts of quantum Special Divine Action is any detailed treatment of what the implications are scientifically and how quantum SDA may be accommodated by the theory.'[10] This does not seem to be a fair criticism of the volumes from the CTNS/Vatican Observatory conferences to which scientists made many detailed technical contributions.

For me, the main problem in Russell's proposal is the idea that before the advent of life God controls all events within the limits set by quantum laws. According to the article quoted above, there is no element of chance or novelty in the inanimate world; everything that occurs is a 'hidden divine action'. In that realm all events are products of the *natural determination* of continuing superpositions (through the laws God established) plus subsequent *divine determination* through the selection of quantum events. This seems to make God fully responsible for the evil and suffering produced by inanimate systems today such as earthquakes, hurricanes, and even the AIDS virus (which is not a form of life). Before the advent of life, God's action through quantum events would have been *bottom–up*, which perpetuates in this realm the reductionistic assumption that the behavior of systems is determined by their smallest parts. Russell says that after the advent of life, God withholds his power to control all quantum events in order to allow creativity, top–down causality within organisms, and finally human freedom. I will indicate later how process thought avoids the discontinuities in the mode of God's operation at different stages of cosmic history, and at different levels in nature today, that are portrayed in Russell's account.

Holism in Quantum Physics

In addition to the challenge of indeterminacy to determinism, the holism of quantum physics has challenged the reductionism that seemed to be implied by classical physics. An impressive form of holism known as *non-locality* is shown in a type of experiment proposed by Einstein and more recently by John Bell. In one version, a source emits two photons, A and B, which fly off in opposite directions – left and right, let us say. One detector at the left measures the spin of A. The spin of B is immediately known; it is equal and opposite to that of A, since the system initially had total spin zero. In a 1997 experiment, the left detector was thirty kilometers distant at the far end of an optical fiber. The orientation of this detector was chosen while A was in flight – too late for a signal to reach B before it arrived at the right detector, assuming that no signal can travel faster than the speed of light, as relativity theory requires.

Quantum theory describes each photon in flight as a mixture ('superposition') of waves representing all possible spin orientations. As we have seen, each set of waves collapses to a single value only when a measurement is made. How could the waves representing B know what is happening to the waves representing A? The connection seems to be instantaneous and does not decrease with distance as most physical forces do. Evidently the two particles originating in one event must be described by a single overall wavefunction, no matter how far apart they are. However, we could not use such a system to send a message faster than the speed of light (in violation of relativity theory) because the spin of A is unpredictable; it can be recorded but not controlled by the experimenter.

Einstein made two assumptions: (1) *classical realism* (individual particles possess definite classical properties at all times, even when we are not observing them), and (2) *locality* (no causal influence can be transmitted faster than the speed of light). Two-particle experiments like the one above show that both of these assumptions cannot be correct. Most physicists conclude that we should follow Bohr here, giving up classical realism and keeping locality. They insist that particles that originated in one event must be regarded as a single system even when they are far apart. Only after an observation can they be regarded as having separate identities and independent existence. But it is possible to maintain a critical realism concerning the probabilistic whole while abandoning classical realism concerning the separate parts.[11] Thus physicist Paul Davies concludes, 'The system of interest cannot be regarded as a collection of things, but as an indivisible, unified whole.'[12] John Polkinghorne writes, 'Quantum states exhibit an unexpected degree of togetherness ... The experiment points to a surprisingly integrationist view of the relationship of systems which have once interacted with each other, however widely they may subsequently separate.'[13]

Bob Russell comments on my conclusions as follows:

> According to Barbour, most physicists follow Bohr by giving up classical realism and retaining special relativity. Barbour then tentatively sides with Bohr and suggests that locality can be combined with critical realism and a limited form of holism. In my opinion Barbour's move does not solve the problem, but it might stimulate us to reconsider the alternatives of either locality or classical realism in slightly different forms. Following other scholars, I believe we should explore a nonlocal form of realism in which quantum non-locality is an indication of an underlying 'non-separable' ontology. Here entangled (once bound) particles now at a (spacelike) distance remain part of an ontological whole. This in turn takes us to the edge of current research and points us ahead to the questions on the horizon: how are we to produce a conceptual framework, or another, through which a nonseparable ontology can be made intelligible? Whether Whitehead's metaphysics will provide such a framework is, in my opinion, an open question, particularly in light of the rather mixed assessment it received by Abner Shimony in relation to Quantum Mechanics.[14]

I am impressed by Russell's interest in a 'non-separable ontology', though I think Whitehead's metaphysics remains a live option. Shimony's article suggests that with some modifications process concepts are consistent with both quantum theory and relativity.[15] Other physicists have defended in detail the compatibility of process thought with these theories.[16]

Russell notes the holism shown in these recent two-particle experiments, but he has not given attention to other holistic features of quantum theory. In my earliest writings I tried to show that *holism* is a pervasive characteristic of the quantum world and I have often returned to this theme.[17] A bound electron in an atom has to be considered as a state of the whole atom rather than as a separate entity. As more complex systems are built up, new properties appear that were not foreshadowed in the parts alone. New wholes have distinctive principles of organization as systems and exhibit properties and activities not found in their components.

The Pauli Exclusion Principle states that in any atom no two orbital electrons can be in identical states (with the same quantum numbers specifying energy, angular momentum, and spin). To this remarkable and far-reaching principle can be attributed the periodic table and the chemical properties of the elements. This 'exclusion' does not resemble any imaginable set of forces or fields. In quantum reasoning any attempt to describe the behavior of the constituent electrons is simply abandoned; the properties of the atom as a whole are analyzed by new laws unrelated to those governing its separate parts, which have now lost their identity. An orbital electron is a state of the atomic system, not an identifiable entity.[18]

The energy levels of an array of atoms in the solid state (such as a transistor) are a property of *the whole system* rather than of its components. Again, some of the disorder–order transitions and the so-called cooperative phenomena have proven impossible to analyze through the behavior of the components – for example, the behavior of electrons in a superconductor. Such system laws are not derivable from the laws of the components. Distinctive explanatory concepts characterize higher organizational levels. Interpenetrating fields and integrated totalities replace self-contained, externally related particles as fundamental images of nature. The being of any entity is constituted by its relationships and its participation in more inclusive patterns.

David Bohm carries the concept of holism even further. He has developed the equations for a quantum potential that acts as an instantaneous pilot wave guiding quantum events. He elaborates an underlying *implicate order* whose information unfolds into the explicate order of particular fields and particles. One analogy he uses is a holographic transparency in which every part has three-dimensional information about the whole object photographed. Bohm's scheme shows a dramatic wholeness by allowing for non-local, non-causal, instantaneous connections. Events separated in space and time are correlated because they are unfolded from the same implicate order, but there is no direct causal connection between them since one event does not itself influence another event.[19]

Bohm's theory does seem to fit well with the experiments on non-locality described above. But in general its predictions are identical with those of standard quantum theory, which most physicists are reluctant to abandon unless it conflicts with experimental evidence. Moreover, Bohm's theory is deterministic. For him, *holism* rather than *indeterminacy* is the distinctive feature of the quantum world. Bohm sees parallels in the holism found in the writings of the Hindu mystic Krishnamurti. In meditation there is a direct experience of undivided wholeness and the basic unity of all things. Fragmentation and egocentricity can be overcome in the absorption of the self in the undifferentiated and timeless whole. The parallels of Eastern mysticism and quantum physics have been presented by many authors since Fritjof Capra's *The Tao of Physics*.[20] In most cases, their worldview is monistic and deterministic. My own conviction is that a more limited holism can allow for a greater pluralism of agents as well as human freedom and individuality.

Holism and God's Action at Higher Levels

Holism at higher levels is significant because unlike quantum indeterminacy it supports the idea of top–down causality. Holism is a feature common to all levels and not unique to the quantum level. Consider first the transition from inanimate to living systems. Most physical and chemical systems will return to the most probable, disordered, equilibrium state if disturbed from it. But sometimes in systems that are unstable and far from equilibrium, a new level of *collective order* will appear and achieve a stable form. Ilya Prigogine won a Nobel prize for his work on dynamic systems far from equilibrium. One of his examples is the sudden appearance of a complex pattern of convection cells in the circulation of a fluid heated from below. In such cases a small fluctuation is amplified and leads to a new and more complex order that is resistant to further fluctuations and maintains itself with a throughput of energy from the environment.[21]

Prigogine has analyzed many inanimate *self-organizing* systems in which disorder at one level leads to order at a higher level, with new laws governing the behavior of structures showing new types of *complexity*. Randomness at one level leads to dynamic patterns at another level. In some cases the new order can be predicated by considering the average or statistical behavior of the myriad components. But in other cases, Prigogine shows, there are many possible outcomes, and no unique prediction can be made. Multiple divergent solutions arise from these non-linear instabilities. The formation of such self-organizing, self-perpetuating systems at the molecular level was perhaps the first step in the emergence of life.

Living organisms exhibit a *many-leveled hierarchy* of systems and subsystems. A level identifies a unit which is relatively integrated, stable, and self-regulating, even though it interacts with other units at the same level and at higher and lower levels. One such hierarchy of levels is identified structurally: quark, nucleus, atom, molecule, macromolecule, organelle, cell, organ, organism, and ecosystem. Others are identified functionally, for example information-processing networks in computers or brains.[22]

Top–down causality is the influence of a system on its subsystems. Higher-level events impose boundary conditions on chemical and physical processes at lower levels without violating lower-level laws. The state of the upper-level system is specified without reference to lower-level variables. Correlation of behaviors at one level does not require detailed knowledge of all its components. Network properties may be realized through a great variety of particular connections. The laws of chemistry limit the combinations of atoms that are found in DNA, but do not determine them. The meaning of the message conveyed by DNA is not given by the laws of chemistry, but by the interaction of the proteins expressed by the DNA within their wider organismic context. Theo Meyering describes top–down causation as follows:

> [Levels] are related by higher-level principles organizing lower-level events into systemic patterns of interaction. As a result, certain context-dependent causal pathways of physical activities will be selectively activated rather

> than others ... Higher-level patterns of organization are themselves
> genuine causal factors actually operative in channeling and orchestrating
> the lower-level flux of microphysical events to yield stable recurrent
> patterns of macrocausation that are self-sustaining or self-reproducing as a
> result of the systemic organization of their parts.[23]

Terrence Deacon has distinguished three kinds of emergence in which holistic
top–down causality is increasingly prominent. In *first-order emergence*, new
properties appear in an aggregate but they can be predicted from lower-level
laws and configurational relationships among the components, without
knowledge of the previous history of the system. For example, the liquidity
of water can be explained by the laws governing hydrogen, oxygen, and their
combination into water molecules. Thermodynamic laws for the behavior of
gases can be derived from the statistical mechanics of gas molecules. In *second-
order emergence*, system-wide configurations change across time and affect
lower-level interactions. Higher-order regularities can become unpredictably
unstable and new causal architectures are formed. Chaos theory and
complexity theory show critical sensitivity to initial conditions and to historical
contingencies.[24]

In *third-order emergence*, according to Deacon, levels of causality are linked
across wider spans of time and space. When features of the state of a system
can be represented as an historical memory, the information can be
repeatedly re-entered at lower levels of the ongoing system. This occurs in
differing ways in the development of an embryo, in biological evolution, and
in the cultural transmission of information. In the continuing interaction
between genes, organisms, populations, and environments, causality is
distributed across time and space, forming multilayered systems of great
complexity. Representation, memory, and reference are crucial features of
cognitive processes expressed in global configurations of neural activity in the
brain. Deacon defends a 'progressive holism' of 'top–down configurational
causes' in addition to bottom–up causes that have a discrete location in time
and space.

The idea of levels of reality can be extended if God is viewed as acting from
an even higher level than nature. In his earlier writing, Arthur Peacocke
proposed that God exerts a *top–down causality* on the world. God's action
would influence relationships at lower levels without violating lower-level laws.
Constraints may be introduced not just at spatial or temporal boundaries but
also internally through any additional specification allowed by lower-level
laws. In human beings, God would influence their highest evolutionary level,
that of mental activity, which would affect the neural networks and neurons in
the brain. Within human beings, divine action would be effected down the
hierarchy of natural levels, concerning which we have at least some
understanding of relationships between adjacent levels.[25] His use of top–
down causality seems to me more problematic in the case of divine action on
inanimate matter; we would have to assume direct influence between the
highest level (God) and the lowest level (matter) in the absence of intermediate
levels – which has no analogy within the natural order.

More recently, Peacocke extends to God the idea of *whole–part constraints* found in nature. He proposes that God as 'the most inclusive whole' acts on 'the-world-as-a-whole'.[26] But this spatial analogy seems dubious because the world does not have spatial boundaries. Moreover the rejection of universal simultaneity in relativity theory makes it impossible to speak of 'the-world-as-a-whole' at any one moment. The whole is a spatiotemporal continuum with temporal as well as spatial dimensions. In such a framework God's action would presumably have to be more localized in space and time, interacting more directly with a particular part rather than indirectly through action on the spatiotemporal whole.

Philip Clayton has traced three stages in evolutionary history and assigns differing roles to God in each:[27]

1. The Physical Level

Though there may be some indeterminacy at this stage, lawfulness predominates and can be seen as an expression of God's constancy. But Clayton insists that Deism can be avoided because, according to the *panentheism* that he defends, God is always present in the world – even if only as the upholder of order and regularity.

2. The Biological Level

Here information, function, and form are crucial. In this context, it makes sense to speak of the role of information as formal causality. Moreover, the historicity of organisms and their changing evolutionary environments is important; Clayton cites Deacon's view of third-order emergence. With more complex living organisms, purposiveness and proto-mentality are present. Clayton holds that divine intentionality can influence the drives and unconscious goals of organisms. He claims that biology shows that purposiveness and proto-mentality are present only *after* the emergence of life.

3. The Human Level

Mental properties differ in kind from properties at lower levels and mental activities exert a distinctive type of causality. Clayton writes, 'I have argued the real existence and causal efficacy of the conscious or mental dimension of human personhood.'[28] Ideas and intentions can change history. God can influence our thoughts and motives at the mental level without violating lower-level laws. Human/divine interaction in religious experience, human history, and culture go far beyond anything previously possible. Prehuman life reveals little of the personal character of the divine, but human life can be an expression of God's personal agency.

Clayton balances continuity and discontinuity in evolutionary history, but for him discontinuity is greatest at the transitions between physical, biological, and human stages. But the transition between these stages appears problematic unless we postulate intermediate steps in the transitions. Clayton's thought resembles process thought in many ways, but by limiting God's role in the physical world to that of upholding lawful regularities, he denies any possibility of direct divine action before the advent of life.

Interiority in Process Thought

Whitehead himself was influenced by *quantum physics* in his portrayal of reality as a series of momentary events and interpenetrating fields rather than isolated enduring bits of matter. The temporality and holism seen in the quantum world were taken to be characteristic of all entities. Process thought rejects determinism, allows for alternative potentialities, and accepts the presence of lawful regularities among events. It shares with *evolutionary theory* the conviction that processes of change are more fundamental than enduring substances and that no absolute line separates human from non-human life, either historically or in the world today. An organism is a highly integrated and dynamic pattern of interdependent events. Its parts contribute to and are modified by the unified activity of the whole. Every event occurs in a context that affects it. The process view is ecological in conceiving of the world as a network of interactions in which every entity is constituted by its relationships.

Process thought envisages two aspects of all events as seen from within and from without. The evolution of *interiority*, like the evolution of physical structures, is characterized by both continuity and change. The forms taken by interiority or subjectivity vary widely, from rudimentary memory, sentience, responsiveness, and anticipation in simple organisms to consciousness and self-consciousness in more complex ones. Interiority can be construed as a moment of experience, though conscious experience occurs only in organisms with nervous systems.[29]

Clayton claims that the findings of science are 'incompatible' with the presence of interiority before the appearance of life.[30] I would agree that the effects of interiority at the physical level are indeed negligible, though indeterminacy, holism, and top–down causality are evident at that level. But I would argue that a minimal interiority can be postulated even at the physical level for the sake of *metaphysical generality*. In Whitehead's definition a category must be universally applicable to all events; the diversity among the characteristics of events must then be accounted for by the diversity of the modes in which these basic categories are exemplified. Mechanical interactions can be viewed as low-grade organismic events (since organisms always have a mechanical aspect), whereas no extrapolation of mechanical concepts can yield the concepts needed to describe subjective experience. Our categories must also represent the continuity of developmental processes and of evolutionary history, and the impossibility of drawing any sharp lines between stages.[31]

Moreover, we have immediate access to *human experience*. I know myself as an experiencing subject. We are part of nature; even though human experience is an extreme case of an event in nature it offers clues as to the character of other events. To be sure, we must avoid the dangers of *anthropomorphism*, the assumption that beings are just like us. But we must also avoid the dangers of *mechanomorphism*, the assumption that other beings are just like machines.

For matter to produce mind, in evolution or in embryological development, there must be intermediate levels, and mind and matter must have some characteristics in common. Process thought interprets lower-level events as simpler cases of higher-level ones, rather than trying to interpret higher-level events in terms of lower-level concepts or resorting to dualism. Yet Whitehead himself was so intent on elaborating a set of metaphysical categories applicable to all events that I believe he gave insufficient attention to the radically different ways in which those categories are exemplified at different levels.

Among thinkers influenced by Whitehead, Charles Hartshorne developed most fully the idea of *a hierarchy of levels* intermediate between the atom and the human self. He held that the basic components of reality are not one kind of enduring substance (matter) or two kinds of enduring substance (mind and matter), but one kind of event with two phases. In the objective phase a unitary event is receptive from the past; in the subjective phase it is creative toward the future. Every event is a subject for itself and becomes an object for other subjects. This view combines dipolar monism and organizational pluralism. It is a form of *monism* because it insists on the common character of all unified events. *Dipolar* makes an ontological claim about the two phases of every event, not merely an epistemological distinction as proposed by some advocates of two-aspect monism. *Organizational pluralism* signals recognition that events can be organized in diverse ways. A stone is merely an aggregate of its components with no patterns of integration at higher levels. But a cell is a complex community with many channels of communication that enable it to act as an integrated unit. Only in advanced life-forms are data integrated in the high-level stream of experience we call mind.[32]

Is the subjective experience that is postulated in process thought accessible to scientific investigation?[33] Does not science have to start from objective data accessible to all observers? Whitehead sometimes stresses *the selectivity of science* and the abstractive character of its concepts. He writes: 'Science can find no individual enjoyment in nature; science can find no aim in nature; science can find no creativity in nature; it finds mere rules of succession. These negations are true of natural science; they are inherent in its methodology.'[34] On this reading, we must accept the limitations of science and supplement it by including it in a wider metaphysical synthesis that integrates diverse kinds of experience. This view would also limit the contribution that process metaphysics might make to science.

A similar view is taken by John Haught in discussing Teilhard de Chardin's concept of 'the within':

> This does not mean that theology must reject science's *methodological* bracketing of the fact of subjectivity in nature. Science has every right to leave out all considerations of subjectivity as long as its practitioners remain aware of this self-limitation. ... It is of utmost importance that a theology in dialogue with science have available to it a metaphysics fully aware that science, in its attempt to be clear and distinct, has left behind

what is truly fundamental in the natural world, including the possibility of a vein of subjectivity inaccessible to scientific objectification.[35]

By contrast, David Griffin has pointed to other passages in which Whitehead says that adequate metaphysical categories are in the interest of science itself and that scientific concepts are after all reformable. Griffin suggests that if every entity is for itself a moment of experience, one would expect this to be reflected in observable behavior. He accepts the idea that the initiative and creativity of organisms have sparked evolutionary changes (the Baldwin effect). He points out that ethologists use explanatory concepts referring to the mental life of birds and animals. As we consider lower levels, he asks, how can we draw a sharp line at any point? He holds, moreover, that scientists adopting a process metaphysics would be likely to redirect research to problems neglected by other scientists, and they might propose new concepts and theories and ways of testing them observationally.[36] I am inclined to agree with Griffin here, though I agree with Haught that we must be aware of the limitations of science and the need to draw from diverse forms of human experience.

God's Action in Process Thought

Let us consider finally the understanding of divine action in process thought. Whereas some theologians stress God's role in establishing and maintaining order, and others see God's hand in violations of order, for Whitehead God is involved in both order and novelty. *Order* arises from God's structuring of possibilities and from the entity's conformation to its past. *Novelty* arises from God's offering of alternative possibilities and from the entity's self-creation. This means that no event can be attributed solely to God. God presents new possibilities to the world but leaves alternatives open, eliciting the response of entities in the world. As the source of novelty God is present in the interiority of every event as it unfolds, but God never exclusively determines the outcome.

According to process philosophy, God does not intervene unilaterally to fill particular gaps in nature like the old 'God-of-the-gaps' whose role was diminished with each advance of scientific knowledge. God is already present in the unfolding of every event, but no event is attributable to God alone. The role filled by God is not a gap of the kind that might be filled by science. The contribution of God cannot be separated out as if it were another external force, for it operates through the interiority of every entity.

God's ability to engender creative change at lower levels seems to be limited. God is always one factor among others and, particularly with respect to low-level beings in which creativity is minimal, this power seems to be negligible. But we must remember that God is not absent from events that monotonously repeat their past, for God is the ground of order as well as novelty. At low levels God's novel action may be beyond detection, though signs of it may be present in the long sweep of cosmic history and emergent evolution.[37]

Even when there is novelty at higher levels, God always acts along with other causes, qualifying but not abrogating their operation. This seems to *limit God's power* severely as compared to traditional ideas of omnipotence. But it is consistent with our understanding of evolution as a long, slow, gradual process over billions of years. Each stage is built on previous stages and supports the next stage. Complex forms presuppose simple ones. Life had to await appropriate conditions. Cosmic history resembles a long trial-and-error experiment more than a detailed, predetermined plan. Process thought holds that God works patiently, gently, and unobtrusively.

If God does not act unilaterally but only through the responses of other beings, we would expect the divine influence to be more effective *at higher levels* where creativity and purposeful goals are more prominent. It is not surprising that the rate of evolutionary change accelerated in early human and then cultural history. In human life and in religious experience, God's influence and human response could occur in unprecedented ways. The Whiteheadian understanding of God is consistent with what we know about cosmic, biological, and human history.

Russell suggests that God has the power to control all quantum events but refrains from using it in the animate world to allow for creativity and human freedom. This theme of divine *self-limitation* or *kenosis* has been developed by many recent authors. Some are motivated by the desire to protect the integrity of nature and human freedom, or to reduce God's responsibility for the suffering and evil in the world. Among Christian writers it also reflects the conviction that God overcomes evil through suffering love, as exemplified in the Cross, rather than by sheer power. Feminist authors have noted that historically our patriarchal culture has given attention to *power* in human relations and correspondingly in God's relation to the world. Feminists have affirmed the importance of care and nurture, which have more often been associated with women in Western history. All of these forms of *kenosis* seem to diminish God's power, but they can better be understood as pointing to a different form of power: not *overpowering* control of another being, but *empowerment* of another being. Creative empowerment is not a 'zero-sum' game (in which one person loses something when the other person gains it), but rather a 'positive-sum' game (in which both parties can gain).[38]

Process thought is distinctive in holding that limitations of divine power arise from *metaphysical necessity* rather than from voluntary self-limitation. In analyzing omniscience, process authors claim that if temporal passage is real for God, and if chance, novelty, and human freedom are features of the world, then the details of future events are simply unknowable, even to God, until they occur. It would make no sense to say that God might have had knowledge of the future but set aside such a capacity. Similarly, process thinkers present a view of reality in which divine omnipotence is in principle impossible.[39]

Charles Hartshorne elaborates a metaphysics in which all reality including God is *inherently social*. Every being has passive and receptive as well as active and causally effective capabilities. No being can have a monopoly of power or effect unilateral control. It is not as if the presence of the world limits God's otherwise unlimited power, since any valid concept of God must include sociality and relationality. Hartshorne says that in some aspects God is temporal and affected by the world, but in other aspects God exemplifies classical divine attributes. God alone is everlasting, omnipresent, and omniscient (in knowing all that can be known). God is perfect in love and wisdom and unchanging in purposes and goals. God offers an initial aim to every entity and orders the world through cosmic laws that limit but do not exclude creaturely freedom. God's power is universal in scope. It 'influences all that happens but determines nothing in its concrete particularity'.[40]

To say that the limitation of God's power is a metaphysical necessity rather than a voluntary self-limitation is not to say that it is imposed by something outside God. This is not a Gnostic or Manichean dualism in which recalcitrant matter restricts God's effort to embody pure eternal forms in the world. If *God's nature* is to be loving and creative, it would be inconsistent to say that God might have chosen not to be loving and creative. We cannot say that God was once omnipotent and chose to set aside such powers temporarily. If behind God's kenotic actions there was an omnipotent God who refrained from rescuing the victims of pain and suffering, the problem of theodicy would be acute. Hartshorne objects to divine omnipotence on *moral* as well as metaphysical grounds. Within a social view of reality, persuasion has a higher moral status than coercion, even if it entails greater risk of evil and suffering. He says that God does all that it would be good for a supreme being to do, though not all that it would be good for other beings to do for themselves. Process thought thus agrees with other proponents of kenotic theology on the limitation of God's power, but grounds it in the social character of reality, including God, rather than on a voluntary self-limitation at some point in cosmic history.

I have not discussed *physical cosmology*, which could be the topic of another dialogue with Bob Russell. I have indicated elsewhere that Whitehead wrote at a time when there was very little scientific evidence concerning the early universe. More recent theories suggest that the Big Bang was an absolute beginning, though it can still be interpreted as the beginning of a new universe among multiverses (in successive cycles of expansion and contraction, or in parallel universes born in quantum vacuum fluctuations or in black holes). Whitehead held that the limitation of God's power arises not only from God's nature but also from the influence of past events on subsequent events. Moreover, in the course of cosmic history events at higher levels of organization express increasing self-determination, culminating in human freedom. These limitations were not present in the early moments of our universe before even quarks existed. The pure potentialities in the primordial nature of God could have been more readily and rapidly realized in those dramatic early moments of the Big Bang than in subsequent history (even in a multiverse scenario) and would represent an essentially unilateral exercise of divine power.[41]

To sum up, process thought differs from Russell's proposal by suggesting how God might act at higher levels, and it develops more fully the themes of holism and top–down causality. Process thought defends ontological openness at all levels, and not just at the level of quantum indeterminacy. It holds that God acts in essentially the same way at all levels, with no discontinuities in the mode of divine action across cosmic history. Process thinkers agree with

Clayton in defending holism, emergence, and top–down causality at all levels. But in contrast to Clayton they allow the possibility of at least a minimal divine influence at the physical level, though not the total determination of quantum events (within the range of probabilistic potentialities) before the advent of life that Russell envisages. In short, I suggest that process thought offers a promising prospect for understanding God's role in nature that is consistent with the findings of science today. We are all greatly indebted to Bob Russell for having exemplified and encouraged wide-ranging reflection on 'Scientific Perspectives on Divine Action' in the years since the founding of CTNS, and we can hope that discussion of this important topic will continue in the future.

Notes

1 Robert John Russell, 'Tributes to Ian Graeme Barbour', *Theology and Science*, 2:1 (April 2004): 5–6.

2 Robert John Russell (ed.), *Fifty Years in Science and Religion: Ian G. Barbour and His Legacy* (Aldershot, UK: Ashgate, 2004).

3 Ian G. Barbour, *Religion and Science: Historical and Contemporary Issues* (San Francisco: HarperSanFrancisco, 1997), 170–73.

4 Robert John Russell, 'Divine Action and Quantum Mechanics: A Fresh Assessment', in *Quantum Mechanics: Scientific Perspectives on Divine Action*, ed. by Robert John Russell, Philip Clayton, Kirk Wegter-McNelly, and John Polkinghorne (Vatican City State and Berkeley, CA: Vatican Observatory and Center for Theology and the Natural Sciences, 2001), 293–328.

5 Ibid., 318.

6 Robert John Russell, 'Barbour's Assessment of the Philosophical and Theological Implications of Physics and Cosmology', in *Fifty Years*, 150.

7 Nicholas Saunders, 'Does God Cheat at Dice? Divine Action and Quantum Possibilities', *Zygon*, 35:3 (2000): 539.

8 Nicholas Saunders, *Divine Action and Modern Science* (Cambridge: Cambridge University Press, 2002), 152.

9 See Robert John Russell, Nancey C. Murphy, and Arthur R. Peacocke (eds), *Chaos and Complexity: Scientific Perspectives on Divine Action* (Vatican City State and Berkeley, CA: Vatican Observatory and Center for Theology and the Natural Sciences, 1995) and Russell et al. (eds), *Quantum Mechanics*.

10 Saunders, *Divine Action*, 125.

11 Barbour, *Religion and Science*, 175–7.

12 Paul Davies, *Other Worlds* (London: Abacus, 1982), 125.

13 John Polkinghorne, *Quantum World* (London: Penguin Books, 1986), 79, 80.

14 Russell, 'Barbour's Assessment', 147. A 'spacelike' interval between two events is one across which no communication is possible without exceeding the velocity of light.

15 Abner Shimony, 'Quantum Physics and the Philosophy of Whitehead', in *Search for a Naturalistic World View: Volume II, Natural Science and Metaphysics* (Cambridge: Cambridge University Press, 1993, reprinted from 1965), 291–309.

16 Timothy E. Eastman and Hank Keeton (eds), *Physics and Whitehead: Quantum, Process, and Experience* (Albany, NY: State University of New York Press, 2004); Michael Epperson, *Quantum Mechanics and the Philosophy of Alfred North Whitehead* (New York: Fordham University Press, 2004).

17   Ian G. Barbour, *Issues in Science and Religion* (Englewood Cliffs, NJ: Prentice-Hall, 1965), 295–7; Barbour, *Religion and Science*, 173–5.

18   Ian G. Barbour, *When Science Meets Religion* (San Francisco: HarperSanFrancisco, 2000), 81–3.

19   David Bohm, *Wholeness and the Implicate Order* (Boston: Routledge and Kegan Paul, 1980).

20   Fritjof Capra, *The Tao of Physics* (New York: Bantam Books, 1977).

21   Ilya Prigogine and Isabelle Stengers, *Order out of Chaos* (New York: Bantam Books, 1984).

22   Barbour, *Religion and Science*, 230–35.

23   Theo Meyering, 'Downward Causation', in *Encyclopedia of Science and Religion*, ed. by J. Wentzel Vrede van Huysteen (New York: Macmillan Reference, 2003), 229.

24   Terrence Deacon, 'The Hierarchic Logic of Emergence: Untangling the Interdependence of Evolution and Self-Organization', in *Evolution and Learning: The Baldwin Effect Reconsidered*, ed. by Bruce Weber and David Depew (Cambridge, MA: MIT Press, 2003), 81–106.

25   Arthur Peacocke, *Theology for a Scientific Age*, enlarged edn (Minneapolis: Fortress Press, 1993), Chapter 3.

26   Arthur Peacocke, *Paths from Science Towards God: The End of all our Exploring* (Oxford: One World, 2001), 108–14.

27   Philip Clayton, 'The Emergence of Spirit', *CTNS Bulletin*, 20:4 (Fall 2000): 3–20.

28   Philip Clayton, 'Neuroscience, the Person, and God', in *Neuroscience and the Person: Scientific Perspectives on Divine Action*, ed. by Robert John Russell, Nancey Murphy, Theo C. Meyering, and Michael Arbib (Vatican City State and Berkeley, CA: Vatican Observatory and Center for Theology and the Natural Sciences, 1999), 211.

29   See Barbour, *Religion and Science*, 287–290.

30   Philip Clayton, 'Barbour's Panentheistic Metaphysic', in *Fifty Years*, 113–23.

31   Ian G. Barbour, *Nature, Human Nature, and God* (Minneapolis, MN: Fortress Press, 2001), 37, 99.

32   Charles Hartshorne, *Reality as Social Process* (Glencoe, IL: Free Press, 1953), Chapter 1.

33   These three paragraphs are adapted from Ian G. Barbour, 'Evolution and Process Thought', *Theology and Science*, 3:2 (2005): 161–78.

34   Alfred North Whitehead, *Modes of Thought* (Cambridge: Cambridge University Press, 1938), 211.

35   John F. Haught, *God After Darwin: A Theology of Evolution* (Boulder, CO: Westview Press, 2000), 178–9.

36   David Ray Griffin, 'On Ian Barbour's *Issues in Science and Religion*', *Zygon*, 23 (1988): 57–81.

37   See Barbour, *Religion and Science*, 295–7.

38   John Polkinghorne (ed.), *The Work of Love: Creation as Kenosis* (Grand Rapids, MI, and London: Eerdmans and SPCK, 2001).

39   Ian G. Barbour, 'God's Power: A Process View', in *The Work of Love*, 1–20.

40   Charles Hartshorne, *Omnipotence and Other Theological Mistakes* (Albany, NY: State University of New York, 1984), 25.

41   Barbour, *Nature, Human Nature, and God*, 114–16.

CHAPTER NINE

Basic Puzzles in Science and Religion

Charles H. Townes

Over the last few decades there has been a steadily increasing amount of useful discussion between the fields of science and theology. Most of it has been done by individuals who are sympathetic and interested in both fields, in an effort to make them more coherent and tolerant of each other. Robert John Russell has played a major role both as an important scholar and in forming the very effective Center for Theology and the Natural Sciences. These developments and discussions have brought out much mutual support between science and religion, and a tendency to view their apparent inconsistencies in ways which are as positive and productive as is practical. I appreciate this approach. But to solve human puzzles or problems, it is also often useful to face them squarely, defining them clearly and as boldly as possible so that we are strongly challenged. Problems and inconsistencies appear in the sciences themselves, and clear statements of them are often helpful in encouraging thought and work, though this can also be frustrating.

The physical sciences are, I believe, increasingly facing both new problems and some long-standing ones, such as: the origin of our universe; the inconsistency between quantum mechanics and relativity; why the physical constants are as they are, and whether they are constant; why zero-point fluctuations are not more evident; and whether there are dimensions other than time and three-dimensional space which we do not directly sense but which have effects on our universe. All this makes me think it useful to state as overtly and clearly as I can some of the important apparent inconsistencies between present science and religion with the hope that we can face them rigorously and continuously while at the same time recognizing that such inconsistencies may be due primarily to our limitations rather than to any ultimate and fundamental clash between these two important fields of human thought and instincts. Such problems and inconsistencies are not new or unknown, but I believe their statement and a bit of discussion may be useful. Five of them follow.

First, a basic question for both science and religion is what initiated our universe, or perhaps whence came its initiator. There is an inherent problem with the nature of a beginning. Even if we assume a set of physical laws or equations which create our universe, why are they that way and what allowed even their possibility?

We can indeed construct some physical laws which created the 'Big Bang', a unique moment for our universe. The result then develops, following physical laws, into just the kind of universe we experience near and far around us. We have recently discovered properties of the background microwave radiation, coming toward us from all directions, which provide many tell-tale characteristics of this event about 14 billion years ago and agree well with certain physical laws. But why did these particular physical laws apply, and why do the physical constants – the force of gravity and electricity, or the size of quanta and characteristics of particles – have the values they do? A partial explanation offered by some scientists is that there were many 'Big Bangs', each creating a different universe, and ours is only one of billions which turned out by chance to have the physical constants it does and make a universe suitable for human life. But why should each universe have a different random set of physical properties? So far, we know no way of contacting the other universes and hence confirming such a hypothesis. Hence this solution does not appear to fit ordinary science, which normally requires the possibility of a test.

Religious individuals can say, of course, that the universe was God's creation. And as we understand more about the expansion of our Universe, the formation and characteristics of stars, or why we have the richness of chemicals on earth and the conditions that can allow life, we recognize that physical laws must be just as they are for us to be here at all. This recognition has produced the idea and phraseology of 'intelligent design', which fits well into the assumption of a creative God. But this has a problem with the real beginning similar to that of science. How did God come about? We can hardly think he created himself and are left only with the same type of problem pure science faces in avoiding any assumption of God. He, or it (the set of physical laws), was just always there and hence our universe could be born.

Second, modern science allows us to understand and explain much of what's happening, so much in fact that it poses a very natural question: is there a place and possibility for God to act in our world?

Some individuals see no way in which God can act or has acted in this world. Others see no room for God in our present universe, but believe he could have planned and created it in such a way that it would develop into the beautiful universe we know. This represents a religious view in some sense; it is a recognition that God's will and creativity surround us always. But it is a step back from the usual religious view of God's continued action among us to focus merely on God's having provided the initial design which we and our universe follow.

Before the twentieth century, science was already remarkably successful and seemed to say that everything happening in our world was completely deterministic. That is, given the particular present situation the laws of science determine completely what will happen at any future time. But in the twentieth century this changed with the study of very small particles and the discovery of quantum mechanics. Science now has fundamental laws predicting the probability of particular things happening, but it is not able to say precisely which of the likely things will actually happen. An electron can never be located at a precise place, nor be known to head in a precise direction.

Particularly for very small objects we can predict only a range of likely behaviors. And, while we can predict the behavior of large objects rather more successfully, though not perfectly, the behaviors of larger objects are sometimes affected in major ways by the unpredictable behavior of smaller ones, such as atoms. For example, quantum mechanics tells us that we can never be sure when a radioactive atom might emit a particle which sets off a switch which blows up a building. Similarly, a genetic mutation, very much affecting a developing life-form, may be due to the basically unpredictable behavior of an atom or molecule.

Early in the history of quantum mechanics, many scientists thought that perhaps the unpredictability of phenomena which had been discovered provided a place where God could and was acting. It is well known that Einstein distrusted the randomness and uncertainty predicted by quantum mechanics, believing there must be some 'hidden force' which determines just what happens, and the problem was simply that we didn't know what the hidden force was or what it was doing. But now such a supposition is generally disproved, again leaving no room for any current 'hidden force' or perhaps no action by a God. This disproof comes from experimental results associated with Bell's theorem. The theorem predicts, for example, the results of measurements on two particles which are initially related, but then separate and have their characteristics measured in separate places. The statistical correlation of characteristics of the two particles allows a test to determine whether there is any unrecognizable force affecting the particles, or only that the quantum mechanics uncertainty principle applies. And the answer demonstrated by a number of independent experiments is that there is no unrecognized force. To most people, this appears to be conclusive proof against Einstein's intuition, and that no God can be affecting an outcome. Only the laws of our science apply even though only the probability of various outcomes can be determined by scientific law, not necessarily a specific result.

Bell's theorem and the associated experiments seem completely logical and conclusive. However, I do not believe this eliminates the possibility of God's action in the world. What it really seems to show is that God did not intervene during the experiments which were done. It is not in fact assumed by most religious people that God intervenes or exerts a determining force in all actions on earth, but rather that he made the laws which generally govern these actions and he takes separate action or intervenes only on occasions when such intervention is needed. How this intervention can occur is a mystery to us, but if it occurs it would hardly be expected to show up in the statistics of a normal physics experiment. God could of course purposely avoid any intervention in such tests, but still occasionally intervene and produce the miracles which many religious people attribute to his action.

Consider even the resurrection of Christ's body, one of the most striking miracles of the Bible. Could God have intervened and affected the quantum mechanical behavior of each atom in Christ's dead body, restoring the body's molecular structure into a living Christ? Bell's theorem doesn't really prove that could not occur. The real mystery to us is how God can intervene. Our scientific experiments do not rule out such intervention.

Is there indeed some spiritual force, an influence on natural materials, of which our science is completely unaware? A similar question comes up in connection with free will, and whether humans really have free will. That a new type of force might exist is not completely contrary to scientific methodology, though it is something we presently do not understand. Some scientific models proposed to understand physical matter, for example, make the assumption that there are other dimensions, in addition to time and the three directions of space, and that these other dimensions affect us substantially even though we do not sense them. Such assumptions are yet to be proven correct, but they are made as part of the scientific method and exploration. And they are not very different from the assumption of a spiritual dimension or a God affecting us which is not sensed in any simple and direct way. But the question remains, does god intervene in our world and, if so, how?

My third question: do humans have free will? That is, can an individual make a decision and take action in a way which is not determined by past experience and present conditions, in accordance with physical laws? And if so, what is this 'thing' or 'spirit' that can make an independent decision?

We all feel that we can make at least some free choices. I know no scientist who does not have and nurture this instinctive feeling, even though it appears contrary to present scientific knowledge and understanding. Free will is of course an inherent religious assumption in the concept of an evil or a good person; something within the person has independence and a character. Yet, as far as we know our bodies are made of atoms which obey the laws of quantum mechanics and each atom must act in accordance with its physical nature and the forces it encounters. What independence can we really have?

One suggestion discussed by religious and philosophically oriented individuals is the so-called 'emergence' principle. This is that when many simple objects which we believe we understand are assembled into a complex whole, new phenomena emerge which we could not have predicted and may not understand. This certainly occurs. A simple case to consider, for example, is water vapor, a gas of individual molecules bumping into and repelling each other. Would we predict that, if the gas density were to become high enough, many of these individual molecules would get together, form water droplets, and flow? And would we predict that, if the temperature is below zero centigrade they would then assemble in an orderly fashion and form solid crystals of ice? Once we see that actually happen, we think we can understand it. But in nature there are many still more complex and surprising phenomena. So why not the occurrence of free will in the enormously complex series of nerve cells which make up our brain?

I do not myself believe that the 'emergence' mechanism can explain free will. This is because free will is contrary to the basic laws that each atom must follow. Within other complex systems in nature, we do not encounter phenomena which are contrary to the basic nature of the components of which the system is made, even though unpredictable behavior may occur. But freedom of decision or action which avoids the dictates of physics on which each atom depends is contrary to basic atomic nature as we understand it, and does not seem logical or possible.

One might also ask, how far back along the evolutionary chain does free will go? Did our chimpanzee-like ancestors have free will? Do worms or single-cell animals have free will? If free will really exists, what is required for this existence and where does it come from?

God, as commonly conceived, involves phenomena which are not describable in terms of the science we presently know. Free will may have some of this same character. As discussed under my second question, perhaps there are other important dimensions in our universe which affect us, but which we cannot sense overtly and directly, as is assumed in some current but exploratory scientific proposals. Perhaps these dimensions or some presently quite unknown scientific principles are involved in free will. When early in the previous century science moved from complete determinism to quantum mechanical uncertainty we went through a rather complete revolution in our scientific thinking and philosophy. Perhaps there will be another such change, explaining the nature of free will (if it is found to exist).

Fourth, what is consciousness? How can it be defined, and to what extent does it occur in species other than humans?

We think we know what is meant by consciousness, and in most cases couple it very closely to the human mind and human characteristics. Yet I have never encountered a satisfactory definition of what it is, or what couples it so strongly to humans. One sophisticated friend defined for me a conscious organism as one which (1) has some purpose or purposes; (2) can sense the world and events around it; and (3) takes action on the basis of its purpose and senses. This sounds rather nicely descriptive, but then, to reveal the difficulty of such definitions in a rather extreme way, can't we say this describes a mouse-trap? There is a purpose, a sense of what's happening, and a snap action resulting from the two – all applying to a mouse-trap.

The problem of defining consciousness is, I believe, closely related to the problem of whether life, or human life in particular, can be essentially duplicated by a mechanism. Some think that eventually, as our technology develops, the equivalence of life will be constructed mechanically. If we understand a particular process, I believe it logical that we can in fact duplicate it with a mechanism. The development of computers, with their enormous number of minute components, has made it more and more obvious that we can mechanize very complex actions if we understand the processes involved. But I have often wondered whether eventually human beings will understand fully how their own mind works. If so, then this could open the way to mechanistic construction of something more or less human. We do understand many other rather complex systems, but it may be that for system A, such as our brain, to understand system B, it must be more complex than system B. In this case something can never completely understand itself. And if so, we shall never in principle be able to mechanize a human and perhaps never understand all the subtleties which we associate with human consciousness. But this is only a supposition.

It may be that our free will and our consciousness, as well as other human aspects associated with spirituality, involve some phenomena and principles that are completely different from any we presently visualize. Additional dimensions, perhaps, as mentioned above, ones which we don't sense but have a powerful effect on us, may indeed be present. As already noted, some scientists are willing to postulate and study possible results of such undetected dimensions in trying to understand the nature of matter. I believe we should be open to such possibilities as contributing to the mysteries of free will, consciousness, and 'spiritual' phenomena. Will we eventually know, in a scientific sense, whether this is real?

Finally, what, where, and when is the human spirit or individual? We instinctively feel that an individual is something existing in the body we see, but what is it and where does it reside? The human spirit or person has at times been connected closely with the heart, or more commonly with the mind, while not being any particular part of either.

It has been made clear that both the heart and mind are critical to human functioning. But now that doctors can install artificial hearts, it's obvious that an individual does not exist within the heart. We know, too, that at least some parts of the brain can stop functioning and still a person exists. Where does the essence of our being exist? And is it indeed something which continues to exist after the body completely stops functioning? Is there something which in itself is immortal? And when is it initiated – at fertilization of an ovum, at birth, or somehow gradually during development? Are we suddenly human and immortal, or does a human develop gradually and then at death disappear, or perhaps just gradually disappear as death approaches?

The science we know now can only allow a human to develop slowly and to eventually exist as an integrated body with the brain as most critical to our thoughts, character, and actions. And when the body is dead, present science would conclude that the individual no longer exists in any form except as his or her actions have affected the world which remains.

A quantum mechanical view of this remnant effect would be that an individual during his or her lifetime has changed and entangled many wavefunctions by observation, force, and action, and after death these wavefunctions last indefinitely, producing effects onward into infinite time which are at least partially determined by the individual's actions. So in some sense the individual lasts forever. However, the wavefunctions, while continuing indefinitely, are very much modified by other events and are very diffuse – hardly the unique spirit as some believe exists after death.

Religion, of course, normally considers the individual as something distinctly beyond body parts and mechanisms, and holds that some integrated being exists after normal death. These two points of view cannot be consistent unless there is much beyond our present understanding, and it should indeed not be surprising for this to be true. But if so, what is it? Again, new hidden forces or dimensions? Can we, as we progress and explore, learn more about the real situation – what, when, and where is the human spirit or individual?

The basic and challenging problems or puzzles which I have selected are of course well recognized by many, and confront any synthesis of science and religion. And they challenge our understanding of either science or religion. One can wonder whether human abilities will ever serve to solve them. But our scientific instincts in particular encourage us to never give up the ultimate possibility of understanding, and to take pleasure in exploring the unknown. Puzzles and unknown territory can be interesting, rather than simply troublesome. As noted, the development of physics has revolutionized our basic ideas, and recent cosmological discoveries are clarifying at least some aspects of our origins. Though we will undoubtedly always be left with mysteries, why shouldn't there be revolutions in our ideas of life, free will, or consciousness? Such revolutions might turn out to simply provide a clear view as to why we basically cannot understand the puzzles in our present framework of thought.

It is notable that typical revolutions in science, while sometimes changing our understanding almost completely, usually leave our old ideas and experience importantly valid as approximations. Our discovery of the atomic and molecular makeup of matter did not change the ways we handle normal materials, but did enrich the possibilities for new and useful materials. Quantum mechanics invoked a thorough philosophical change from our previous Newtonian mechanics and determination. Yet Newtonian mechanics in most circumstances works very well, describes much of our world, and we teach it to our students as a remarkably accurate and excellent description of human experience. I believe that whatever new, basic, and fascinating discoveries we will hopefully make in connection with the deep questions raised will likely be similar. They may radically change our viewpoints, but leave our present best and workable ideas still effective, useful, and hence real from a practical point of view. I personally feel strongly and believe that spirituality, free will, and the human sense of personality and consciousness are indeed reality, and am eager for any additional understanding.

CHAPTER TEN

Quantum Theology

John Polkinghorne

Robert John Russell – or Bob, to use a more familiar form of address – has been an active figure in the world of science and religion for about a quarter of a century. The Center for Theology and the Natural Sciences (CTNS) at Berkeley, which Bob founded and which he has directed throughout its existence, celebrates its quarter-centenary in 2006, a year which, by happy coincidence, is also that of Bob's sixtieth birthday. This conjunction affords an admirable opportunity for Bob's friends and colleagues to express their appreciation of his contribution to our discipline of science and theology.

Bob is a scientist–theologian and, like all of us who fall into this category, the style and content of his work has inevitably been influenced by the scientific context of his formation. In Bob's case this was physics, and much of his thinking might be classified under the rubric of quantum theology. Quantum theory was brought fully to birth in those remarkable years 1925–26, and it undoubtedly represents the greatest revolution in our understanding of the nature of the physical world since the pioneering discoveries of Isaac Newton. Quantum physics is quite different from classical physics, and its under-standing calls for modes of thought that are counter-intuitive to the habits formed by everyday experience. Those like Bob, who both know this and (in a Russell phrase) want to hold science and theology in 'creative mutual interaction', have work to do. Bob has devoted his professional career principally to this task.

Russell (now that we get down to academic detail, a more formal style of reference becomes appropriate) is internationally known and respected for the conferences he has organized in collaboration with George Coyne, SJ, of the Vatican Observatory, and for the carefully edited volumes that report their proceedings and which constitute a major resource in the literature of science and theology. The first of these meetings took place in 1987, on the occasion of the third centenary of the publication of Newton's *Principia*. The wide scope of the conference is indicated by the title of its proceedings, *Physics, Philosophy, and Theology*.[1] Russell contributed a long article on 'Quantum Physics in Philosophical and Theological Perspective', which adumbrated many of the ideas and issues with which his subsequent work has largely been concerned.

First, he surveyed the basic ideas of quantum physics. In this section an interesting feature is the emphasis laid on quantum statistics, the mutual behaviour of members of assemblies of identical quantum particles, which behave according either to Fermi statistics (in which case no two particles can occupy the same state) or to Bose statistics (in which case there is a propensity for particles to crowd together in the same state).[2] Russell saw this as a sign of the intrinsic relationality of the quantum world. The significance of quantum relationality had been greatly enhanced in the early 1980s by the experimental confirmation of the property of non-locality, the mutual entanglement of two quantum entities that have once interacted, a property expressing an influence between them which is preserved over spatial separation, however great. Russell also discussed the cloudy and fitful character of quantum physics, manifested by its intrinsic unpredictability and unpicturability. He summarized all these characteristics by describing the quantum world as 'gossamer' and as 'surprise and [possessing a] hidden nature'.[3] Turning his attention to philosophical issues, Russell then raised the question of ontology. There is agreement about quantum epistemology (the limitations on the knowledge of quantum systems imposed by the uncertainty principle), but the variety of conflicting interpretations of quantum theory that remain matters for argument indicates that there are considerable disagreements about its ontological implications. In common with most scientist–theologians, Russell inclines to some form of realist position, while acknowledging that simple local realism is an option ruled out by entanglement.[4]

Two themes were particularly significant in Russell's theological discussion. One was complementarity,[5] not at all invoked as a facile way of wriggling out of paradox, but as an analogical resource for cautious use by theology as it wrestles with its many dichotomies, such as grace and free will, humanity and divinity in Christ, numinous and mystical encounter with the divine. Yet more important, and foreshadowing a continuing concern for Russell, was the second theme of how quantum indeterminism (itself recognized to be a particular interpretation of quantum theory) might relate to thinking about divine action within creation. Could it be that at least part of the 'causal joint' for providential action is located in the exercise of a divine providential power to determine naturally indeterminate outcomes? Referring to an earlier pioneer who had addressed this issue, Russell wrote, 'Moreover, as William Pollard has argued extensively, we understand something about divine activity in the world if we view God as influencing our choices without violating the lawful processes which govern them. Moreover, from the quantum perspective, providence is not so much a time-independent or fixed *telos*, as a constant persuasive re-directing of our desires through creative divine immanence in all processes and events.'[6]

In this passage, two ideas are expressed that are frequently to be found in the writings of scientist–theologians on divine action. One is a theological necessity to understand providential agency as being exercised interactively, within the grain of nature, and not interventionally, against that grain. The fundamental reason for this stance lies in the recognition that God is the ordainer and sustainer of the laws of nature, so that any notion of their arbitrary and fitful setting aside would seem to imply the theological incoherence of God acting against God. The second idea is a corollary of this integrity of nature, that the unfolding history of creation is to be understood as a continuous process of open development, rather than the inexorable execution of a divine plan predetermined in every detail from all eternity. Closely related to this latter point is the recognition that the act of creation is an act of kenosis on the part of God, a divine self-limitation in allowing the created other truly to be itself and to make itself.[7] A very delicate balance of thought is required here, enabling one to steer a path between two theologically unacceptable extremes: the deistic God who does nothing and is simply the spectator of the process of the cosmos, and the Cosmic Tyrant, whose creation is a puppet theatre in which all that happens is determined by how the divine Puppet-Master pulls the strings. In striking this balance, it seems necessary to suppose that God acts through something like 'a constant persuasive re-directing'. I believe that this can be consistent with the attainment of specific ends, even though they have to be achieved through historically contingent paths.

The 1987 conference was such a success that it led to a sequence of five further conferences, organized jointly by CTNS and the Vatican Observatory, each approaching issues of divine action from the perspective of a particular area of science. Their proceedings constitute a substantial and significant contribution to contemporary literature on science and theology.[8] Bob Russell played a leading role in the organization of these creative encounters, acting also as a major contributor and as Editor-in-Chief of the proceedings.

Before going on to consider Russell's contributions in some detail, it will be helpful to consider some general matters relating to the causal nexus of the world as far as natural science is able to contribute to our understanding of it. The first thing that needs to be clear is that questions of causality ultimately demand metaphysical answering. Physics certainly constrains metaphysics, but it does not determine it. There are always matters for decision that can only be settled by appeal to metaphysical critique and argument. The case of quantum theory provides a transparent demonstration of this fact. Although the interpretation most widely accepted in the physics community understands quantum unpredictability as a sign of metaphysical indeterminism, there is an alternative, and equally empirically adequate, interpretation due to David Bohm,[9] whose metaphysical character is deterministic. In the Bohm case, unpredictability arises simply from unavoidable ignorance of the values of certain 'hidden variables'. Because of their empirical equivalence, the choice between these two radically different pictures of quantum reality can only be made on the grounds of criteria held to reflect metaphysically desirable properties, such as economy and lack of contrivance. Russell referred to this kind of issue when he wrote with Wesley Wildman (in fact about chaos theory),

> Now we may pose the basic metaphysical question: which metaphysical scenario – determinism or indeterminism – offers the best explanation that non-randomness and two kinds of randomness appear in the mathematics and apparently also in nature? Even with the distinction introduced up until now, this question is poorly framed, because it begs the question of the relation between chaos in mathematics and chaos in nature. This question must be raised before it is possible to raise the deeper question of the relation between chaos and an ultimate account of nature such as metaphysical determinism.[10]

They go on to state that it would be a 'mistake' to conclude that 'since mathematical equations for chaotic systems are deterministic, nature *must* be metaphysically deterministic if chaos occurs in nature'. (The possibility of an open interpretation of chaotic dynamics is one that I have myself consistently pursued in connection with ideas about divine action.[11]) Behind all this lies the philosophical issue of how epistemology (in this case, unpredictability) relates to ontology. Clearly there is no logical entailment between the two. However, a realist will suppose the two to be closely aligned.[12] In the case of quantum theory, this attitude surely underlies the common assumption in the physics community that Heisenberg's uncertainty principle (discovered as an episte-mological limitation on what can be measured) is to be interpreted ontologically, as a principle of indeterminacy rather than merely as a principle of ignorance.

It is important to recognize that, from the theological point of view, the key metaphysical issue is openness – that is to say, the acknowledgement of there being room for the action of additional causal principles over and above those described by a methodologically reductionist science – and it is not an irrational indeterminism that the theologians desire. The principle of sufficient reason is not lightly to be set aside.[13]

The problem of gaining some understanding of divine agency cannot be expected to be solved quickly or with final certainty. After all, we are far from understanding the processes by which we ourselves are able to act as agents in the world. Discussion of these matters, whatever approach is taken to them, will inevitably be exploratory. A modest – but valuable and realistic – ambition is (as Ernan McMullin said at one of the conferences) to 'defeat the defeaters', to show that taking science seriously does not automatically condemn us to a view of the universe as so totally causally self-enclosed as to make the notion of a deistic spectator the only respectable option open to theology. I think that the chief achievement of the five CTNS–Vatican Observatory conferences was to make it clear, through a variety of tentative options discussed, that an honest science certainly does not forbid theology to speak of God's providential interaction within the unfolding history of creation. Russell expressed this modest evaluation of attainable conclusions when he wrote in relation to his own work, 'I am not in the least suggesting this as an explanation of *how* God works, nor even as the argument *that* God acts. It is only a claim that *if* one believes for theological reasons that God acts in nature, quantum physics provides a clue to one possible location or domain of action.'[14]

Matters are further complicated by the patchy nature of science's actual account of the causal properties of the world. Behaviour is well understood within certain well-defined domains, but the relations between different domains are still matters of perplexity and dispute. A prime example is provided by considering the realms of quantum physics and classical physics. A particular focus is the still-unresolved measurement problem.[15] How does it come about that the cloudy and fitful quantum world, on each occasion of its interrogation by classical measuring apparatus, is found to yield a definite result, though not usually the same result on each such occasion of making the same measurement on similar systems? The frank answer is that we do not know. Various proposals, mutually inconsistent with each other, have been made, but none has achieved universal acceptance and none is entirely free from difficulty. It is the greatest paradox of quantum theory that the act of measurement, so central to experimentally based science, still remains theoretically perplexing eighty years after the great initiating discoveries.

The frontier between the quantum domain and the classical domain is not a simple linear divide between 'small' and 'large', despite Planck's constant providing a natural scale for the definition of these terms. Rather, the boundary is subtle and fractal-like. An admirable example of the niceties involved is provided by quantum chaology. At first sight, it might seem an attractive proposition to produce a theory of universal openness at both micro- and macrolevels, by appealing to the generally accepted open character of quantum processes together with the established sensitivity of chaotic systems to the fine detail of their circumstances, since very soon the future behaviour of chaotic systems comes to depend on details lying below the level of Heisenberg uncertainty. Thus one might think that embedding quantum theory within chaos theory would provide a means to amplify micro-indeterminacy to produce openness in macro-processes. However, the idea does not work, at least not in any straightforward way. The reason is that quantum theory and chaos theory do not fit onto each other in a coherent fashion. There are several ways of seeing why this is so. Quantum systems characteristically have associated with them a discrete set of frequencies (such as those corresponding to the spectral lines of an atom), which give an overall periodic behaviour. Chaotic systems, on the other hand, are intrinsically aperiodic. Another related contrast concerns scaling behaviour. Planck's constant sets a scale for quantum theory, but chaotic behaviour is fractal and so scale-free.

A consequence of this incompatibility is that, in fact, quantum effects in themselves tend to suppress chaotic effects. However, even that rule of thumb is subject to further qualification because of an environmental influence that also has to be considered. It is called decoherence and it arises from interactions between quantum systems and the ambient environment of low-grade radiation that is normally present, coming from the Sun and from the cosmic background radiation. In its turn, the effect of decoherence is to suppress the quantum effects, including their suppression of chaos.[16] Physicists are far from being able to propose a general integrated story of causal factors that takes all these subtleties into account.

These considerations of multiple causal complexity impinge on theological proposals to use quantum theory as at least a partial component in a conjectured picture of the character of divine action. Those who seek to appeal to quantum theory in this regard quite often speak of 'quantum events' without always giving an adequate acknowledgement of how problematic that concept in fact is.[17] The most obvious class of quantum happenings that lead to macroscopic consequences is measurements. As a matter of fact, these are the only occasions, according to the conventionally accepted interpretation of quantum theory, in which discontinuity and indeterminism are manifested. At all other times, the wavefunction evolves smoothly according to the prescription of the Schrödinger equation, in a manner that is perfectly continuous and fully determined. It is a long-standing problem in the meta-interpretation of quantum theory to understand the proper status of the extra condition, imposed on the quantum formalism from outside itself, which is needed in order to represent discontinuous measurement effects. Yet these are the only points at which quantum physics would appear open to the possibility of non-interventionist divine action.

I have emphasized that measurement events only occur from time to time so that, if they are the primary locus of the causal joint of divine activity, that activity will be episodic in its character.[18] Russell has responded by emphasizing, correctly of course, that 'measurements' are not simply events occurring in a laboratory at the behest of a conscious observer, but they correspond to any irreversible macroscopic registration of the state of affairs of a microscopic quantum system. Such registrations will certainly occur across the universe, from time to time and in place to place. Russell therefore proposes that, while they are clearly not ubiquitous, they should be described as 'pervasive', rather than episodic.[19] Personally, I do not think that this verbal change removes the theological difficulty about conceiving of divine action as occurring periodically rather than continuously.

A particular irreversible registration of a quantum effect that has clear and significant macroscopic consequences is genetic mutation induced by micro-processes such as photon interactions. Russell has used this fact as the basis for his proposition of how to give meaning to the idea of theistic evolution.[20] An interesting issue here is whether God is supposed to settle the matter for all open quantum outcomes,[21] or only in the case of some, presumably critically significant, instances.[22] The former option might seem to make God overly determining in relation to creation, exercising a strict control through what one might call quantum occasionalism. The latter option might seem to make God unduly opportunistic. These problems are the quantum counterpart of a very general theological issue in relation to any account of divine action. The nature of creation as involving a kenotic gift by a loving creator who bestows freedom on creatures, will always run up against the classical conundrum of how to strike a balance between the operations of grace and of free will. Some kind of accommodation, in which God interacts with creation without totally overruling creatures, is always going to be called for. In respect of quantum theory ideas, Russell proposed a judicious compromise: 'My suggestion is to start with the scenario that God acts in all quantum events in the universe until the rise of life and consciousness anywhere. God then increasingly refrains from determining outcomes, leaving room for top–down causality in conscious and self-conscious creatures.'[23]

The first volume of conference proceedings on divine action focused on a different kind of setting to which quantum theory is relevant and where theological issues can be brought into play. Russell has always been very interested in cosmology, and the principal concern of that first conference was the quantum cosmology of the very early universe. Scientifically, the discussion would have needed to be based on a well-articulated theory of quantum gravity. General relativity (the modern theory of gravity) is always important in cosmology, and at the very earliest epoch (less than the Planck time of 10^{-43} seconds away from the Big Bang), the universe is so small that quantum theory must also be applied to it as a whole. Unfortunately, however, even at the beginning of the twenty-first century these two great twentieth-century discoveries in fundamental physics still remain imperfectly reconciled with each other. In fact there is no consistent and agreed way known in which their marriage may be consummated. In consequence, quantum cosmology remains a highly speculative subject, in which a variety of hypotheses compete with each other.

General relativity relates to the structure of spacetime, and quantum theory, because of uncertainty, allows fluctuations in which transient bursts of energy can appear from the vacuum. Some cosmologists therefore considered whether our universe might not be one such fluctuation, blown up to huge size and long duration by another hypothetical, but plausible, process known as inflation. Such a notion was held by some to indicate that science could now achieve something that theology had only aspired to understand: creation of the universe *ex nihilo*, out of nothing. A moment's reflection, however, leads to the recognition that a quantum vacuum, which is an active and structured medium, is very far from being the vacuity that could properly be termed *nihil*. Among the competing quantum cosmologies on offer is one proposed by Jim Hartle and Stephen Hawking and conveyed, at least in principle, to the general public in Hawking's celebrated book, *A Brief History of Time*.[24] It implies that in the very early universe, time became essentially space-like, with the initial tip of spacetime rounded off. As a result, there would be no identifiable 'first moment', any more than there is a 'top point' defined on a sphere, other than by convention.

Russell gave careful consideration to these issues. He emphasized that the Hartle–Hawking (HH) model corresponded to 'a finite creation without a beginning' and deemed, rightly I believe, that this was all that was needed to relate to a theological assertion of creation *ex nihilo*.[25] He also compared the HH model with a less sophisticated version of cosmic origin from quantum fluctuation. What is of interest here is that Russell believed that there was a theological reason for preferring the HH model, because it seemed to him to correspond to 'nothing' understood in Greek terms as *ouk on* (absolute nullity), rather than merely *me on* (unstructured potentiality).[26] I am not sure that this judgment is correct, for both speculations assume the laws of gravity and quantum mechanics as givens and that gift, however understood, does not look like anything that science could properly call *nihil*. What interests me specially in this particular piece of Russell's thought is a hankering, which he has quite often expressed, that theology should exercise some discriminating influence on science, at least at the meta-level.

This necessarily brief survey will at least have given some indication of the diversity and interest of Bob Russell's contributions to the exchange between science and theology, particularly along the physics section of the border. These contributions have been made through his own writing, through the stimulating conferences he has organized, and through the educational and research activities of the Center for Theology and the Natural Sciences that he founded. It is a privilege to join others in our field in expressing gratitude to Bob and to CTNS, and to wish them both vigorous and continuing activity into the future that lies ahead.

Notes

1   Robert John Russell, William Stoeger, SJ, and George V. Coyne, SJ (eds), *Physics, Philosophy, and Theology* (Vatican City State: Vatican Observatory, 1988).
2   Ibid., 344–6.
3   Ibid., 355–8.
4   Ibid., 353–4.
5   Ibid., 359–61.
6   Ibid., 362.
7   See John Polkinghorne (ed.), *The Work of Love* (London and Grand Rapids, MI: SPCK and Wm. B. Eerdmans, 2001).
8   Robert John Russell, Nancey C. Murphy, and Chris J. Isham (eds), *Quantum Cosmology and the Laws of Nature: Scientific Perspectives on Divine Action* (Vatican City State and Berkeley, CA: Vatican Observatory and Center for Theology and the Natural Sciences, 1993); Robert John Russell, Nancey C. Murphy, and Arthur R. Peacocke (eds), *Chaos and Complexity: Scientific Perspectives on Divine Action* (Vatican City State and Berkeley, CA: Vatican Observatory and Center for Theology and the Natural Sciences, 1995); Robert John Russell, William R. Stoeger, SJ, and Francisco J. Ayala (eds), *Evolutionary and Molecular Biology: Scientific Perspectives on Divine Action* (Vatican City State and Berkeley, CA: Vatican Observatory and Center for Theology and the Natural Sciences, 1998); Robert John Russell, Nancey Murphy, Theo C. Meyering, and Michael A. Arbib (eds), *Neuroscience and the Person: Scientific Perspectives on Divine Action* (Vatican City State and Berkeley, CA: Vatican Observatory and Center for Theology and the Natural Sciences, 1999); Robert John Russell, Philip Clayton, Kirk Wegter-McNelly, and John Polkinghorne (eds), *Quantum Mechanics: Scientific Perspectives on Divine Action* (Vatican City State and Berkeley, CA: Vatican Observatory and Center for Theology and the Natural Sciences, 2001).
9   David Bohm and Basil Hiley, *The Undivided Universe* (London: Routledge, 1993).
10 Russell et al. (eds), *Chaos and Complexity*, 77.
11 See John Polkinghorne, *Belief in God in an Age of Science* (New Haven, CT: Yale University Press, 1998), Chapter 3.
12 I like to express this stance in the slogan, 'Epistemology models Ontology'.
13 Cf. the discussion of 'gaps' by Russell in *Evolutionary and Molecular Biology*, 216–18; *Quantum Mechanics*, 293–6.
14 *Evolutionary and Molecular Biology*, 216; see also *Quantum Mechanics*, 295.
15 See John Polkinghorne, *Quantum Theory: A Very Short Introduction* (Oxford: Oxford University Press, 2002), 44–56.
16 Michael Berry, 'Chaos and the Semiclassical Limit of Quantum Mechanics (Is the Moon There When Somebody Looks?)', in *Quantum Mechanics*, 43–54.
17 See also Nicholas Saunders, *Divine Action and Modern Science* (Cambridge: Cambridge University Press, 2002), 139–44.
18 John Polkinghorne, 'The Metaphysics of Divine Action', in *Chaos and Complexity*, 152–3.
19 *Evolutionary and Molecular Biology*, 211–12; *Quantum Mechanics*, 310.
20 *Evolutionary and Molecular Biology*, 191–223.

21 Nancey Murphy, 'Divine Action in the Natural Order: Buridan's Ass and Schrödinger's Cat', in *Chaos and Complexity*, 338–44.
22 Thomas F. Tracy, 'Particular Providence and the God of the Gaps', in *Chaos and Complexity*, 316–22.
23 *Quantum Mechanics*, 318.
24 Stephen Hawking, *A Brief History of Time* (New York: Bantam, 1988).
25 *Quantum Cosmology and the Laws of Nature*, 295.
26 Ibid., 318–21.

CHAPTER ELEVEN

Robert John Russell's Theology of God's Action

Wesley J. Wildman

This essay explains and analyzes Robert John Russell's theory of divine action. Russell's proposal has exercised significant influence on others working in the area of science and religion with interests in Christian systematic theology. It would be valuable to trace the lines of that influence, but I do not have space to do that here. I can testify to his influence in more personal terms, however. For years I was Bob's semi-regular passenger as he drove to work in his storied old green Volvo. We spent countless hours discussing theology and science, divine action, and every topic under the sun in that car; not even engine fires distracted us. He was then and continues to be a marvelous conversation partner. He sees deeply and broadly, registering connections across disciplines as easily as within them. It is in such conversations that I most appreciate his Gilbert-and-Sullivan ability to talk quickly: there is a lot to say when you see as much as he does all at once. I have always treasured his insight, support, and friendship, and I am honored to continue our conversations in this critical and appreciative reflection on his theory of divine action.

It would be possible to start in on Russell's network of theological ideas from any point and thereby contextualize his theory of divine action. I shall begin with his theory of special divine action and then work outward to his sensitive theodicy, his Trinitarian understanding of God, and his theological interpretation of history, including the creation and consummation of the universe, though I have space only to situate these later ideas. Along the way I will try to press Russell's personalist theological perspective from my own more mystical perspective of God as ground and power of being. I do not seek to convert him to my way of thinking because the spiritual resonances and intellectual structure of our two views are quite different and I know he likes his more. Nevertheless, I do intend to make a serious challenge to him. In particular, I want to invite him to give the ancient Greek heritage of Christian doctrine more weight in his theology, which seems to me too much in thrall to biblical portrayals of God as a divine person instead of to the unchanging God of the philosophers, to Jerusalem instead of to Athens. I would never expect him to follow me as far as I go toward Athens. I would be happy to know, however, that he was inspired by this latest of our conversations to contemplate adjusting the balance.

The main focus of my attention will be on Russell's contributions to the Divine Action Project, a series of research conferences and publications jointly sponsored by the Vatican Observatory and Russell's own organization, the

Center for Theology and the Natural Sciences in Berkeley, California.[1] These volumes are partly the result of Bob's organizational imagination and are an ongoing testimony to his determined fascination with the idea of divine action.[2]

Russell's Theory of Divine Action in Context

For the sake of placing Russell's theory of divine action in the broader context of theological discussions of divine action, consider the following division of theories of how God acts in created reality. On the one hand, we have the compatibilist theories. Their defenders assume that a theory of divine action can work as well in a causally closed universe – one with no ontological gaps in which we might imagine a divine being acting – as in an ontologically indeterministic universe. Compatibilist theories easily adapt to changing scientific descriptions of the world because they are not dependent on an incomplete scientific account of the causal web of nature, so the science and the theology pass by each other without much traction. For instance, it doesn't make much sense to speak of miraculous violation of the laws of nature on this view of divine action because God can do anything God wants in perfect consistency with the ordinary operations of nature, whatever they might be. It follows that compatibilist theories of divine action do not enjoy the concrete intelligibility of views that deliberately take up positions science could falsify. Yet they can harmonize with the natural sciences by means of large-scale consonance and detailed coverage of scientific topics. Thomas Aquinas articulated a compatibilist theory of divine action according to which God (as primary cause) acts through other events by upholding the actions of created agents (secondary causes). It is scientifically bulletproof in the sense that science can never contradict it, but theologians continue to debate whether that is a good strategy for theology. In our own time, Arthur Peacocke has developed a compatibilist theory of divine action that is as sensitive to the science of our day as Thomas was to the Aristotelian science of his.[3]

On the other hand, we have the incompatibilist theories. Their proponents believe that a case for special divine action in our world demands a demonstration that science has room for such a phenomenon, even though (most agree) science could never prove that it occurs. Whereas the compatibilist sees no contradiction in principle between scientific accounts of the causal web of reality and religious claims about divine action, the incompatibilist thinks the two realms can conflict with one another. Incompatibilist theories of divine action are of two basic sorts. Interventionist theories accept that the laws of nature reflect the deep ontological structure of reality as God created it and are happy to imagine that God might act in nature by ignoring or violating those laws of nature. This is the miracle approach to divine action and is implicit or explicit in much modern evangelical theology. Some theologians are bothered by the interventionist approach to an incompatibilist theory of divine action, however. They resist the idea of God creating the world one way and then having to set aside that arrangement in order to get specific things done in the world, seeing it as deeply inconsistent and reflecting poorly on God's wisdom in the original act of creation. Thus, they seek a non-interventionist approach to the incompatibilist's challenge, which involves showing that science leaves ontological room for God to act in this world without breaking God's own rules for its operation.

The incompatibilist, non-interventionist family of divine action theories is quite diverse. Among them, I judge Russell's to be a rather theologically textured one. As such it is worthy of close attention and I shall try to do justice to it in this essay. The fact that I can even entertain describing Russell's theory in these terms also indicates his importance as an intellectual; it is no small achievement to elaborate a scientifically nuanced and theologically rich theory of divine action. I shall present evidence of these virtues as we follow Russell's theory across a wide range of theological doctrines, all of which he brings to bear on his theory of divine action.

We can consider the more precise classification of Russell's theory of divine action that he himself offers with the aid of a complex set of distinctions. This will also serve to introduce the basic terminology Russell uses in his theory.[4]

First, Russell makes a methodological distinction to clarify what he is doing in his theory of divine action. He calls his approach 'constructive theology' and sometimes indicates that he is paying special attention to a constructive theology of nature. He contrasts this with natural theology and physico-theology and the design argument, all of which seek to argue for theological conclusions on the basis of the way nature is. This means that Russell's approach is essentially confessional, drawing his theological motivations and doctrines from his religious community and its theological traditions, and rational in the sense of *fides quaerens intellectum*, existing faith seeking rational understanding of itself in the deepest and richest way possible. A constructive theology that includes a theology of nature in following this approach in our time will necessarily have to engage the natural sciences. Because this is his approach to a theological understanding of divine action, Russell insists that he is not explaining *how* God acts[5] and certainly not arguing *that* God acts, but only seeking to make the theological claim of divine action rationally intelligible and credible.

Second, Russell distinguishes between objective and subjective divine action (see *CC*, 10–12). Objective divine action affects the physical world in ways that are intelligible in principle, even in the absence of conscious interpreters to make sense of them. Subjective divine action refers to the hermeneutical achievement of discerning God's acts in history and nature, an act of conscious interpreters, and in principle independent of whether or not God actually acts objectively in the world. Russell associates subjective divine action with the miracle-as-life-changing-event view of some liberal Christian theologians and objective divine action with the miracle-as-objective-sign-and-violation-of-natural-laws view of some conservative Christian theologians, which he calls the 'traditional view' (*CC*, 10). He thinks that the subjective approach surrenders intelligibility crucial for the credibility of Christian faith claims, but also does not like the theological inconsistency of objective miracles, in the sense of violations of the laws of nature as created by God. Thus, he sees his non-interventionist proposal for objective divine action as a *tertium quid*, transcending the impasse between liberal and conservative theologians, and making the Christian faith more credible at the same time. This distinction between objective and subjective recurs for Russell in the question of whether one needs religious presuppositions to discern non-interventionist objectively special divine action.

Third, Russell distinguishes direct from indirect divine action, though affirming both. Direct divine action is caused by God's objective action, whereas indirect divine action refers to subsequent ramifications of direct divine acts. In Russell's view, God intends and plans for the providential results of divine action and direct divine acts are the means by which God brings about these results.[6]

Fourth, Russell distinguishes among three ways to deploy the idea of divine action (see *QM*, 294): in agential models closely related to scientific ideas of nature and causation, in agential models worked out in relation to elaborate metaphysical schemes (he gives process philosophy and neo-Thomism as examples), and in embodiment models (here he is thinking of proposals such as Grace Jantzen's on the world as God's body). Russell says that he follows the first approach, though he does not seem inimical to the alternatives.

Fifth, within the strategy that deploys the idea of divine action in agential models closely related to scientific ideas of nature and causation, Russell distinguishes three approaches: via top–down causality, whole–part constraint, and bottom–up causality (*QM*, 294). He thinks that a fully satisfying theological account of divine action would involve all three approaches but also asserts that a bottom–up component in any theory of divine action is indispensable (*QM*, 300). He develops his own proposal in relation to bottom–up causality.[7]

Finally, with virtually all theologians, Russell distinguishes between general and special divine action. By special divine action he seems to mean intentional acts of a personal divine being at particular places and times in our world (though sometimes he imagines that these events might be universal). Interestingly, Russell avoids the term 'general divine action', whereas he uses the term 'special' in relation to providence and divine action frequently. I think the reason for this is that, unlike many theologians, and to his credit, Russell sees the blending of the two forms of divine action, and this in three ways. First, on Russell's account, any action of God, including the general activity of ontologically sustaining the universe in being, is not an automatic or mechanistic operation of the divine being but involves deliberate intentions and divine awareness of the specifics of reality, all of which suggest that we might fruitfully think of general divine action as a universal form of special divine action. Second, whenever God acts in a particular place and time, this must be in harmony with so-called general activities such as sustaining the universe's being. Third, the very idea of *creatio continua*, or continual creation, though usually assigned to the 'general' category, could equally well be understood as special divine action toward a generally applicable end. Because of these considerations, the category of general divine action is more difficult to make out than we might expect. I have not seen a place where Russell walks through this argument, but I think this explains why he uses the term special far more often than general in describing divine action.

These distinctions form the background for Russell's working classification of positions on divine action (see Figure 11.1, which reproduces the table from the introductions to *CC* and *QM*), which I reproduce here.

	Creation	Uniform Divine Action		Objectively Special Divine Action		
		Sustenance	Subjectively Special	Interventionist	Noninterventionist	
					Apparent with religious presuppositions	Apparent without religious presuppositions
Atheism						
Deism	X					
'Theism'	X	X				
'Liberal'	X	X	X			
'Traditional'	X	X	X	X		
Theology and Science:						
(1) Top-Down or Whole-Part (e.g., mind/brain)	X	X	X		X	?
(2) Bottom-Up (e.g., quantum indeterminacy)	X	X	X		X	?
(3) Lateral Amplification (e.g., chaos)	X	X	X		X	?
(4) Primary/Secondary	X	X	X		?	?

Figure 11.1

The table in Figure 11.1 is both a neat representation of major options in the contemporary science-and-religion debate over divine action and a helpful summary of Russell's own way of thinking about the alternatives.[8] Its defining characteristic is the nine views on the left, and the various columns of the diagram serve to distinguish most of those views from one another.[9] In the terms of this diagram and the distinctions introduced above, Russell's contribution is an incompatibilist, non-interventionist theory of objectively special, direct, bottom–up, mediated divine action. He does affirm creation, of course, but I will not discuss the specifics of his view of creation here.[10]

Motivations for Russell's Approach to Special Divine Action

Having located Russell's theory of divine action in the wider debate, let us begin the exposition of his theory with the reasons that Russell prefers an incompatibilist, non-interventionist approach, and indeed why he defends special divine action at all. Precisely because there are several other significantly different strategies that he might have adopted, understanding why he chose the approach he did should illumine basic motivations for, and pervasive constraints on, his theological reflection. I think at least the following three considerations are relevant.

First, why speak of special divine action at all? Our theological era has been extraordinarily diverse on the question of special divine action in the sense of intentional acts of a personal divine being at particular places and times (and not others) in our world. A small number of theologians, including Maurice Wiles, Robert Neville, and me, reject this kind of action. Wiles does so especially because of theodicy concerns. In my words: a God who can act in this way but does not in fact intervene to help and guide us in situations of massive injustice and evil is a God we have no reason to trust and every reason to resist, regardless of the futility of resistance. Neville rejects the personalist notion of God as incoherent; for him it is a mythological fiction that theologians accept, or hesitate to de-shroud, because of its prominence in the Bible and in personal religious piety. I reject special divine action for both reasons. Many more theologians allow vague talk of special divine action but refuse to explain what they really mean. Some probably have other theological interests and just never get around to analyzing theological language about God's acts. I suspect that a few secretly believe that they could never make sense of claims about divine action but can't bring themselves to say this openly because they believe that theology is supposed to be one of the religious activities of Christian churches. Still other theologians look at the range of world religions, several of which do not even mention God, let alone God acting in history and nature. To them, this confirms its mythological status and makes a theory of divine action seem like a culturally parochial artifact, a backward step in the theological quest for a cross-culturally viable interpretation of ultimate reality.

Against this range of alternatives, Russell presupposes that God is a personal being in the sense of responsive and intentional with the capacity to act, and that God does in fact act in history and nature, in conformity with the claims of the Bible and his understanding of the life of prayer. Whence this starting confidence? I think Russell takes divine action in this straightforward sense to be a central affirmation of his religious community, which is at once decidedly Protestant, generously ecumenical, intellectually liberal, biblically oriented, pietistically inspired, and a creative achievement through a lifetime of relationships with spiritually diverse companions. Moreover, for Russell, theology is a confessional, spiritual act on behalf of this community of fellow travelers. It is not everyone's cup of tea, which means that it must be someone's calling, and Russell is one of those who feel called to articulate in the most intellectually rigorous way the faith of a Christian community. Theology for him is simultaneously a work of spiritual self-exploration and arduous labor on behalf of a tradition he loves, a tradition fleshed out in lives of service and acts of worship and moments of prayer. The basic reason Russell advances a theory of divine action, then, is that his community believes this about God, his own spiritual journey inspires and justifies this belief, and his calling as a theologian demands that he give an account of his faith.

This much could be said of many planks in the faith platform of Russell's religious community. But why has he spent so much time and energy on the particular question of divine action rather than on other of the myriad issues theologians ponder? I think the motivation here is essentially evangelical. In an era and a culture skeptical of traditional claims about divine action – an era in which not only atheists but also some theologians surrender the idea of a God who deliberately answers prayers – there is a crisis for traditional Christian faith. Russell has diagnosed this situation clearly and with equal clarity has seen that divine action must be a point of attack for the evangelical Christian committed to the intelligent, cutting-edge defense of traditional religious claims. This is evangelism in the classical sense of making the Christian vision of the world credible in the terms of the day. It is apologetics, but not in the sense of presenting just enough evidence with a strong enough personality to convince insecure adolescents that God is real and answers prayers. Rather, this is apologetics in the sense of ancient Christians such as Justin Martyr, who took on the cultural luminaries of their day rather than the easy targets for conversion, and who articulated Christianity in an intellectually robust way and made it credible even when it did not produce conversions. This evangelical impulse runs deep in Russell's formation as a Christian intellectual, as deep as his confessional commitment to pursue a theological calling on behalf of his religious community.

With our second consideration, we move from Russell's motivation for defending the idea of special divine action to the reasons he adopts his incompatibilist, non-interventionist strategy. I think he chooses this particular approach to special divine action in part because he believes that it will maximize in his theological assertions the characteristic of concrete intelligibility, which he takes to be a great virtue in theological work. He shares with most scientists an appreciation for propositions that are robust in the sense of specific enough to be falsifiable. In most forms of scientific activity, a proposition does not pass muster unless it has this sort of robustness: we know a proposition means something when we know what would falsify it. Logical positivists such as A. J. Ayer were right about this even if they went too far in tying the meaning of assertions exclusively to their falsifiability principle.[11] The emphasis on intelligibility through falsification-in-principle has been a consistent emphasis of subsequent philosophy of science, albeit in a wide variety of ways. Theology rarely displays this degree of concrete intelligibility and some theological propositions are so vague that they are consistent with virtually any state of affairs in the world. Indeed, some theologians regard this opposite strategy as theoretically virtuous.[12] Compatibilist theories of divine action, for example, are by definition compatible with science, whatever science may say, which makes them less concretely intelligible than Russell would like. We can say the same for miracles understood as violations of natural laws: though more immediately intelligible than compatibilist theories, interventionist theories easily set aside the structures and patterns of nature, spurning the intelligibility they bring to theological claims. To maximize the virtue of concrete intelligibility, therefore, we would have to develop a theory of divine action within the constraints furnished by an incompatibilist strategy and the refusal of miraculous exceptions to the laws of nature. This is precisely what Russell does.

I think the attractiveness of concrete intelligibility for Russell derives especially from his training as a physicist. Of course, other scientists, including physicists such as Russell's friend William Stoeger, have adopted compatibilist approaches to divine action. Yet the virtue of striving to make theology compatible with anything the sciences could ever possibly discover about reality seems almost alien to Russell. So Russell's original training as a scientist is insufficient as an explanation for his love of maximal traction between theology and the natural sciences. It may come down to the specifics of professional training and spiritual formation. Stoeger is a Jesuit deeply imbued with the compatibilist approach to God and divine action developed by Thomas Aquinas, as the great doctor sought to adapt Aristotle's philosophy to his own Christian purposes. Stoeger is also a theoretically oriented astronomer. Russell is a Protestant Christian with less tolerance than most Roman Catholics for elusiveness in theology, and an experimental physicist trained to maximize traction between theory and experiment. Whatever the explanation, there is no question that Russell has sought long and hard for a satisfying incompatibilist, non-interventionist theory of special divine action.

A third motivational consideration bears on another intellectual virtue in Russell's theory of divine action: he wants to maximize consistency with a theology of nature that integrates all aspects of contemporary knowledge. The background intellectual affinities here are with ontological realism, a critical attitude to human knowledge that retains confidence in human rationality to discover the way nature is, trust in the feedback mechanism of nature that we rely on to correct our hypotheses about it, faith in the value of testing and debating theories about reality in the broadest possible interdisciplinary contexts, and the abiding belief that God created one world that demands an integrated theoretical interpretation. I have no space here to dwell on the epistemological and ontological commitments that constitute Russell's working theory of inquiry. I am content here to point out the effect of these commitments on his theory of divine action.

These epistemological and ontological commitments entail that Russell's conversation partners for theological theorizing will include scientists of every stripe as well as philosophers and theologians. The published volumes of the Divine Action Project bear this out. Each is the result of a dialogue over the constraints on and possibilities for special divine action in relation to a particular domain of scientific inquiry, from physics and cosmology to quantum mechanics, and from chaos theory and complexity theory to evolutionary biology and neuroscience. For Russell, any adequate theory of special divine action needs to take its bearings eventually from all of these disciplines (and others) simultaneously, as well as from traditional theological resources. There is one world, created by God, so only the deepest and most unified account of this world can serve as the environment for constructing an optimal theory of divine action. It is precisely because all treatments of divine action since that of Thomas Aquinas have fallen short of this vision of comprehensive inquiry that Russell has worked so hard with the Vatican Observatory to create the Divine Action Project.

Russell's Theory of Special Divine Action

With this discussion of motivations for Russell's incompatibilist, non-interventionist, interdisciplinary approach to special divine action in place, we can proceed to the theory itself. I will make every effort to explain Russell's approach clearly, fully, and as generously as possible. I will also analyze it to some extent as I go, placing it in what I think is its strongest philosophical, theological, and scientific light, which at times includes speculative extrapolations of Russell's proposal that he himself does not broach but that seem entailed by what he does say.

Like other theories of the incompatibilist, non-interventionist, objective, bottom–up type, Russell's method is to locate ontological openness in nature, realms within which God might work without violating natural laws, understood as mathematical descriptions of ontologically basic structures of reality. Neither a compatibilist approach nor an interventionist approach would require ontological openness in nature, but Russell's strategy must locate God's action in ontologically indeterminate regimes of nature if it is to maximize traction with the sciences in the way needed to realize the theoretical virtues discussed above.

Newtonian physics offered more possibilities for ontological indeterminism than many realized at the time. All of these possibilities turn on imagining that Newton's laws of motion were very close but not infinitely accurate approximations to the ontologically basic laws of nature. It is testimony to the excitement surrounding Newton's mathematical model of mechanical and dynamical motion both that so few pointed out this possibility and that a kind of positivistic reductionism came to rule the imaginations of philosophers and theologians of that era. 'Approximate laws' is not a far-fetched idea. People in the seventeenth century were quite used to approximations in a host of realms of life. Moreover, the actually demonstrated predictive power of the Newtonian mechanics was unimpressive, owing to the lack of computers, precise measuring equipment, and the gross approximations involved in rendering extended objects as point masses. No one had used it to land people on the moon, or to deliver intercontinental ballistic missiles to their intended targets, let alone to model truly complex natural systems. The discovery of chaotic dynamical systems in mathematics promised to extend the explanatory potential of Newton's mechanics, but modeling complex systems in nature using mathematical chaotic systems can never work well in principle because the eventual unpredictability of chaotic systems blocks testing of models.[13] So the advent of chaos theory actually does little to shift the debate between determinism and indeterminism one way or the other.

The vision of God acting freely in the indeterministic (albeit constrained) reality beneath our approximations to the laws governing the deep structure of nature is an appealing one. This is essentially Sir John Polkinghorne's proposal for special divine action,[14] and he is quite correct to defend it both as a logical possibility and as a feasible interpretation of the incompatibilist, non-interventionist type. Russell also acknowledges that our best physics, whatever its state of development, might only yield approximations to the ontological deep structure of nature. Being unconvinced by Polkinghorne's chaos-oriented proposal for the causal joint of divine action, however, Russell turns to quantum mechanics, intending to articulate a *possibility* for a causal joint between God and the world as precisely as current physics allows, while accepting that physics may eventually leave his speculations about causal joints far behind.

To that end, Russell investigates the quantum realm for signs of ontological indeterminacy. Always a conscientious interpreter of science, Russell is careful to point out that quantum mechanics is an overwhelmingly deterministic theory. Both the Schrödinger equation and its relativistic equivalent, the Dirac equation, are time-reversible, deterministic equations that, given initial conditions, predict the development of wavefunctions forward and backward in time with infinite precision. There are no incompatibilist, non-interventionist possibilities for God to manipulate wavefunctions, unless we relax the status of these wave equations as ontologically basic laws of nature. As I have said, Russell is willing to entertain this but, for the sake of the concrete intelligibility of his theory of special divine action, he also wants to explore causal joints on the hypothesis that the laws of nature really are the way the wave equation describes them. Thus he rejects divine manipulation of wavefunctions as a serious option for a non-interventionist theory of God's action (see *CC*, 296).

Like other thinkers exploring incompatibilist, non-interventionist theories of special divine action in the quantum realm, therefore, Russell turns his attention to quantum measurement events in search of ontological indeterminacy. He works basically from the standard interpretation, which is one of many feasible and experimentally indistinguishable ontological interpretations of the highly successful quantum formalism. The standard interpretation asserts: (1) that 'interactions' trigger quantum measurement events (while remaining vague about precisely what sort of interactions will do this, which is a huge problem in the interpretation of quantum mechanics); (2) that measurement events trigger the wavefunction's non-reversible collapse from its initial state onto one and only one of the (measurement-dependent) basic states that exist in superposition within the initial state (this is the projection postulate); and also (3) that the final state resulting from the measurement event is not caused by any deterministic mechanism but rather is wholly a matter of chance, constrained only by statistics flowing from the projection postulate, in which the probability of any final state is related to the weighting that state has in the superposition of states that is the initial wavefunction immediately prior to the measurement event. Within this hypothetical framework, Russell's search for ontological openness that might provide ontological room for God to act without violating laws of nature leads in two directions.

First, with others such as Thomas Tracy[15] and Nancey Murphy,[16] Russell speculates that God might step in where chance plays its role in determining the final state of a quantum measurement event. This involves assuming both that God collapses the initial, pre-measurement state onto one basic state of the operator corresponding to the measurement being made, and that God can select outcome states in such a way as to promote divinely providential ends. Russell rejects the possibility that God changes the probability of outcome states, thereby allowing chance to settle the measurement question with divinely weighted dice, as it were (see *QM*, 296).[17] This would violate the statistical laws governing ensembles of measurement events and Russell is not prepared to sacrifice an ontologically robust interpretation of the laws of nature – even of stochastic laws – because of the theoretical virtues he nurtures: concrete intelligibility and traction with the natural sciences. Rather, he speculates that God may act in the ontological openness furnished by the operation of chance in determining outcome states by divinely selecting one particular outcome state, or perhaps limiting the range of outcome states and allowing chance to finish the selection within the narrower parameters.

Russell assumes that God can do this without manipulating measurement probabilities. How is this possible? Though I have seen no detailed discussion of this issue, Russell's view probably has to construe statistical laws governing quantum events in a particular way. Quantum statistics govern the outcomes of repeated measurement events of the same type, and Russell accepts that those statistical laws reflect underlying ontological structures of reality. But which structures? Laws governing the statistics of quantum measurement are ontologically basic in the sense that, without God's influence, chance would determine the outcome of measurement events in conformity with those laws. Yet they are not as ontologically constraining as the wave equation because it really is chance that settles measurement outcomes when God is not involved. There is neither determinism nor unconstrained randomness but chance operating within constraints. The best and only way we have to express both the role of chance in measurement events and the patterns of constraint on the operations of chance, is by means of statistical laws. It is logically impossible to break laws that express constraints on the operation of chance so long as God selects from among permissible states that have a non-zero probability of resulting from the measurement in question, and the laws are understood as constraining ensembles of measurement events rather than individual measurement events. Adjusting probabilities is fiddling with the constraints, and thus is interventionist and unacceptable to Russell. Acting in place of chance respects constraints and thus is a non-interventionist mode of divine action. (It is worth restating here that Russell's proposal assumes philosophical interpretations of the quantum formalism that affirm ontological openness and a role for chance.)

Russell's hypothesis, therefore, is that God acts in the ontological indeterminacy of quantum measurement events while respecting the constraints on that ontological indeterminacy, and thus not violating laws of nature, stochastic or otherwise. This view may be credible in the context of individual measurement events, but how does it translate in the situation of scientists running experiments to gather quantum statistics? We can only ever test statistical laws in the context of large ensembles of particles, in which the same sort of measurement is made repeatedly. So only in such experimental situations can statistical laws ever meaningfully contradict a non-interventionist theory of divine action at the quantum level. Russell's view appears to require that God must pay particular attention to situations where scientists are actually running experiments to test quantum statistics, and make sure that the numbers come out close enough to predictions that quantum theory can have the status it enjoys (thanks especially to quantum electrodynamics) as the most accurate theory in the history of physics.

This piece of contrivance risks the awkward theological specter of a God whose activities are limited not only by divinely created laws of nature, which any non-interventionist theory counts as a virtue, but also by human decisions about when to run experiments to gather quantum statistics. In those situations, God must rig things in just the right way or else just leave the events being measured completely alone. Of course, it is possible to argue that God could not possibly have any reason to be fiddling with quantum events of the trivial sort that quantum statistics measure, anyway. In fact, this argument could be strengthened to the claim that quantum statistics could never be gathered on any quantum events that are of providential interest to God. This last piece of speculation sets up a principled and sharp distinction between two non-overlapping realms of reality: the realms where God acts at the quantum level and the realms where we could never in principle gather quantum statistics. But the principle behind the distinction is not truly theologically satisfying and still seems to leave the impression that God is just lucky that experiments don't cramp the divine style.

Another principle that we might invoke to justify this otherwise bizarre divine behavior – and a thoroughly Russellian one – is God's loving desire for human beings to discover the regularities and the deep structures of nature whenever they set about looking for them. To that end, we might imagine that God refrains from messing with the quantum statistics in experiments in order not to trick or confuse creatures whose enlightenment God prizes. Yet again, we might speculate that God acts regardless of whether anyone is gathering quantum statistics from experiments, and that experimenters disregard the effects as noise, as statistical aberrations, or as within the error limits of the apparatus. This scenario suggests an experiment for detecting special divine action, by gathering quantum statistics in an experimental setup focused on something of importance to God's providential plans. But it is difficult to imagine a practical design for such an experiment.

The second way in which Russell imagines non-interventionist divine action at the quantum level is more controversial and has a more complex history within Russell's thought. In *PPT* and *EMB*, Russell entertains the possibility that God might initiate quantum measurement events. He even preserves this language in the latest summary of his proposal, at a number of places. For example, in the first paragraph of the *QM* statement, Russell writes,

> [I]f quantum mechanics is interpreted philosophically in terms of ontological indeterminism ..., one can construct a bottom–up, non-interventionist, objective approach to mediated direct divine action in which God's indirect acts of general and special providence at the macroscopic level arise in part, at least, from God's objective direct action at the quantum level both in sustaining the time-development of elementary

processes as governed by the Schrödinger equation and in acting with nature to bring about irreversible interactions referred to as 'quantum events'. (*QM*, 293)

God acting to 'bring about irreversible interactions' certainly suggests what is also evident in other passages and in other essays, that Russell entertains the possibility that God triggers measurement events. It is puzzling, therefore, to find an explicit rejection of this possibility in the same summary essay from *QM*, where Russell denies the idea 'that God ... makes measurements on a given system' (296). This last-quoted statement is so clear that there can be no question about Russell's most recent official view on the matter. He may have changed his mind or clarified an obscurity in earlier formulations. Either way, I think there is some justification in pausing to consider whether the possibility of divine initiation of measurement events has a credible non-interventionist formulation.

Non-interventionist divine triggering of quantum events would require at least some possibility of indeterminism associated with the initiation of measurement events. There is almost as much disagreement over what counts as a measurement event and what triggers measurement events as there is conflict over the best ontological interpretation of the quantum formalism, so there appear to be real chances for stabilizing some sense in which the trigger might be indeterministic. For example, Ghirardi, Rimini, and Weber have proposed adding a stochastic element to the Schrödinger equation to steer around the problem of quantum measurement. These continuous spontaneous localization theories explicitly posit a probabilistic trigger for measurement events, related to the complexity of the associated quantum interactions. These theories have problems deriving from the fact that they are not in perfect agreement with the projection postulate. The projection postulate itself may be an approximation, but it is strange that so weirdly beautiful a concept as the projection postulate should be involved at all if it is not an exact law. Well, even if this approach to finding indeterminacy in the triggering of measurement events fails, other possibilities may exist.

If it proves intelligible to posit an element of chance in the triggering of measurement events, then it is feasible to imagine that God could trigger measurement events without violating laws of nature. The same argument about statistical laws of nature would apply in this case that we referred to in explaining Russell's conjecture that God may act in determining the outcomes of quantum measurement events. The downside is similarly perplexing: whatever statistical laws govern the triggering of measurement events would have to be sustained whenever anyone is gathering statistics from experiments. While it seems that Russell is no longer interested in exploring this possibility for non-interventionist divine action, I cannot quite see why he does not affirm it, at least until we arrive at a more compelling understanding of quantum measurement events than we have presently.

Having laid out the basics of Russell's theory of divine action, it is important to stress that he never imagines that God might act exclusively in the quantum realm, nor is he averse to imagining that our present laws of nature may be mere approximations to the ontological deep structure of reality. But Russell also explores his speculative proposal within the hypothetical framework of existing science for the sake of bringing concrete intelligibility to his theory of divine action, even while remembering that the whole speculative enterprise is contingent on and relative to the contemporary state of science.

The final step in Russell's theory of divine action concerns an innovative approach to the question of the scope of divine action, and this in two senses. The first concerns whether God acts in all measurement events or just some. Murphy has defended a view of special divine action in every quantum measurement event, and imagines that God is an essential or constitutive part of each measurement event. Tracy has expressed a preference for special divine action in only some measurement events, arguing that this is more consistent with a robust interpretation of the laws of nature as reflecting the ontological deep structure of nature. Contrary to both of these alternatives, Russell has a hybrid view. He pictures God potentially acting in every event, but never in a constitutive fashion, in the sense that God would not have to act in order for nature to function independently of special divine action. Moreover, Russell's assertion that God acts in every event is subject to the principle that God acts everywhere and at all times in creation to draw forth its full potentiality, including by sustaining the wondrous regularities of nature. Because this overriding purpose for God's action determines whether God will act, rather than any requirement of the operations of nature itself, God may not act in events that do not serve divine ends. Thus, if God does act in all 'events', then it is a case of universal but contingent action, rather than action necessary for the operations of nature.

The second scope issue relates to human freedom. For Russell, it would be inconsistent for God to act in such a way as to override human freedom or undermine moral responsibility, qualities that God worked presumably long and hard to draw forth from nature. To act in a way that interferes with human freedom would be contrary to God's providential love. Thus, Russell proposes a contraction of the divine sphere of influence in domains of free, moral, and spiritual creatures, such as human beings and, perhaps much earlier in the evolutionary process, those with any degree of consciousness. This move is unique among the prominent theories of divine action and indicative of Russell's sensitivity to the broad range of factors – both theological and scientific – that must condition any adequate theory of special divine action.

We could try to express Russell's theory of special divine action without reference to causal joints so as to bring out the overall theological and cosmological import of his proposal. Many theologians, from Plato and Aristotle[18] to Alfred North Whitehead[19] and Pierre Teilhard de Chardin,[20] have conceived of God acting universally as the principle that knits all of reality together or as the visionary that draws forth from reality its full potential. Russell does the same, though the particular way he renders this ongoing divine design project is quite unusual. To begin with, he emphasizes the personal and concretely intentional character of God, which none of those just mentioned entertained in anything like the same way. He also stresses the contingent character of God's action, which also expresses specific, tailored divine intentions, whereas each of these four philosophical theologians imagined that God's action was reflexively immediate, automatic, necessary, and eternal, even when it is also free, as it is especially in Whitehead. In common with them, however, Russell envisages God as a vital aspect of the universe's development, without which it might function, but in less interesting ways. He pictures God as creating and sustaining a universe with an ongoing role for God to draw forth from nature the full richness of its created potential. Whereas Aristotle imagines this in an organic, systematic way, Russell thinks in the dynamic terms of cosmic and biological evolution. And whereas Whitehead imagines that God is not an omnipotent creator but merely the creative performer of a vital function within the vast eternal organism of reality, Russell pictures God as a creator who designs creation with ontological openness suitable for ongoing providential and creative activity.

This is a grand vision indeed, and deserves to be compared with the other world pictures I have mentioned. It is also extremely bold. For example, Russell's view predicts that God acts to enhance the efficiency of the evolutionary process, as measured by the standards of God's creative and providential will. This entails that, if standard naturalistic evolutionary assumptions prove sufficient for explaining the world as we encounter it (and we may never decide this question), then Russell's view of special divine action will be in trouble and his theological vision in need of recasting. But such an outcome would be possible only because of the traction that Russell seeks to create between his theological claims and the natural sciences. It is the flip side of the virtue of concrete intelligibility and precisely what Russell tries to build into his theological proposals.

Evaluating Russell's Theory of Special Divine Action

Russell's theory of special divine action has its critics. The most aggressive, though also an appreciative, critic has been Nicholas Saunders, whose strident criticism of all incompatibilist, non-interventionist theories of special divine action applies squarely to Russell's contribution.[21] Other critics of quantum-level proposals for God–world causal joints point out that the notion of 'quantum event' is highly problematic and, in consequence, argue that speculative work on causal joints is getting too far ahead of known science.[22] Related criticisms are that quantum-level divine joints are incapable of having providentially relevant macroscopic effects and that quantum measurement events are too infrequent to allow God enough opportunities for providentially relevant action.

Russell has gone to great lengths to answer many of his critics. He has given examples of macroscopic effects of quantum events, particularly in the evolutionary process, and he has argued that macroscopic effects are also possible through the accumulation and amplification of quantum events to the macroscopic level.[23] He has urged that the quantum measurement events familiar from laboratory experiments occur all the time in ordinary interactions in nature, thereby allowing sufficient opportunities for providentially relevant divine action.[24] And he has argued (prior to Saunders's later critique) that his view of God's acting in quantum indeterminacies is not interventionist.[25]

I consider Russell's replies to these criticisms adequate, but there are four other challenging issues that go beyond mere questions of consistency of formulation. They concern the futility of quests for causal joints, the opacity of religious language, the problem of theodicy, and the nature of God. I shall present these questions in what follows and discuss Russell's approach to them, where one exists.

First, centuries of philosophical discussion have shown that causal joints for human action are elusive. We can argue that they must exist, point vaguely to them, and even adduce constraints on what we can say about them, but the joint itself typically remains conceptually intangible. Why is this? Immanuel Kant's answer was that it is because of an apparently unavoidable disjunction between categories of freedom and categories of causality in any rational analysis of action. Following David Hume's reflections on this subject, Kant developed his critique of pure reason to account for this strange incapacity of human reason to argue soundly from causal features of the world to a metaphysical theory of freedom. Kant readily admitted that freedom is a transcendental condition of human moral life, but thought it had to be postulated because it could not be demonstrated within a causal account of the world. In other words, we can never isolate causal joints for free moral agents. Although Kant could not have put it the following way, this incapacity of human reason to reconcile categories of causation and freedom is as significant as our inability to harmonize the familiar determinism of the Schrödinger equation and the weird world of quantum measurement, with its tantalizing suggestions of indeterminism. It is a mistake, therefore, to expect too much in the way of specification of causal joints, either for human action (Kant's concern) or for divine action (Russell's concern). More precisely, we must be attentive to this issue when we try to decide exactly how much we can reasonably expect from debates about causal joints and speculative proposals for causal joints such as Russell's.

Russell's theory of special divine action reflects this complex philosophical debate in two ways, each a sign of good philosophical judgment. First, he tries to be as precise about causal joints for special divine action as existing scientific interpretations of the causal nexus of nature permit, but then he also refuses to stipulate that God can only act in the specified way. Second, his speculations about God-world causal joints do not pretend to be infinitely precise or conceptually fully satisfying. We have statistical laws governing quantum measurement events, for example, so even on the standard interpretation of the quantum formalism, the ontological openness that Russell's theory depends on is heavily constrained. On the one hand, to avoid a conflict with quantum statistics, Russell has to choose between weakening their status as natural laws or contriving to have God make sure quantum measurement statistics always come out right whenever a scientist performs a relevant experiment – neither is a desirable outcome. On the other hand, if Russell merely alludes to an incompatibilist, non-interventionist causal joint for special divine action, then he sacrifices the prized virtue of concrete intelligibility in theology, all because he anticipates the eventual futility of specifying how divine freedom operates within the causal nexus of nature.[26]

I am confident that Russell would say that he has judiciously and perhaps optimally balanced the difficulties that accrue as one pushes toward precision in speculative theorizing about God-world causal joints. I am not so sure. From my point of view, we distort the problem of divine action when we fail to acknowledge the limitations on any causal joint speculations. It is far clearer to acknowledge that all of our causal joint speculations are no more than gestures toward the indecipherable than to speculate away and merely append caveats about this not being the only way God might act. Without explicit and regular reminders of the ultimate futility of the task – such as we read in Austin Farrer's impeccably restrained reflections on divine action[27] – causal joint speculations risk promising more in the way of theological intelligibility than they have any right to promise. They also risk representing God as far more an actor alongside other created actors than is theologically prudent, given that God is supposed to be the all-surpassing creator. We are all in this boat together as theologians, of course, but I suspect that clearer acknowledgement of the rational limits of causal joint speculation would enhance rather than detract from Russell's theory of special divine action, making it more plausible, and rendering its attempt at concrete intelligibility less strained.

Second, while the limitations of human reason appear in a peculiar way in causal joint speculations, they also show themselves in more generic ways throughout the range of human efforts to speak about ultimate reality. The problems of theological language are well known among theologians as well as their detractors and they have been much debated on all sides. My question in this case pertains less to solving the problem than to clear recognition of it. Has Russell sufficiently acknowledged the difficulty of speaking of God's intentional activity in his theory of special divine action? The Bible speaks freely of God's activity, and surely it is this biblical testimony that most powerfully inspires Christian intellectuals to find a way to make spiritual and theological sense of the idea of divine action. It is worth remembering, however, that the anthropomorphic pattern of biblical speech about God is also periodically disrupted in theophanies and impenetrable events that leave God's will and even the divine character obscured in darkness. The world of the Bible is not utterly familiar, after all, but strange and new, as Karl Barth reminded us.

In theological terms, the problem is how to speak of what we do not know – God's action and God's nature – when we have at our disposal only human words and ideas as the building blocks for our extraordinary, and frequently overactive, imaginations. Russell rejects exhaustive reliance on revelation, for such a path thinks very poorly of causal joint speculations and more generally of seeking to establish the concrete intelligibility of theological claims in relation to the plausibility conditions of contemporary scientific knowledge. Likewise, he rejects the path of natural theology, being convinced that natural reason cannot reproduce in its own terms the historic importance of concrete revelatory events. Operating between these extremes, Russell's *fides quaerens intellectum* approach is essentially confessional in its starting-point and subsequently seeks to understand rationally what is believed and lived out in Christian communities of faith. On this path, the theologian receives words and ideas, events and histories, stories and doctrines, all filled with a variety of meanings, and all in their various ways pointing beyond themselves to an ultimate reality that passes full understanding. Or does it? Perhaps, as Charles Hartshorne argued, we can speak literally of God and God's actions and goals, because God is a being, enough like us to make our concepts serviceable for the task. All we need is the right metaphysics. But Russell does not hold this; he walks the wide middle path of Christian theology that both affirms the infinite transcendence of God while accepting biblical testimony to God's self-revelation.

Perhaps Russell will turn his hand to this problem and develop an analogical theory of God language that can make sense out of the exercise of seeking a God-world causal joint. He needs to, I think, because the entire venture would seem ill-conceived if we were to conclude (as I do) that our extremely useful language about divine action cannot be taken as referring to a divine being with intentions and the power to act on them. But Russell cannot accept such literal reference either, neither on revealed (for example, biblical) nor on rational (for example, Hartshorne's metaphysical) grounds, so he is in need of a theory of religious language that justifies taking the idea of God as intentional actor so literally as to make questing for a causal joint a meaningful task.

Third, Russell has been uniquely clear among exponents of theories of special divine action about the way such theories worsen the problem of theodicy. In a memorable sentence, he writes, 'I believe the problem of theodicy is stunningly exacerbated by all the proposals, including my own.'[28] He is quite correct, of course, because a God who is aware of what goes on in our world, who can form intentions to act relative to envisaged values and goals, and who has the power to act is also clearly able to act to relieve suffering even when this does not appear to happen. All theodicies run aground on this problem. Theologians such as Jürgen Moltmann have pointed out that the keel really digs into the reef with the Shoah: if God did not act to prevent the Holocaust, then God does not possess the power decisively to stop evil in any situation. Moltmann explores his own version of process theology, as a result, but strikingly Russell does not follow him. He also does not follow the kenotic evacuation of divine power commended to us by John Polkinghorne, George Ellis, and Nancey Murphy in their theories of special divine action. While I understand the kenotic impulse, I concur with Russell's avoidance of it, because kenosis in these cases merely restates the problem: it is God's arbitrary self-restriction that could be lifted at any moment. Such a God is not to be trusted, for we human beings are not wise and we need more education than we are getting, while God politely refuses the task on the grounds of some self-imposed and utterly arbitrary metaphysical principle. I would rather have God's love in the form of guidance and protection, in the way I try to guide and protect my children, even if it means blunt intervention when ignorance threatens to lead to destruction of self or others. Russell also refuses to rely too much on the Stoic theodicy that God knows what is best, a desperately weak move that shores up trust in God at the expense of human moral intuition and power.

In contrast to these approaches, Russell's response to the 'stunningly exacerbated' problem of theodicy is a sustained attempt to make sense of God's goodness through the Cross. In a grand vision of history and nature, Russell conjoins the events of the crucifixion and resurrection of Jesus with a robust doctrine of the Trinity to frame and empower an aggressively optimistic view of history, both as theistic evolution (looking backward), as eschatological consummation (looking forward), and as faithful waiting and witness in the present, with the crucifixion deeply entangling the Holy Trinity in the suffering of the created world. I respect the orthodoxy of Russell's approach to the problem of theodicy enormously, as well as this vision of the meaningfulness of creation and history that some forms of Christianity commend to the rest of the world. It was one of the luminous moves of early Christian theologians and preachers to vest in the rationally and morally impenetrable crucifixion all the surds of history and nature, promising ultimate meaningfulness as incipiently present in the blood-streaked waters of history and (somehow, through the Cross and resurrection) yielding eventually to consummation of every potential, the wiping away of all tears, the righting of all wrongs, and the resolution of all confusions. It is not easy to know how this is all supposed to happen, as the struggles within theological interpretation of the key elements of this vision have shown, but it is breathtaking nonetheless. And it is a narrative of consummate power, rivaling the samsaric visions of South Asian religions.

I do not begrudge Russell this approach to the problem of theodicy. Rather I commend him for acknowledging that a theory of special divine action demands a response of just such bold proportions. Moltmann was driven by his sensitivity to the Shoah decisively to abandon key elements of this picture of reality, however, and process theologians are numerous in our time for similar reasons. So my question to Russell in this case is as deep as the tears of suffering, unendingly sympathetic, strained with moral self-doubt, and deeply personal for both of us: can he really surrender himself to this vision? Is not such surrender to wrap oneself in delusion for the sake of self-comfort and communal belonging in face of vast moral aporia and cosmic anomia? Might not another strand of theology – for example, process theology, mystical theology's God who passes moral comprehension, or even Christian atheism or a Christian form of religious naturalism – have better resources for a morally effective and intellectually compelling response to the problem? We all share this problem in one way or another, in the form of a problem of suffering if not a problem of theodicy. Since none escapes, none should gloat. Yet, like Moltmann, one can despair of waiting, and rewrite God's nature, or else, like me, re-evaluate divine morality so as to render divine neglect as the automatic operation of partly life-giving natural principles, and to reconstruct human morality as the responsibility to make our own moral choices, to create a loving and just world that is possible because we can imagine it, even if it is not divinely envisaged or ordained or encouraged. This question, then, is an infinitely gentle one, a cry from heart to heart.

Finally, there is the question of God's nature. Russell's personalistic theism is of the distinctively modern kind, which sprang up when the seeds of the Hebrew Bible's anthropomorphism germinated in the fertile soil of an increasingly literate culture filled with bibles from the newly invented printing press. It is a distinctively Protestant deviation from the mainstream Christian view, preferring the Jerusalem to the Athens side of the famous tension that has dominated Christian theology from the beginning. I freely confess to favoring the Athens side of the balance, but my own bias will not stop me from calling Russell back to the center, and pressing on him the question that knits together the previous three questions: should not the classical traditions of Christian theology be allowed greater authority in his view of God? Of course, Russell is a Trinitarian theologian, but his God is also a being among other beings, whose action in the world is properly subject to the quest for its mechanism, the causal joint that links the divine intentions to the created world. What happened to the classical doctrines of aseity and immutability, the affirmations that God is self-contained and does not change through acting or feeling? What happened to God as the ground of being or being itself, as pure act and first cause? How does Russell deflect the classical intuition that God as a being can be no God at all but merely an idol of the human imagination?[29]

I admit that a call to centrist classical Christian orthodoxy from an unregenerate Athens-style philosophical theologian such as myself is a move in bad faith. But such a call has two saving graces. On the one hand, it is fun to remind other theologians of where the Christian theological traditions' centerlines run, especially when one does not walk upon them oneself. On the other hand, and far more seriously, personalist theism is as weak philosophically as it is biblically congenial, and so it is not for nothing that the mainstream of Christian theology has maintained a greater tension between Athens and Jerusalem than Russell does.

Notes

1 The volumes of what I am calling the Divine Action Project are as follows (with a volume from the Capstone conference in 2003 yet to appear): Robert John Russell, William R. Stoeger, SJ, and George V. Coyne, SJ (eds), *Physics, Philosophy, and Theology: A Common Quest for Understanding* (Vatican City State: Vatican Observatory Publications, 1988) (referred to as '*PPT*' in this essay); Russell, Nancey Murphy, and Chris J. Isham (eds), *Quantum Cosmology and the Laws of Nature: Scientific Perspectives on Divine Action*, vol. I (Vatican City State and Berkeley, CA: Vatican Observatory and Center for Theology and the Natural Sciences, 1993; Russell, Nancey C. Murphy, and Arthur R. Peacocke (eds), *Chaos and Complexity: Scientific Perspectives on Divine Action*, vol. II (Vatican City State and Berkeley, CA: Vatican Observatory and Center for Theology and the Natural Sciences, 1995) ('*CC*'); Russell, William R. Stoeger, SJ, and Franscisco J. Ayala (eds), *Evolutionary and Molecular Biology: Scientific Perspectives on Divine Action*, vol. III (Vatican City State and Berkeley, CA: Vatican Observatory and Center for Theology and the Natural Sciences, 1998) ('*EMB*'); Russell, Nancey Murphy, Theo C. Meyering, and Michael A. Arbib (eds), *Neuroscience and the Person: Scientific Perspectives on Divine Action*, vol. IV (Vatican City State and Berkeley, CA: Vatican Observatory and Center for Theology and the Natural Sciences, 1999); and Russell, Philip

Clayton, Kirk Wegter-McNelly, and John Polkinghorne (eds), *Quantum Mechanics: Scientific Perspectives on Divine Action*, vol. V (Vatican City State and Berkeley, CA: Vatican Observatory and Center for Theology and the Natural Sciences, 2001) ('*QM*').

2 I will pay most attention to Russell's most recent work on the topic of special divine action at the quantum level. See 'Divine Action and Quantum Mechanics: A Fresh Assessment', in *Quantum Mechanics*, 293–328. Other relevant essays are 'Quantum Physics in Philosophical and Theological Perspective', in *Physics, Philosophy, and Theology*, 343–74; the introduction to *Chaos and Complexity*, especially because Russell had a hand in, and often refers to, the typology presented there (this typology also appears in the introduction to *Quantum Mechanics*); his essay with me entitled 'Chaos: A Mathematical Introduction with Philosophical Reflections', in *Chaos and Complexity*, 49–90; and his essay entitled 'Special Providence and Genetic Mutation: A New Defense of Theistic Evolution', in *Evolutionary and Molecular Biology*, 191–223. As far as his work on general divine action is concerned, the definitive expression to date is 'Finite Creation without a Beginning: The Doctrine of Creation in Relation to Big Bang and Quantum Cosmologies', in *Quantum Cosmology and the Laws of Nature*, 293–329.

3 Arthur Peacocke, *Theology for a Scientific Age*, 2nd enlarged edition (London: SCM Press, 1993), especially Chapter 9.

4 Of the two basic distinctions introduced above, Russell uses that between interventionist and non-interventionist accounts of divine action but not that between compatibilist and incompatibilist approaches. This latter distinction has proved crucial in the philosophical analysis of human action and freedom and I think that it can play the same clarifying role in debates over divine action. Russell should incorporate it into his already large set of working distinctions accordingly. See Wesley J. Wildman, 'The Divine Action Project, 1988–2003', *Theology and Science*, 2:1 (April 2004): 31–75.

5 This claim seems odd, at first glance, because Russell certainly does seem to explain the 'how' of at least one way that God acts. But I think it makes sense, and in two ways. On the one hand, Russell does not explain *exhaustively* how God acts with his theory of divine action, and freely allows that God may act in ways other than those he discusses. On the other hand, Russell seems to be denying that he is identifying precisely the causal joint or mechanism of divine action, but rather only positing a location for that mechanism in nature.

6 A closely related distinction is that between mediated and unmediated divine action (see *Quantum Mechanics*, 296, note 12). Mediated divine action is 'in, through, and together with the processes of nature' and thus in harmony with the order of nature as God created it, and Russell affirms this side of the distinction. By contrast, he rejects unmediated divine action, which he describes as unilateral and occasionalist, which means that God's action is really what keeps nature going in its orderly fashion, despite the appearance of natural causes and the usefulness of mathematics and science for describing causal regularities. I am not sure that this distinction is stable because 'unmediated' divine action seems reducible to interventionism far more obviously than to occasionalism, and existing distinctions take account of both ideas.

7 This distinction begs complicated questions about the ontological status of top–down and bottom–up causation. Are they ontologically distinct forms of causation or rather merely convenient devices for describing the ways that complex systems mediate ordinary causes and their effects up and down levels of organization in complex systems? I think the latter is the right way to understand the way nature works – this is the mono-causal hypothesis in conjunction with a theory of complex systems that can constrain and coordinate ordinary causation at a variety of levels. Russell at places appears to entertain an ontological interpretation of the distinction between top–down and bottom–up causality, however, particularly when thinking of the causal powers of conscious creatures such as human beings. See *Quantum Mechanics*, 300–301, for example, where Russell asks what top–down causation could mean prior to the evolution of conscious creatures.

8   I know others worked with Russell in creating this diagram, but I do not know the details. In *Chaos and Complexity*, Russell does say the following: 'Since its inception in 1991, the typology has been developed further through conversations with a number of scholars including Nancey Murphy and Thomas Tracy' (9).

9   The disadvantages of the table are that it leaves out bona fide theories of divine action (not discussed here), that it obscures different assumptions that these various views make about the divine nature, that it conceives everything in theistic terms (even atheism) and so is insensitive to other theological and philosophical alternatives (from Neoplatonism to religious naturalism), that its handling of the primary-secondary causation models is awkward (due in part, I think, to neglect of the compatibilist versus incompatibilist distinction), that it contrives to treat subjectively special divine action under the category of uniform divine action, and that it renders the chaos option as lateral amplification (which is misleading, covering only the role of chaos theory in imagining how quantum events may produce macro effects, and neglecting the way some, such as John Polkinghorne, use chaos theory to articulate an alternative view of ontological openness in nature). For these reasons, I prefer another approach to classifying theories of divine action, which I presented in 'The Divine Action Project'.

10 See Russell, 'Finite Creation without a Beginning'.

11 See A. J. Ayer, *Language, Truth, and Logic* (London: Gollancz, 1936; 2nd edn, 1946).

12 Robert Neville, for example, intends his doctrines of God and creation to be consistent in principle with anything the natural sciences could ever possibly discover about reality. He takes this to be the very meaning of metaphysics: propositions that would be true in any possible world. See *God the Creator* (Chicago: University of Chicago Press, 1968).

13 For an explanation of this, see Wildman and Russell, 'Chaos', especially 73–4, 80–82.

14 See John Polkinghorne, 'The Metaphysics of Divine Action', in *Chaos and Complexity*, 147–56.

15 See Thomas F. Tracy, *The God Who Acts: Philosophical and Theological Explorations* (University Park, PA: Pennsylvania State University, 1994). See also Tracy's contributions to the Divine Action Project: 'Particular Providence and the God of the Gaps', in *Chaos and Complexity*, 289–324; 'Evolution, Divine Action, and the Problem of Evil', in *Evolutionary and Molecular Biology*, 511–30; and 'Creation, Providence, and Quantum Chance', in *Quantum Mechanics*, 235–58.

16 Nancey Murphy's key essay on divine action is 'Divine Action in the Natural Order: Buridan's Ass and Schrödinger's Cat', in *Chaos and Complexity*, 338–44.

17 Importantly, Russell must hold that stochastic laws governing quantum measurement events – however understood – constrain ensembles of events, not individual events. Otherwise, God's action in the indeterminacy of measurement events would amount to intervening in probabilistic laws of nature, and this would defeat Russell's goals. This question – whether stochastic laws governing quantum measurement events constrain individual events or only ensembles of events – is one of the key controversies in theories of divine action; see Wildman, 'The Divine Action Project', 54–5.

18 See, among many other works, Plato's *Republic* and Aristotle's *Metaphysics*.

19 See, among many other works, Alfred North Whitehead, *Process and Reality*, corrected edn, ed. by David Ray Griffin and Donald W. Sherbourne (New York and London: Free Press and Collier Macmillan Publishers, 1978; 1st edn, 1929).

20 See, among many other works, Pierre Teilhard de Chardin, *The Phenomenon of Man* (1959), *The Divine Milieu* (1960), and *Hymn of the Universe* (1965).

21 See Nicholas Saunders, *Divine Action and Modern Science* (Cambridge: Cambridge University Press, 2002), especially Chapter 6, 'Does God Cheat at Dice?' Saunders develops criticisms expressed by John Polkinghorne in 'The Metaphysics of Divine Action', in *Chaos and Complexity*. I discussed Saunders's criticisms in 'The Divine Action Project'.

22 See especially the dissertation of Christoph Lameter, 'Divine Action in the Framework of Scientific Thinking: From Quantum Theory to Divine Action' (Ph.D. diss., Fuller Theological Seminary, 2004).

23 See Russell, 'Special Providence and Genetic Mutation'.

24 See Russell, 'Divine Action and Quantum Mechanics'.

25 See ibid.

26 Critiques of special divine action sometimes take advantage of this difficulty with specifying causal joints. Saunders, for example, ventured a round-house attack on all existing proposals for the causal joint of special divine action that crucially depends on the expectation that the goals of the incompatibilist, non-interventionist program should include unlimited precision in the specification of the causal joint. Because this is not possible, in principle, it is unsurprising that all existing proposals in one way or another fail to reach Saunders's high standards for them. Saunders argues that all theories presenting non-interventionist accounts of a causal joint for special divine action fail because they arbitrarily massage the interpretation of natural laws to enable the proposed causal joint to avoid conflict with the laws of nature, interpreted in a robust ontological way. But the only vision we can get with the laws of nature is a causal one, and the more comprehensive our theories become, the closer we will approach a causally closed picture of nature. In order to make good on the promise for divine action of ontological indeterminism within nature, even within the quantum realm, it will be necessary either to accept vagueness in the formulation of the causal joint or to adjust conveniently our interpretation of the laws of nature. Since facing this choice is unavoidable, its occurrence cannot be a sign of theoretical failure.

27 See, among many other works, Austin Farrer, *Finite and Infinite* (Westminster: A. & C. Black, Dacre Press, 1943; 2nd edn, 1949; reissued New York: Seabury Press, 1979).

28 Russell, 'Special Providence and Genetic Mutation', 216.

29 On all of these questions, see the remarkable work by Thomas G. Weinandy, *Does God Change? The World's Becoming in the Incarnation*, Studies in Historical Theology, vol. IV (Still River, MA: St Bede's Publications, 1985), which deserves far wider distribution. Weinandy's approach seems roughly compatible with Russell's theological instincts.

III

Cosmology and God's Action in Nature's World

CHAPTER TWELVE

Today's Playing Field: Theology and Science

George V. Coyne, SJ

It would appear to me to be rather rash to attempt to describe today's playing field without some overview of how the game has been played over the centuries. There is the temptation to view the theology–science dialogue as a phenomenon of our times, a young and exciting field of interdisciplinary studies born from the marvelous recent advances in the natural sciences and the openness of philosophers and theologians to take seriously the impact of those advances on fundamental matters of religious faith. If yielded to, that temptation could eviscerate the dialogue itself, making it an enjoyable game but not a very meaningful one. So please allow me to spend the first part of my essay on a review of the game as it has been played up to the birth of modern science.

The great intellectual and spiritual currents of science and faith run through our civilization from its very beginning. Sometimes they have seemed to be in opposition. More often they have worked together as inseparable elements of a common human quest for understanding. Their mutual relationships have at times been very conspicuous, at other times obscure, but never absent. Some of them are presented here.[1]

The Age of Mythology and the Greek Awakening

All ancient civilizations in Egypt, Mesopotamia, Greece, and many other parts of the world have left evidence of an early stage of intellectual development at which the discourse about nature was framed in the ordinary language of interpersonal communication between human beings. Consequently, nature was conceived as a kind of all-embracing society or state the rulers of which were a number of more or less powerful gods, spirits, and demons.[2] The arbitrary will of the gods of nature was behind everything, serving man as a reasonable, or at least intelligible, explanation of all phenomena. There was no split between nature and culture.

The old mythological conception of nature gradually began to yield to the new idea that the phenomena of nature did not appear as a consequence of the free decisions of its gods, but because they had to appear as a consequence of an inner necessity which forced them to do so. This was a stark denial of the wisdom of all previous ages and as such it provoked an intellectual upheaval compared with which all later 'scientific revolutions' appear as mere ripples on the surface of that ocean of thought which was first stirred by that band of innovators who have become known as the pre-Socratic philosophers. This was a Greek movement, but over the last hundred years the history of science has been able to shed much new light upon the achievements of the earlier great civilizations[3] and, even if we cannot always trace the channels through which Eastern knowledge percolated into Hellas, there is no doubt whatever that many individual features of the Greek intellectual world from about 600 BCE were not conceived here but in earlier cultures. If this is so, there arises the question as to why the Ionian philosophers along the coast of Asia Minor were able to accomplish an intellectual breakthrough on this formidable scale. An answer may be sought in the very different structure of societies. In Egypt the king was divine, and in Babylon he was the highest representative of his people *vis-à-vis* the heavenly court. In neither country could a process of demythologization set in without disturbing the very political order. In Ionia the situation was different after the expulsion of the kings or tyrants and the establishment of some kind of government by the people. It is worth remembering that Thales is said to have been active both in philosophy and in politics.

Looking back upon this development which ultimately changed the intellectual outlook of a great part of all mankind one cannot help but be struck by the sheer linguistic difficulties of the whole undertaking. At the bottom was the groping insight that the phenomena of nature were not arbitrary, but necessary. In what kind of language could this insight be expressed? The Ionian thinkers grappled with this problem and tried to solve it in two very different ways: by metaphor and by mathematics. Throughout the centuries the Greek philosophers pursued numerous experiments in the metaphorical use of ordinary language. The result was a new vocabulary of technical terms, the metaphorical origin of which went into oblivion in the course of the long process which gradually made the Greek world familiar with the idea of a non-mythological account of the ways of nature. A very different solution was discovered by the Pythagoreans. This discovery of a mathematical alternative to the metaphorical discourse about nature had far-reaching consequences. Since then science has never forgotten that nature contains necessary, internal connections which only mathematics is able to disclose and express. However, this new insight had to fight for its survival.

Aristotle had already fought this special conception of the mathematical discourse on nature on several fronts. In the final chapter of the *Metaphysics* he raised his voice against numerological speculations in a rhetorical manner in marked contrast with his usual style, as if he were almost emotionally involved in this question.[4] This stems from Aristotle's particular concept of philosophical knowledge in general and natural knowledge in particular. Here the key word is 'cause'. The point is that any account of nature must remain incomplete if it ignores one or more of the four causes. If a philosopher does not discover them he has not reached his goal. While the mathematician is not concerned with final causes, the natural philosopher is obliged to study all the four types of causation.[5] When all is said and done, Aristotle would have refused to admit not only the mathematician but also the mathematical physicist to the kingdom of final causation, with the obvious inference that the purely mathematical discourse on nature contributes nothing to the quest for wisdom and is unable to shed any light upon the ultimate questions of human existence. Aristotle succeeded inasmuch as he was able to identify his God not only with the Prime Mover and Supreme Cause of the world but also with the Supreme Good and Life as such, making Him the source of both the unity of the universe and the moral existence of man. Nevertheless, one has to admit that the God of Aristotle remained a purely rational construction which was unable to appeal to the religious consciousness of the great masses.

However, it is impossible to realize what happened in both Hellenistic and later science without admitting the existence of another great tradition which may be properly named after Archimedes. This tradition is characterized by a consistent use of the language of mathematics and by a general disregard of causal and teleological explanations. The Archimedean approach was fruitfully adopted by medieval scholars and both Galileo and Kepler used it to lay the foundations of modern mechanics and astronomy. So, even if Archimedes failed to comply with Aristotle's insistence on causal explanations as the hallmark of a scientific description, it is impossible to ignore the fact that over the ages the Archimedean tradition was able to produce an ever-increasing body of insights into the connections of the phenomena of nature, insights that were obtained thanks to mathematical discourse and could not have been obtained or expressed in any other way. And it gives food for thought that Archimedes' results in mechanics are valid even today, whereas Aristotle's causal explanations have largely fallen into oblivion.

In summary, the Greek cosmos was a rational construction based on the fundamental assumption that the regularities of natural phenomena were grounded upon necessary connections or relationships inherent in nature itself, and that apparent irregularities must in some way be reducible to necessary and regular laws. Consequently, the task of the natural philosopher was to find means of expressing the material necessity in nature by a logical necessity in the discourse on nature.

Among the later philosophico-religious systems the most important from a historical point of view was the 'natural theology' of the Stoics. Their view of the world carried the Aristotelian discourse on nature to an inevitable conclusion in the form of a universal determinism from which perhaps only the human mind had a slender chance of escaping through its deliberate acceptance of the inevitable. Never before had the problem of human freedom versus universal causality been so clearly grasped or its ethical implications so seriously envisaged. The result was an impressive structure of thought in which man became more intimately related to nature than in any previous system.

The Age of Christianity

Into this world torn by conflicting views on the proper discourse on nature and the true relations between God and human beings Christianity emerged from its obscure origin in Palestine. At first sight it would seem that it must stay out of the philosophical battle as a non-combatant who was singularly uninterested in the scientific achievements of the Greeks. There is no treatise on cosmology in the New Testament and extremely few references to particular elements of the Greek account of the universe. All efforts are spent on the proclamation of the belief that the birth, life, death, and resurrection of Jesus had radically changed the way in which the relations between God and the world should be envisaged.

From the religion of Israel Christianity also inherited the belief that the one Lord of the world is also its Creator.[6] Time and again the Old Testament underlines the fact that the world is created. This is almost always understood in the sense that it has come into being independently of man and without human assistance. 'Where were you when I laid the foundations of the earth?',[7] was God's question to Job. The biblical doctrine of creation seems to be marked by a paradox. On the one hand, there is a chasm between God and His creatures. Nothing in nature is divine. On the other hand, the created world is said to testify to the divinity of its creator. God must be present within it in such a way that man can recognize it as created. The beginning of the Gospel of St John indicates a solution to this dilemma: 'In the beginning was the *logos*, and the *logos* was with God, and the *logos* was God. He was in the beginning with God. All things came into being through him, and without him not one thing came into being.' Here the Pauline proclamation of Jesus as the redeemer of the world is supplemented by a specific Johannine discourse on Jesus as the divine *logos*.

When the fourth Gospel opens by saying, 'In the beginning was the *logos*', it looks at first sight like the introduction to a Greek philosophical treatise on the *arche*, or *principium* of the universe.[8] To use the word in a Christian context was an important step towards assimilating the conception of the world as a rational structure according to the basic tenet of Greek philosophy. It is difficult to reject the idea that by describing Christ as the universal and divine *logos*, and as such the ground of all creation, Christianity was prevented, at least in principle, from rejecting the Greek conception of the universe as a rational structure.

Despite its apparent ignorance of all matters scientific the New Testament presented Christianity in a way that contained a number of seminal ideas out of which the future relationships between the scientific discourse and the Christian theology would develop. The belief in One God implied a demythologization of the discourse on nature. That nature was created meant that its inner connections were established independently of the human mind which had to respect them when they were discovered. The transcendence of God would eventually remove the fear of trespassing upon the forbidden ground or the sacred by subjecting nature to scientific investigation. Finally the *logos* Christology made the idea of an all-permeating rationality at home in a religion which hailed Christ as the Lord of the World. It is difficult not to see a connection between this insight and the emergence of experimental methods in science.

What is new, for instance, in Thomas Aquinas is his insistence that the natural knowledge of God must be acquired in the same way as all other knowledge. This means that 'it does not go beyond that kind of knowledge that is acquired through the senses'.[9] Bonaventure represented a much more traditional theology which gave natural reason a more limited scope.[10] We have here a clash between two different attitudes. Bonaventure is imbued with the Augustinian notion of the interior light by which God illuminates the soul so that it cannot look at the world except as something which is related to Him. This was consciously a polemical stand against Aquinas, who upheld the autonomy of human reason within its proper bounds without the special assistance of grace.

Another great tradition in Christian thought is that of Duns Scotus. Aristotle had found the ultimate happiness of man in the intellectual knowledge of the Divine. Duns Scotus was well aware of this; but he also maintained that this kind of knowledge is not identical with the Good News of the Gospel about salvation from sin and life in the beatific vision of God, being fully aware that this was a strictly theological position which cannot be founded upon purely philosophical reasons. The believer simply knows something which the pure philosopher ignores. This becomes manifest when we consider the doctrine of creation. The philosopher is unable to describe creation except in terms of cause and effect, with the consequence that the world derives from God by necessity. On the other hand, the theologian knows that the world came into being through a free act of God just as man is saved by a free gift of grace. This meant that the laws of nature are such as they are because of a free decision by God. If God had so willed, they might have been different. The recognition of the laws of nature as contingent upon the Divine will was more than a theological subtlety. It had implications of immediate importance for the scientific approach to nature.

The Birth of Modern Science

The increasing use of mathematical arguments in the fourteenth century went hand-in-hand with a new awareness of how thought experiments based on common sense and everyday experience could contribute to the critical re-examination of the discourse on nature. No previous scientist had ever been able to carry this type of mathematical approach to nature to a similar perfection with such a methodological freedom and open-mindedness as did Johannes Kepler. More than anyone else, it was Kepler who became the herald of a new era in which mathematical physics would go from strength to strength. With Kepler the Book of Nature[11] reached the summit of its metaphorical life as the vehicle of the self-understanding of a first-rate scientist who was deeply committed to the Christian faith. But with Galileo the Book of Nature was confronted with the Book of Scripture in a dramatic encounter which has ever since been regarded as one of the most decisive interactions between the world of science and the world of belief. Many polemicists have even taken it as the final proof of the alleged incompatibility of these two worlds and evidence of an essential enmity between the Catholic Church and the scientific attitude. The setting of this 'affair' was the first half of the seventeenth century when Europe was torn by many conflicts, some of which were caused by the struggle for power over the European dominions beyond the ocean, while others had originated in the Reformation one hundred years earlier. While these events shook the political and ecclesiastical world it became Galileo's fate to shake the foundations of the inherited discourse on nature. In this he was not alone. But in the course of events he came to occupy a more conspicuous position than that of the other great pioneers of modern science. After many years of quiet work at Pisa and Padua, Galileo suddenly rose to European fame in 1610 when he published the first results of his epoch-making astronomical observations with the telescope he had constructed. All the world was amazed at the mountains on the moon, the innumerable fixed stars, the resolution of the Milky Way into separate stars, and the four satellites revolving around the planet Jupiter.[12] The framework of traditional cosmology had no room for such discoveries and would collapse under their weight.

The Galileo affair raises the inevitable question of how it was possible that the highest doctrinal office of the Church with Pope Urban VIII in the chair could make a decision which was wrong and truly fatal, since it contributed over the coming centuries to alienate people from the faith by exposing the Church as the enemy of scientific progress. What was it that went wrong? Here we remember that in the fourteenth century radical innovators of cosmology had risen to high positions in the hierarchy, and that one hundred years later the even more revolutionary ideas of Nicholas Cusa had not prevented him from getting a Cardinal's hat. Why should everything be so different in the seventeenth century?

In the course of time, there have been many answers to this painful question.[13] Some have said that it was just typical of the Church to try to check the progress of science, although this claim simply disregards the historical evidence of the long period before Galileo. Still others underline that after all nobody knew at the time whether the Copernican system was true or false. This is correct, but it is not what the Holy Office said; it said it was false, and said it without listening to the evidence which the other part was prepared to offer. Consequently, the 'Galileo Affair' cannot be seen as a genuine meeting or interaction between Christian faith or theology and natural science, for science was not represented at the table.

The results of Kepler and Galileo provided a completely new point of departure for the science of mechanics. The philosophers were duly impressed and as soon as 1637 Descartes proposed a general theory of the universe in terms of purely mechanical interactions between various types of fundamental particles supposed to fill all space and influencing each other by their mutual collisions. On the other hand, more mathematically inclined scientists became increasingly aware that Descartes had built his physics on shaky foundations. In Book I of the *Principia*, Newton showed how all problems of motion could be mathematically stated on the basis of a few fundamental axioms, Newton's Laws, so that their solutions would depend only on appropriate mathematical techniques. This victory made a strong impact on the minds of the eighteenth century. Voltaire hailed Newton as the great rationalist in whom human reason had defeated the intellectual darkness of all previous ages, a picture which also satisfied the positivistic philosophers of science in the nineteenth century.

In recent years scholars have delved more deeply into the great mass of theological writings left in manuscript form, with the result that we now have to concede a place to Newton in the history of theology. With his usual reluctance to publish any connected exposition of his religious views Newton chose to explain his ideas on God and nature in an appendix or *General Scholium* added to the second edition of the *Principia*. First and foremost it is manifest that Newton admitted the necessity of a Divine Revelation. In the *Principia* he had described a System of the World which purported to give a coherent account of the fundamental principles governing the physical universe. He had also stated, 'it belonged to natural philosophy to discourse of God from the appearances of things'. However, this account was incomplete. It ignored human history, which was imbedded in the physical universe but not explained by its laws. It seems that Newton's life-long occupation with historical and exegetical questions was motivated by a desire to subject the human world to the same kind of essential order and clarity which the *Principia* had lent to the physical universe.

Newton argued that nature exhibits a number of mechanical phenomena for which no theoretical explanation could be found within a theory that was designed to comprehend all the motions of the bodies in the whole universe. From these premises he had constructed his argument for the existence of a Deity whose direct intervention would explain the gaps in the theoretical discourse. But this manner of reasoning made Newton's natural theology extremely vulnerable. His argument would clearly lose its force at the moment when this discourse itself became sufficiently advanced to close the gaps by its own force. In astronomy this situation had arisen already towards the end of the eighteenth century, when a number of French mathematical physicists of no common genius had utilized Newton's laws of motion to create a highly sophisticated celestial mechanics which seemed to solve those problems which Newton's own account had left unanswered. In the beginning of the nineteenth century the work of Laplace and his colleagues produced a growing feeling that at long last Newtonian mechanics itself had become able to stop the gaps in which Newton had found room for the Deity. This is the background of the popular anecdote of Laplace replying to Napoleon, 'Sir, I have no need of that hypothesis', when the Emperor asked him why God did not figure in his *Mécanique céleste* (1799 CE and later).[14]

Today's Playing Field

From this historical overview we can garner the following characteristics of the playing field which today's game must not ignore. In the age of mythology there was no split between nature and culture. For the Pythagoreans nature contains necessary, internal connections which only mathematics is able to disclose and express. While Aristotle insisted that nature could only be understood by searching out the four causes, Archimedes emphasized that knowledge of nature came through sense experience and experimentation with the use of mathematics. The Stoics carried the emphasis on causality to its limit by proposing a universal determinism, thus challenging human freedom. The human being was intimately related to nature but only to her/his detriment, being caught in a web of universal causality. Christianity at its very birth asserted that the Lord and Saviour was also the Creator of the world and, through the *logos* theology of John, that there was a rational structure in creation which derived from the very triune nature of the Creator. Thus, the world of the senses was worth investigation through the experimental method. The question arose, however, as to whether there is a necessary connection between the Creator and the rationality of the universe or whether God freely chose that rational structure. With the birth of modern science the delicate balance between the search for the objective rational structure of the universe and the more subjective religious experience of faith was threatened. John Paul II represents, though not exclusively, one way of playing the game in this field.

From the very beginning of the papacy of John Paul II one can discern a new view on the relationship of science and faith. One aspect of this relationship is the part that science plays in the search for 'ultimate meaning', a phrase found many times in the encyclical *Fides et Ratio*. It will be helpful first to summarize three periods which together set the background for judging what is new in this new view from Rome: (1) the rise of modern atheism in the seventeenth and eighteenth centuries; (2) anticlericalism in Europe in the nineteenth century; and (3) the awakening within the Church to modern science in the twentieth century. In the misappropriation of modern science in the seventeenth and eighteenth centuries to establish the foundations for religious belief we find the roots from which sprung the divorce between science and faith and, thus, atheism. We have seen this in Newton's 'proofs' for the existence of God as presented in the *General Scholium* to the *Principia*. As to the influence of nineteenth century anticlericalism on the development of the relationship between science and faith, a good example is seen in the founding of the Vatican Observatory in 1891 by Pope Leo XIII. His words show very clearly the prevailing mistrust of many scientists for the Church and his rather hostile response:

> So that they might display their disdain and hatred for the mystical Spouse of Christ, who is the true light, those borne of darkness are accustomed to calumniate her to unlearned people and they call her the friend of obscurantism ... but we have in the first place put before ourselves the plan [in founding the Vatican Observatory] ... that everyone might see that the Church and its Pastors are not opposed to true and solid science, whether human or divine, but that they embrace it, encourage it, and promote it with the fullest possible dedication.[15]

The awakening of the Church to modern science during the twentieth century is best seen in the personage of Pope Pius XII, who had an excellent gentleman's knowledge of astronomy and, as Pope, frequently discussed astronomical research with the staff of the Vatican Observatory. However, he was not immune from a certain apologetic tendency and sought to identify the beginning state of the Big Bang cosmologies with God's act of creation. Georges Lemaître, a respected cosmologist and President of the Pontifical Academy of Sciences, had considerable difficulty with this view of the Pope. Lemaître insisted that the *Primeval Atom*, of which he was the author, and the Big Bang hypothesis should be judged solely as physical theories and that theological considerations should be kept completely separate.[16]

From what has been said of these three historical periods we can conclude the following. First, as an inheritance from the origins of modern atheism in the seventeenth and eighteenth centuries, there had been within the Church a tendency to associate scientific research with atheism. Second, a type of 'siege' or hostile mentality characterized the thinking of the Church at the time of the foundation of the Vatican Observatory. Third, when enlightened to the magnificent progress in scientific research in the twentieth century, the Church wished too hastily to appropriate the results of science to its own ends. In the papacy of John Paul II we see a view of the science–faith relationship which contrasts in a significant way with each of these antecedent views.

The views of John Paul II on the relationship of science and faith and on the search for ultimate meaning can be found in many of his messages to university communities and to scientists. Two of these are of key importance: the message written on the occasion of the tricentennial of Newton's *Principia Mathematica*, and published as an introduction to the proceedings of the meeting sponsored by the Vatican Observatory to commemorate that same tricentennial,[17] and the encyclical *Fides et Ratio*.[18]

The newness in what John Paul II has said about the relationship between science and religion consists in his having taken a position compellingly different than the one he had inherited. This statement is justified principally in the message on the occasion of the tricentennial of Newton's *Principia Mathematica*. John Paul II clearly states that science cannot be used in a simplistic way as a rational basis for religious belief, nor can it be judged to be by its nature atheistic, opposed to belief in God. Furthermore, he expresses uncertainty as to where the dialogue between science and faith will lead. The Pope raises the question, 'Can science also benefit from this interchange?' It takes a great deal of openness to ask that question and it does not have a very clear answer. In fact, it is very difficult to see what the benefits to science as such might be. In the papal message it is intimated that the dialogue will help scientists to appreciate that scientific discoveries cannot be a substitute for knowledge of the truly ultimate. In what way, however, do scientific discoveries participate, together with philosophy and theology, in the quest for that ultimate? This is a serious and open question.

Fides et Ratio and the Search for Ultimate Meaning

In the encyclical *Fides et Ratio* the dialogue continues and a serious attempt is made to lay the foundations for dialogue with the sciences. The principal thrust of John Paul II's encyclical *Fides et Ratio*, which in the twilight of his papacy summarized his thinking on the relationship of faith and reason, is a plea that we not lose the search for ultimate truth. He writes, for instance:

> She [the Church] sees in philosophy the way to come to know fundamental truths about human life. ... I wish to reflect upon this special activity of human reason. I judge it necessary to do so because at the present time in particular the search for ultimate truth seems often to be neglected.[19]

How are we to define ultimate truth? For my purposes the answer to this question is of utmost importance, since I wish to propose that the natural sciences, together with philosophy and other ways of knowing, contribute to this search for ultimate truth. I prefer to construct a definition from the words of the encyclical:

> people seek an absolute which might give to all their searching a meaning and an answer – something ultimate which might serve as the ground of all things. In other words, they seek a final explanation, a supreme value, which refers to nothing beyond itself and which puts an end to all questioning.[20]

In this search there are various ways of knowing and among them philosophy has a privileged role. The Pope then contrasts philosophy with other ways of knowing and especially with the natural sciences. It is clear that philosophy and the natural sciences must each have their autonomy:

> St. Albert the Great and St Thomas were the first to recognize the autonomy which philosophy and the sciences needed if they were to perform well in their respective fields of research.[21]

A further contrast between science and philosophy is given when he writes:

> Reference to the sciences is often helpful, allowing as it does a more thorough knowledge of the subject under study; but it should not mean the rejection of a typical philosophical and critical thinking which is concerned with the universal.[22]

While its principal focus is not upon the natural sciences, the encyclical makes a serious attempt to lay the foundations for dialogue with the sciences in the search for ultimate meaning. However, the view presented of the natural sciences, as a participant in the search, is somewhat limited. Scientific research, especially in our day, cannot be excluded from the search for ultimate meaning. Today scientists, within their own well-determined methodology, are asking the following questions. Why is there anything rather than nothing? Is the universe finite or infinite in time and in space? Is the universe fine-tuned to the existence of intelligent life? Did humans come to be through necessary processes, chance processes, or some combination of the two in a universe fecund to allow both processes together to fructify? Such questions as these bring me to a discussion of a new view of modern physics, applicable also to the other sciences, which makes ever more significant its role in the search for ultimate meaning. My attempt will be to indicate that science cannot be characterized as depending exclusively, or even principally, on sense experience, but that, like philosophy, it has an important speculative and universal element to it. Science should, therefore, be seen as a true partner in the search for ultimate meaning.

The New Physics and the Search for Ultimate Meaning

The newness of the new physics cannot really be appreciated without some remarks on the history which brought about the new physics. At the birth of modern science in the sixteenth and seventeenth centuries, there was the persistent idea, as there had been for the Pythagoreans, that physicists were discovering some grand transcendental design incarnate in the universe. In fact, it is claimed that one of the essential factors in the birth of modern science was the Christian theology of creation and of the Incarnation. In the latter case, the concept in St John's Gospel of the *logos* becoming incarnate was particularly appropriate and hailed back in some way to Platonic and Pythagorean concepts of the world of eternal ideas and of the transcendental character of mathematics. Indeed, Newton, Descartes, Kepler, and others can be cited as viewing physics and mathematics in this way. Kepler, for instance, saw geometry as providing God with a model for creation. He went so far as to see the circle as transcendentally perfect, the straight line as the totally created and incarnate, and the ellipse as a combination of the two, an incarnation in this world of what would have been the perfect geometry for the motion of the heavenly bodies in an ideal world. Newton was the epitome of this manner of thinking as he called upon the Deity as the only explanation of why the universe, dominated by the law of gravity, did not collapse. And yet the simple equations in which he expressed that law of gravity and the laws of motion redirected for future centuries the role of mathematics in physics. No longer was mathematics simply a description of what was observed; it was a probe of the very nature of what was observed.

As usual in scientific revolutions, what was happening with this mathematization of physics only came to full realization after it had occurred. A three-layered conception of the universe, only partially inherited from the Platonic–Pythagorean tradition, came to be accepted implicitly, and only slowly did it come to consciousness. There was the layer of the true mathematics, the mathematical structures of which the world is truly made. Then there was the second layer, the mathematics of we humans, structures which were in a Platonic sense only the shadows of the first layer. Finally there were at the third layer the images in concrete reality of the true mathematical structures which we humans attempted to understand with our shadow mathematics. However, there is a subtle development, described well by Michael Heller,[23] in which at the second layer mathematics is not only the language or the interpretative tool of physics (the formal object in scholastic terminology) but becomes also the 'stuff' of the ideal world of physics (material object in scholastic terminology).

For the present this 'stuff' remained under the control of empirical verification; that is, the third layer, the images in concrete reality, remained the test of how true the human mathematical structures were.

The rise of quantum mechanics and of relativity theory at the beginning of the twentieth century soon weakened the connection between the second and third layers described above and, in fact, re-emphasized the connection between the second and first layers. The images in concrete reality made very little, if any, sense as a test of mathematical 'stuff' of the ideal world of physics. There are no natural images or representations which correspond to Hilbert spaces, the mathematical 'stuff' of quantum theory. And while general relativity has passed all of the experiments yet made to test its empirical predictions, there are no adequate images or representations which correspond to motions at relativistic velocities or under very large gravitational forces. In its 'purest' form the physics of both the sub-quantum world and the world 'beyond-relativity' is strictly mathematical in the tradition of Plato and Pythagoras and has little to do with any sensory component.

There is another significant element in the new physics. The study of the dynamics of non-linear systems has given birth to the fields of chaos theory and complexity. This represents, in some sense, a return from quantum physics to the world of macroscopic physics and it is, in another limited sense, a vindication of Aristotle's view that the world of the senses is too rich to be limited to or comprehended by mathematics. From what we have said about the new physics, there appear to be two strains in modern science which are in tension with one another. On the one hand, there is the mathematization of physics and the diminished connection to sense experience. On the other hand, there is the recognition that the world of sense experience has an innate unpredictability which prevents it from being subject to ultimate mathematical analysis. These characteristics of the new physics may make it a significant ally of philosophy and theology in the search for ultimate meaning.

Theology and the New Physics in Dialogue

The methodology of modern science is evolving and that is why I call it a new physics. The methodology of theology must also be in flux. As an effort at coming to a rational understanding of revealed truth, theology is subject to all of the vagaries of human thought. And revealed truth, granted that it first occurred at a privileged time and to chosen persons, is continuous and incarnate. What is revealed is deeply imbedded in the way we think and the understanding of it is, therefore, evolving. Furthermore, all rational knowledge of God is analogous and it would, therefore, be appropriate that concepts from the new physics be taken as analogies in the search to understand God. The methods of theology have always been greatly determined by prevailing philosophies and Christian theology in particular has since the Middle Ages been very much attached to the Aristotelian–Thomistic tradition, and especially to the concept of final cause. Thus such notions as purpose and design have been dominant. Might theology not apply itself to an attempt to understand God, the creator of a universe, where purpose and design are not the only nor even the dominant factors, but where spontaneity, indeterminacy (even at a macroscopic level), and unpredictability have contributed significantly to the evolution of a universe in which life has come to be? After all, we are products of an evolutionary universe and are still evolving. It would appear to me that our understanding of the universe, using the best methods of modern science, would also contribute to an understanding of ourselves and thus of our relationship to God, the Creator of the universe.

I think we must beware, however, of a serious temptation of the new physics. Within the culture of the new physics God is essentially, if not exclusively, seen as an explanation and not as a person. God is the ideal mathematical structure, the theory of everything. God is Mind. It must remain a firm tenet of the reflecting believer that God is more than that and that God's revelation of Himself in time is more than a communication of information. Even if we discover 'the mind of God' we will not necessarily have found God. The very nature of our emergence in an evolving universe and our inability to comprehend this even with the new physics may be an indication that in the universe God may be communicating much more than information to us.

There will, of course, always be a tension between science and theology because of the transcendental (beyond reason) character of the latter, but considering the somewhat Platonic quest in the new physics for the 'mind of God', for ultimate meaning, that very tension could be the source of a quite creative dialogue. It need not be excluded that such dialogue could take place even on the level of ultimate meaning.

Summary

Against the background of previous centuries the thought of John Paul II on the relationship of science and faith can be characterized as new. Science is seen by the Church as a partner in dialogue. Although *Fides et Ratio* is only indirectly concerned with the natural sciences, it welcomes further dialogue on the partnership of the sciences with philosophy and theology in the search for ultimate meaning, the true focus of the encyclical. From the historical roots of modern science one can come to an appreciation of a new physics which contains highly speculative and universal elements. An understanding of these elements is necessary for evaluating the role of the natural sciences in the search for ultimate meaning. Furthermore, the intrinsic unpredictability in the evolutionary history of the universe as investigated by the sciences appears to open up questions which are concerned with an understanding of ourselves in the universe and ultimately of our relationship to God, the Creator. In *Fides et Ratio* John Paul II states that the 'ultimate truth about human life' is a 'gift' and that 'every truth attained is but a step toward the fulness of truth'.[24] He, furthermore, reiterates in the encyclical what he had stated in an address in Krakow to celebrate the six hundredth anniversary of the Jagiellonian University:

Scientists are well aware that the search for truth, even when it concerns a finite reality of the world or of man, is never ending, but always points beyond to something higher than the immediate object of study, to the questions which give access to mystery.[25]

Notes

1 I am very much indebted to the lifelong research of Olaf Pedersen (deceased in 1997) for this historical survey. I am preparing the posthumous publication of his voluminous work, *The Two Books*, a brief presentation of which is given in *The Book of Nature* (Vatican City: Vatican Observatory Publications, 1992).

2 Thorkild Jacobsen, 'The Cosmos as a State', in *Before Philosophy*, ed. by H. Frankfort, H. A. Frankfort, J. A. Wilson, and Th. Jacobsen (Harmondsworth: Penguin, 1949; 1st edn, Chicago: University of Chicago Press, 1946), 137–99. A large number of relevant texts (in English translation) are found in J. B. Pritchard, *Ancient Near Eastern Texts Relating to the Old Testament*, 3rd edn with supplement (Princeton, NJ: Princeton University Press, 1969).

3 M. L. West, *Early Greek Philosophy and the Orient* (Oxford: Clarendon Press, 1971).

4 See the posthumous work by T. L. Heath, *Mathematics in Aristotle* (Oxford: Clarendon Press, 1949), in which almost all mathematical passages in the works of Aristotle have been collected and translated into English.

5 Aristotle, *Physics*, II, 7, 198a.

6 See R. J. Clifford, 'Creation in the Hebrew Bible', in *Physics, Philosophy, and Theology*, ed. by R. Russell, W. Stoeger, and G. Coyne, 2nd edn (Vatican Observatory: Vatican Observatory Publications, 2000), 151–70. Cf. the various essays in B. A. Anderson (ed.), *Creation in the Old Testament* (Philadelphia, PA: Fortress, 1984).

7 Job 38:4.

8 See W. Kelber, *Die Logoslehre von Heraklit bis Origenes* (Stuttgart: Urachhaus, 1958).

9 *Summa contra Gentiles*, III, 47. Cf. I, 3 quoted above.

10 *Itinerarium mentis in Deum*.

11 The metaphor of the Book of Nature goes back to the age of the Fathers, but it took quite a long time before it got off the ground. Its prehistory is as old as theology itself since the fundamental idea had already been expressed by St Paul's assertion that the works of God disclose His divinity, invisible being and eternal power (Rom. 1:18–20). How this should be understood was not specified and it became a problem in the early Church of how to solve this issue.

12 *Sidereus Nuncius*, Venice, 1610, in Galileo Galilei, *Opere*, 20 vols, ed. by A. Favaro (Firenze, Tip. di G. Barbèra, 1890–1909), III, 55–96. English translation in Stillman Drake, *Discoveries and Opinions of Galileo* (Garden City, NY: Doubleday, 1957), 21–58.

13 See A. Fantoli, *Galileo: For Copernicanism and for the Church*, 3rd edn, trans. by G. V. Coyne, SJ (Vatican City: Vatican Observatory Publications, 2003), from the original Italian, *Galileo: Per Copernicanesimo e Per la Chiesa*, 2nd edn (Vatican City: Vatican Observatory Publications, 1997).

14 It is very difficult to trace the origin of this story, which is found mentioned for the first time in Rouse Ball's *A Short Account of the History of Mathematics* from 1888, 4th edn (London and New York: Macmillan, 1908). Probably it is a clever invention on a par with Galileo's *Eppur si muove*. It has given place to some highly polemical discussions of Laplace's own religious attitude; see G. Sarton, 'Laplace as a run of the mill Catholic', *Isis*, 33 (1941): 309–12, and J. Pelseneer, 'Laplace as a non-Christian materialist', *Isis*, 36 (1945): 158–60. Cf. R. Hahn, 'Laplace's religious views', *Archives Internationales d'Histoire des Sciences*, 30 (1958): 38–80.

15 Leo XIII 1891, *Motu Proprio, Ut Mysticam*, in Sabino Maffeo, SJ, *The Vatican Observatory: In the Service of Nine Popes*, trans. by G. V. Coyne, SJ (Vatican City State: Vatican Observatory Publications, 2001), 315–19, from the original Italian, *La Specola Vaticana: Nove Papi Una Missione* (Vatican City State: Vatican Observatory Publications, 2001).

16 G. Lemaître, 'The Primeval Atom Hypothesis and the Problem of Clusters of Galaxies', in *La Structure et L'Evolution de l'Universe* (Bruxelles: XI Conseil de Physique Solay, 1958), 7.

17 Russell et al. eds, *Physics, Philosophy and Theology*, M3–M14.

18 John Paul II, '*Fides et ratio*', *Origins*, 28:19 (1998): 317–48.

19 Ibid., no. 5.

20 Ibid., no. 27.

21 Ibid., no. 45.

22 Ibid., no. 69.

23 M. Heller, *The New Physics and a New Theology*, trans. by G. V. Coyne, SJ (Vatican City State: Vatican Observatory Publications, 1996).

24 John Paul II, '*Fides et ratio*', no. 2.

25 'Address of John Paul II at the Jagiellonian University, June 8, 1997', *L'Osservatore Romano* (June 9–10, 1997): 12.

CHAPTER THIRTEEN

Emergent Realities with Causal Efficacy – Some Philosophical and Theological Applications[1]

Arthur Peacocke

Those who have been long engaged in the dialogue between theology and the natural sciences have good cause to be permanently grateful to Robert John Russell. For he has not only headed and orchestrated the magnificent enterprise of the Center in Berkeley of which he is Founding Director but has also been an inspiration to and coordinator of the unique, interdisciplinary conferences on 'Scientific Perspectives on Divine Action' which have been convened over the last decade or so in cooperation with the Vatican Observatory. He has himself been the Editor-in-Chief of the five (six with the initiating) state-of-the-art volumes emerging from these essentially research enterprises. As the continuing Editor of these volumes, he has contributed to all but one a remarkable series of 'Introductions' which manifest omnivorous reading, insightful and fair judgments, the highest quality of scholarship, and an ability to create a comprehensive overview shared by hardly anyone else in the field.

His own particular research contributions to those volumes, and elsewhere, have been characterized by a sustained attempt to relate divine action, in general, and biological evolution and human thought processes, in particular, to what we know about the quantum level of physical reality. I have been one of those who has not fully agreed with his proposals but have had to recognize the cogency and integrity of his arguments for them. The following essay, which I gladly offer for this Festschrift to celebrate his sixtieth year, develops a way of thinking about emergent realities, including human mental capacities, which I surmise provides a context to which all proposals about divine action may have to relate, not least his own challenging and stimulating ones. I hope he will receive it as a recognition of my indebtedness to him and to his work.

In this essay I shall attempt to extend the concepts necessary for the understanding of relationships between the various levels of organization, and so of description, that have developed in recent years from scientific analyses of complex physico-chemical and biological systems to wider issues in philosophy and theology.

Hierarchies of Complexity, and Emergentist 'Monism'

The natural and human sciences more and more give us a picture of the world as consisting of a complex hierarchy (or hierarchies) – a series of levels of organization and matter in which each successive member of the series is a whole constituted of parts preceding it in the series.[2] The wholes are organized systems of parts that are dynamically and spatially interrelated – a feature sometimes called a 'mereological' relation. Furthermore, all properties also result, directly in isolation or indirectly in larger patterns, from the properties of microphysical entities. This feature of the world is now widely recognized to be of significance in relating our knowledge of its various levels of complexity – that is, the sciences which correspond to these levels.[3] It also corresponds not only to the world in its present condition but also to the way complex systems have evolved in time out of earlier simpler ones.

I shall presume at least this with the 'physicalists': all concrete particulars in the world (including human beings), with all of their properties, are constituted only of fundamental physical entities of matter/energy manifest in many layers of complexity – a 'layered' physicalism. This is indeed a *monistic* view (a constitutively–ontologically reductionist one) that everything can be broken down into whatever physicists deem to constitute matter/energy and that no extra *entities or forces*, other than the basic four forces of physics, are to be deemed to be inserted at higher levels of complexity in order to account for their properties. However, what is significant about natural processes and about the relation of complex systems to their constituents now is that the concepts needed to describe and understand – as indeed also the methods needed to investigate each level in the hierarchy of complexity – are specific to and distinctive of those levels. It is very often the case (but not always) that the properties, concepts, and explanations used to describe the higher-level wholes are not logically reducible to those used to describe their constituent parts, themselves often also constituted of yet smaller entities. This is an epistemological assertion of a non-reductionist kind.

When the epistemological non-reducibility of properties, concepts, and explanations applicable to higher levels of complexity is well established, their employment in scientific discourse can often, *but not in all cases*, lead to a putative and then to an increasingly confident attribution of reality to that to which the higher-level terms refer. 'Reality' is not confined to the physico-chemical alone. One must accept a certain 'robustness'[4] of the entities postulated or, rather, discovered at different levels and resist any attempts to regard them as less real in comparison with some favoured lower level of 'reality'. Each level has to be regarded as a cut through the totality of reality, if you like, in the sense that we have to take account of its mode of operation at that level. New and distinctive kinds of realities at the higher levels of complexity may properly be said to have *emerged*. This can occur with respect either to moving, synchronically, up the ladder of complexity or, diachronically, through cosmic and biological evolutionary history.

Much of the discussion of reductionism has concentrated upon the relation between already established theories pertinent to different levels. This way of examining the question of reductionism is less appropriate when the context is that of the biological and social sciences, for which knowledge hardly ever resides in theories with distinctive 'laws'. In these sciences, what is sought is more usually a *model* of a complex system which explicates how its components interact to produce the properties and behaviour of the whole system – organelle, cell, multi-cellular organism, ecosystem, and so on. These models are not presented as sentences involving terms which might be translated into lower-level terms for reduction to be successful but, rather, as visual systems, structures or maps, representing multiple interactions and connecting pathways of causality and determinative influences between entities and processes. When the systems are not simply aggregates of similar units, then it can turn out that the behaviour of the system is due principally, sometimes entirely, to the distinctive way its parts are put together – which is what models attempt to make clear. This incorporation into a system constrains the behaviour of the parts and can lead to behaviour of the systems as a whole which is often unexpected and unpredicted. As W. Bechtel and R. C. Richardson[5] have expressed it: 'They are *emergent* in that we did not anticipate the properties exhibited by the whole system given what we knew of the parts.' They illustrate this by an historical examination of the controversies over yeast fermentation of glucose and oxidative phosphorylation, how the understanding of a system

> in which the contributions of the parts are recognized, but the organization is understood to generate unanticipated behaviours in the whole system, usually develops later, after those pursuing the more reductionistic path discover that the parts are insufficient to explain the behaviour of the system and turn to examining how the organization of the system might affect the activities of the parts (p. 267).

What is crucial here is not so much the unpredictability, but the inadequacy of explanation if only the parts are focused upon rather than the whole system: 'With emergent phenomena, it is the interactive organization, rather than the component behaviour, that is the critical explanatory feature' (p. 285).

There are, therefore, good grounds for utilizing the concept of 'emergence' in our interpretation of naturally occurring, hierarchical, complex systems constituted of parts which themselves are, at the lowest level, made up of the basic units of the physical world. I shall denote this position as that of *emergentist 'monism'*.[6]

Whole–Part Influence (or Causation)

If we do make such an ontological commitment about the reality of the 'emergent' whole of a given total system, the question then arises how one is to explicate the relation between the state of the whole and the behaviour of parts of that system at the microlevel. It transpires that extending and enriching the notion of causality now becomes necessary because of new insights into the way complex systems, in general, and biological ones, in particular, behave.

A more substantial ground for attributing reality to higher-level properties and the entities associated with them is the possession of any distinctive causal (I would say, rather 'determinative') efficacy of the complex wholes which has the effect of making the separated, constituent parts behave in ways they would not do if they were not part of that particular complex system (that is, in the absence of the interactions that constitute that system). For *to be real is to have causal power*.[7] New causal powers and properties can then properly be said to have *emerged* when this is so.

Subtler understanding of how higher levels influence the lower levels allows application in this context of the notion of a determining ('causal') relation from whole to part (of system to constituent) – never ignoring, of course, the 'bottom–up' effects of parts on the wholes which depend on their properties for the parts being what they are, albeit now in the new, holisitic, complex, interacting configurations of that whole. A number of related concepts have in recent years been developed to describe these relations in both synchronic and diachronic systems – that is, both those in some kind of steady state with stable characteristic emergent features of the whole and those which display an emergence of new features in the course of time.

In particular, the term '*downward causation*' or '*top–down causation*' was employed by Donald Campbell[8] to denote the way in which the network of an organism's relationships to its environment and its behaviour patterns together determine in the course of time the actual DNA sequences at the molecular level present in an evolved organism; even though, from a 'bottom–up' viewpoint of that organism once in existence, a molecular biologist would tend to describe its form and behaviour as a consequence of those same DNA sequences. Other systems could be cited,[9] such as the Bénard phenomenon: at a critical point a fluid heated uniformly from below in a containing vessel ceases to manifest the entirely random 'Brownian' motion of its molecules, but displays up and down convective currents of literally millions of molecules in columns of hexagonal cross-section, while the individual molecules themselves continue to obey the normal laws covering their motion and interaction. Moreover, certain auto-catalytic reaction systems (for example, the famous Zhabotinsky reaction and glycolysis in yeast extracts) display spontaneously, often after a time interval from the point when first mixed, rhythmic temporal and spatial patterns, the forms of which can even depend on the size of the containing vessel. Indeed Harold Morowitz has, in fact, identified some twenty-eight emergent levels in the natural world.[10]

Many examples are now known also of dissipative systems which, because they are open, a long way from equilibrium, and non-linear in certain essential relationships between fluxes and forces, can display large-scale patterns in spite of random motions of the units – 'order out of chaos', as Prigogine and Stengers dubbed it.[11]

In these examples, the ordinary physico-chemical account of the interactions at the microlevel of description simply cannot account for these phenomena. It is clear that what the parts (molecules and ions, in the Bénard and Zhabotinsky cases) are doing and the patterns they form are what they are *because* of their incorporation into the system-as-a-whole – in fact, these are patterns *within* the systems in question. The parts would not be behaving as observed if they were not parts of that particular system (the 'whole'). The state of the system-as-a-whole is influencing (that is, acting like a 'cause' on) what the parts, the constituents, actually do. Many other examples of this kind could be taken from the literature on, for example, not only self-organizing and dissipative systems but also economic and social ones; and Terrence Deacon has usefully categorized different kinds of emergent levels.[12]

A wider use of 'causality' and 'causation' than Humean temporal, linear chains of causality as previously conceived (A→B→C ...) is now needed to include the kind of whole–part, higher- to lower-level relationships that the sciences have themselves recently been discovering in complex systems, especially the biological and neurological ones. One should perhaps better speak of 'determinative *influences*' rather than of 'causation', as having misleading connotations. Where such determinative influences of the whole of a system on its parts occurs, one is justified in attributing reality to those emergent properties and features of the whole system which have those consequences. Real entities have influence and play irreducible roles in adequate explanations of the world.

Here the term *whole–part influence* will be used to represent the net effect of all those ways in which a system-as-a-whole, operating from its 'higher' level, is a determining factor in what happens to its constituent parts, the 'lower' level.

With arrows representing such influences, the determining relations between the higher (H) and lower (L) levels in such systems and their succession of states (1, 2, 3 ...) may be represented thus:

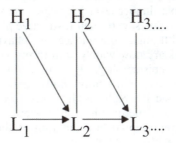

Figure 13.1

The vertical lines here represent the mereological relation between the state of the whole system H and the entities of which it is constituted at the lower level L at particular times (1, 2, 3 ...). The diagonal arrow is meant to indicate that the holistic state H_2, which is composed of constituents L_2, is determined by (is 'caused by', is a consequence of) the holistic state H_1 *jointly* with L_1. How might this understanding of the relation of 'higher' to 'lower' levels in complex physical, physico-chemical, and biological systems contribute to our understanding of the relationships in other complex realities? I suggest there are both philosophical and theological applications.

Philosophical Applications

Mind–Brain–Body Relation

Much of the discussion of the relation of higher- to lower levels in hierarchically stratified systems has centred on the mind–brain–body relation, on how mental events are related to neurophysiological ones in the human-brain-in-the-human-body – in effect, the whole question of human agency and what we mean by it. In this context a hierarchy of levels[13] can also be delineated, each of which is the focus of a corresponding scientific study, from neuroanatomy and neurophysiology to psychology.

The still-intense philosophical discussion of the mind–brain–body relation has been, broadly, concerned with attempting to elucidate the relation between what are colloquially regarded as the 'top' level of human mental experience and the 'lowest', bodily physical levels. The question of what kind of 'causation', if any, may be said to be operating from a 'top–down', as well as the obvious and generally accepted 'bottom–up', direction is still much debated in this context.[14]

I suggest a clue to this problem is available from the foregoing discussion concerning the general relation of wholes to constituent parts in a hierarchically stratified complex system of stable parts. I used the term 'whole–part influence'[15] and maintained that a non-reductionist view of the predicates, concepts, laws, and so on, applicable to the higher level could be coherent. Reality could, it was argued, putatively be attributable to that to which these nonreducible, higher-level predicates, concepts, laws, and so on, applied; and these new realities, with their distinctive properties, could properly be called 'emergent' and thought to influence the behaviour of their constituent parts. Mental properties are now widely, and in my view rightly, regarded by many philosophers as epistemologically irreducible to physical (that is, neurological) ones. In the mind–brain–body case the idea that mental properties can be 'physically realized' has also been much deployed[16] in association with the 'non-reductive physicalist' view of the mind–brain issue.

This view is usually represented in a diagram of the form (what M and P might refer to is discussed further below):

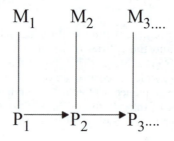

Figure 13.2

Kim has argued[17] that this concept is paradoxical for, if it is taken to mean that a microstructure physically realizes a mental property by being a *sufficient* cause for that property, then in the physicalist perspective there is complete causal closure at the physical level alone such that mental properties cannot, in fact, have real causal powers irreducible to physical ones. However, if for mental properties to be real is for them to have new, irreducible causal powers, then the *non-reductive* physicalist is thereby committed to downward causation from the mental to the physical levels. S. D. Crain has succinctly summarized these conclusions of Kim: 'the *non-reductive* physicalist cannot live without downward causation, and the non-reductive *physicalist* cannot live with it'.[18]

What light can be thrown on this particular impasse for non-reductive physicalism by the above treatment of relations between higher- and lower-level states in many natural complex systems? I suggest that it is Kim's assumption that when a physical microstructure 'physically realizes' a higher-level property (in this case, putatively, a mental one) then a *sufficient* description of the causal relations can be given in terms of microphysical events in the realizing level entirely (if only eventually) explicated by the laws and theories of physics. However, as I have argued above, in the wider range of physical, biological, and other systems previously discussed, the determining effects of the higher levels on the lower ones were real but different in kind from the effects the parts had on each other operating at the lower level. The patterns of the higher levels make a real difference to the way the constituents behave. Hence what happens in these systems at the lower level is the result of the *joint* operation of both higher- and lower-level influences. The higher and lower levels could be said to be *jointly* sufficient determinators of the lower-level events, a proposition which has also been developed philosophically in terms of higher- and lower-level properties by Carl Gillett.[19] This proposal of the recognition of the existence of *jointly* sufficient determinators of lower-level events by *both* higher- and lower-level influences can illuminate, I suggest, the paradox in non-reductive physicalism, as normally propounded, which Kim has accurately identified with respect to the mind–brain issue.

How can we apply this recognition to the relationship between the levels that operate in the mind–brain–body complex? Three graded possibilities suggest themselves, working 'upwards', as it were, from the purely physical.

1   Levels H are states of the brain; levels L are individual neuronal events.
2   Levels H are mental-with-brain states; levels L are individual neuronal events.
3   Levels H are mental states; levels L are brain states.

Here, by a 'state of the brain' is meant the 'temporarily coherent functional units distributed through different maps and nuclei'[20] – that is, it is the spatial and temporal *patterns* of activity at the brain level, as can be observed externally by empirical techniques, to which reference is being made. I have discussed these possibilities more fully elsewhere.[21] Suffice it to say here that 1 is an example of the same kind of purely physical systems involving whole–part influence that we have discussed above. In 2, mental states are regarded as brain states under another description (a dual-aspect or even an identitist understanding) and would therefore involve mental causation. Possibility 3 involves a recognition that mental states are an emergent property of the physical system of the brain and involves an extrapolation from understood physical systems to the non-understood, the mental. In all three cases a *joint* influence of the higher and lower levels on the succession of coincident higher- and lower-level states is regarded as operative, so that there is higher to lower-level causation (H → L) as well as lower to lower-level causation (L → L). Most 'non-reductive physicalists', particularly in their talk of the 'physical realization' of the mental in the physical when not supplemented by any further discussion of whole–part influences, hold a much less realistic view of these higher-level mental properties than I wish to affirm here in this emergentist monist perspective;[22] and also do not attribute determinative (causal) powers to that to which higher-level concepts refer. Just as the complex brain states can be said to emerge from the states of the individual neurones, so similarly mental states can coherently be regarded as emergent from brain states, as having causal efficacy and so as also being real. The content of 'consciousness' then putatively becomes how we describe to ourselves the holistic higher-level state of the component neurones, and so on, of our brains. Perhaps the capacity of mentalistic language to self-refer to its own activity in the experience of consciousness may one day be understood but, meanwhile, it is legitimate to postulate, with respect to human persons, a whole–part determinative influence (top–down causation) of holistic mental states via lower brain states on the 'microphysical' neuronal level, and so on the body. For *that* mental events, such as intentions – whatever they are ontologically – have causal efficacy in the physical world can scarcely be doubted in view of the ability of human agents to act in that world (for example, the intending, then effecting, of the picking up of an object); *how* this might be so, consistently with well-understood relations in complex systems, is the issue to which the preceding discussion is addressed.

Persons

Up to this point, I have been taking the term 'mental' to refer to that activity which is an emergent reality distinctive especially to human beings. But in many wider contexts, not least that of philosophical theology, a more appropriate term for this emergent reality would be 'person', and its cognate 'personal', to represent the total psychosomatic, holistic experience of the human being in all its modalities, conscious and unconscious, rational and emotional, active and passive, individual and social, and so on.

There is a strong case for designating the highest level, the whole, in that unique system which is the human-brain-in-the-human-body-in-social-relations as that of the 'person'. Hence to speak only of mental states as having downward causal efficacy on lower-level brain and neuronal events does not do justice to the rich complexity of the actual higher level of the *person*, namely, of the human-brain-in-the-human-body-in-social-relations. Now persons as such experience themselves as *inter alia* causal agents with respect to their own bodies and to the surrounding world (including other persons), so that the exercise of personal *agency* by individuals transpires to be a paradigm case and supreme exemplar of whole–part influence. They can, moreover, report with varying degrees of accuracy to themselves (and by language also to others) on aspects of their internal mental states and so implicitly on their brain states concomitant with their actions. In other words, 'folk psychology' is unavoidable and the real reference of the language of 'personhood' is justified.

Theological Applications

In natural complex systems, including that of the human person, we have seen that there is much evidence that new realities can emerge when new relationships occur within the system and that these realities can often be shown to have a determinative ('causal') influence on the component elements of the complex. Moreover, non-reducible language is required to describe these emergent realities which are thereby characterized by concepts expressed in a language distinctive to that level of complexity (for example, that of psychology in relation to that of neurophysiology; or that of biology in relation to that of the physico-chemical). These relationships between the language and concepts referring to higher and lower levels of complexity arise both synchronically (when comparing a hierarchy of complexes as they exist at present) and diachronically (when considering systems that evolve over the course of time from lower to higher levels of complexity).

It is this cluster of notions which I think can be relevant to theology. I suggest that the existence of such relationships in the language and concepts referring to the natural world can serve to clarify the nature of theological language and concepts in their reference to theological realities.[23] For theological language and concepts refer to what one might well call the apex in human experience of the hierarchy of complexity – namely, the threefold interaction of nature, persons and God. When human beings are exercising themselves in religious (or should one better say, today, 'spiritual'?) activities they are in fact operating at a level in the hierarchy of complexity that is more intricate and cross-related than in any of the subsystems of the natural and social sciences. In those religious activities whole human persons (representing multiple levels of the natural world – 'body, mind, and soul', traditionally) utilize every facet of their being in interacting with each other and with the natural world; and, as they discover the meaning in these interactions, they can further encounter and experience the presence of the transcendent yet immanent Creator who is the source of all-that-is. It seems to me that no higher level of integration in the hierarchy of natural systems can be envisaged than this; and theology is about the conceptual schemes that articulate the content of this integrated activity. Theology therefore refers to this most holistic level we know in the hierarchy of natural and human relationships and so it should not be surprising if the theories and concepts which it develops to explicate the nature of this activity, both as experienced and as intellectually articulated, are uniquely specific to and characteristic of this level. It should not be surprising, too, if special methods, techniques, and languages had to be developed to describe this supremely integrating and highly complex activity. Moreover, it could also be the case that the pattern of relationships between higher and lower levels which we have been elaborating might serve to model relationships which are the focus of interest in theology. Some possible areas of theological concern that might be illuminated by these considerations are as follows.

God's Interaction with the World

A major, critical question in contemporary theology is: in a world that is a closed causal nexus, increasingly explicated by the sciences, how might God be conceived of as influencing particular events, or patterns of events, in the world without interrupting the regularities observed at the levels the sciences study?[24]

I have proposed[25] a model which is based on the recognition that the omniscient God uniquely knows, over all frameworks of reference of time and space, everything that it is possible to know about the state(s) of all-that-is, including the interconnectednesss and interdependence of the world's entities, structures, and processes. By analogy with the operation of whole–part influence in natural systems, the suggestion is that, because the 'ontological gap(s)' between the world and God is/are located simply *everywhere* in space and time, God could affect holistically the state of the world (the whole in this context). This is a pan*en*theistic[26] perspective, for it conceives of the world as, in some sense, being 'in' God who is 'more' than the world, so that the world can be subject to divine determinative influences not involving matter or energy (or forces). Thence, mediated by such whole–part influences[27] on the world-as-a-whole (as a *System*-of-systems) and so on its constituents, God could cause particular events and patterns of events to occur which express God's intentions. These would then be the result of 'special, divine action', as distinct from the divine holding in existence of all-that-is, and would not otherwise have happened had God not so intended.

This unitive, holistic effect of God on the world could occur without abrogating[28] any of the laws (regularities) which apply to the levels of the world's constituents by analogy with the exercise of whole–part influence in the natural systems already discussed. Moreover, this action of God on the world may be distinguished from God's universal creative action, in that particular intentions of God for particular patterns of events to occur are effected thereby and the patterns could be intended by God in response *inter alia* to human actions or prayers.

The Incarnation

We have seen that new levels of reality can emerge in natural systems and that, when they do so, new concepts and languages have to be used to explicate these new realities. Although there is a natural continuity with the systems from which the new have emerged, there is a discontinuity in the conceptual resources utilized in explaining the new situation. This has seemed to me[29] to provide a pointer to making intelligible traditional Christian affirmations about the relation of the human to the divine in Jesus, that is, the doctrine of the 'Incarnation'.

The basic starting-point for the Christian theist should, I suggest, be that creation is in God and that God is the agent of its events and processes – that God is *semper Creator*, giving existence to all-that-is in all time. In Jesus his followers encountered, especially in the light of his resurrection, a dimension of that transcendence which, as good monotheists, they attributed to God alone. But they also encountered him as a full human person and in his personhood they experienced an intensity of God's immanence in the world. The fusion of these two aspects of awareness of the presence of God in the person of Jesus led to the conviction that something new had appeared in the world, and they ransacked received concepts to try to give expression to this *dis*continuity – to that new non-reducible distinctive mode of existence, eventually designating it *inter alia* as 'incarnation'. We can now properly, I am suggesting, regard Jesus as a new kind of reality, an 'emergent', for that manifestation of God in a human life must have been both a manifestation emanating from within creation and a fulfilment of its inherent God-given potentialities. Because of the continuity of the creative activity of God throughout time acting through the inherent creativity of the world, it seems to me that we can come to see Jesus as a unique manifestation of a possibility always inherently there for human beings by virtue of their potential nature being created by God. The 'incarnation' which is then said to have occurred in Jesus can be regarded as an example of that emergence-from-continuity that characterizes the processes of the created order. There is continuity with all that preceded him, yet with him a new mode of human existence emerges through a new openness and obedience to God – for this new relationship of God–humanity creates a new emergent reality. That openness to God could arise only from his human response to an experienced initiative from God, so that he was, as it were, a God-informed human being.[30] Hence God was, in this sense, *acting* in the incarnation through the immanent processes of Jesus human consciousness and will, and the fusion of the two engendered a new kind of reality.[31] Yet, for Christians, Jesus also manifests a unique *dis*continuity with what preceded him, in that titles employing new, non-reducible language – of Christ (= Messiah, Anointed), *logos* (= Word), Lord, Son of God – had to be applied to his person to represent the new kind of reality experienced in him.

All of this I find very congruent with the kind of *logos*-Christology represented in the Prologue to the Gospel of John: 'In the beginning was the Word ... and the Word was God ... All things came into being through him ... What has come into being in him was life, and the life was the light of all people ... He was in the world. ... yet the world did not know him ... and the Word became flesh and lived among us, and we have seen his glory.'[32]

Worship

The nature of relationships of persons to God may also be illuminated by our understanding of the emergence of new realities in complex systems. For in many situations where God is experienced by human persons we have by intention and according to well-winnowed experience and tradition complexes of interacting personal entities, material things, and historical circumstances which are epistemologically not reducible to concepts applicable to these individual components. Could not new realities C and so new experiences of God for humanity C be seen to emerge in such complexes and even to be causally effective?

I am thinking, for example, of the Church's Eucharist (Holy Communion, the Mass, the Lord's Supper), in which there exists a distinctive complex of interrelations between its constituents. These latter could be identified *inter alia* (for the Eucharist is many-layered in the richness of its meanings and symbols) as follows.

1 Individual Christians are motivated by a sense of *obedience* to the ancient, well-authenticated historically, command of Jesus, the Founder of their faith, at the actual Last Supper to do *this* – that is, to eat the bread and to drink the wine in the same way he did on that occasion and so to identify themselves with his project in the world.

2 Christians of all denominations have been concerned that their communal act is properly *authorized* as being in continuity with that original act of Jesus and its repetition, recorded in the New Testament, in the first community of Christians. Churches have differed about the character of this authorization, but not about its importance.

3 The physical 'elements', as they are often called, of bread and wine are, of course, part of the matter of the world and so representative, in this regard, of the created order. So Christians perceive in these actions, in this context, and with the words of Jesus in mind, that a *new significance and valuation of the very stuff of the world* is being expressed in this action.

4 Because it is bread and not corn, wine and not grapes which are consecrated, this act has come to be experienced also as a new evaluation of the work of *humanity in co-creating with God in ordinary work*.

5 The broken bread and poured-out wine were explicitly linked by Jesus with his anticipated self-sacrificial offering of himself on the Cross, in which his body was broken and blood shed to draw all towards unity of human life with God. Christians in this act consciously acknowledge and identify themselves with Jesus' *self-sacrifice*, thereby offering to reproduce the same self-emptying love for others in their own lives and so to further his purposes of bringing in the Reign of God in the world.

6 Christians are also aware of the promise of Jesus to be present again in their re-calling and re-making of the historical events of his death and resurrection. This 'making present' (*anamnesis*) of the Jesus who is

regarded as now fully in the presence of and is, in some sense, identified with God is a unique and spiritually powerful feature of this communal act.

7 The creative *presence of God*, as transcendent, incarnate, and immanent.

8 The action is to be undertaken in the community of the Church and both forms and strengthens it – a determinative influence.

Here do we not have an exemplification of the emergence of a new kind of reality, since this complex situation is epistemologically not reducible? For what (if one dare so put it) 'emerges' in the eucharistic event *in toto* can only be described in special non-reducible terms such as 'Real Presence' and 'Sacrifice'. A new kind of reality is attributable to the eucharistic event, for in it there is an effect on both the individual and on the community that creates specifically Christian personhood and society. That the Eucharist has a causal efficacy in enhancing the spiritual life of the participants has been the concern of that branch of study called 'sacramental theology', which has developed to interpret this special reality and the human experience of it. Since God is present in, with, and under this holistic eucharistic event, in it God may properly be regarded as acting distinctively through it on the individual and community – an exemplification of God's non-intervening, but specific, 'whole–part' influence on the world.

I have taken the Eucharist as one example, but I propose that the principle involved in trying to make clear what is special about this particular spiritual situation is broadly applicable to many other experiences of worship, prayer, and of 'grace' (with its implications of determinative, 'causal', efficacy) that are of theological concern and interest, both historical and contemporary. The concept of emergence can contribute not only to a release for theology from the oppression of excessively reductionist interpretations by the sciences, such as psychology, but also to a making accessible of theological language and concepts to the general exchanges of the intellectual life of our times. As I have indicated elsewhere,[33] would it be too much to suggest that these new, emergentist monist insights into the inbuilt creativity of our world through its complexifiying and self-organizing capacities open up a vista of continuity between the physical, the mental, and the spiritual which could, in this new century, break down the parallel barricades mounted in the last, not only between the 'two cultures' of the sciences and the humanities but also between the developed experiences of nature and of God, that is, between the sciences and of religion?

Notes

1 A revised version of a paper presented at a symposium on 'Reduction and Emergence: Implications for the Science/Theology Dialogue', at San Francisco University, October 2003. Parts of this paper follow some of the text of another paper of mine, mainly on the mind–brain–body problem rather than on theological issues, namely, 'Emergence, Mind and Divine Action: The Hierarchy of the Sciences in relation to the Human Mind–Body–Brain', in *The Re-emergence of Emergence*, ed. by Philip Clayton and Paul Davies (Oxford: Oxford University Press, 2006).

2 Conventionally said to run from the 'lower', less complex to the 'higher', more complex systems from parts to wholes so that these wholes themselves constitute parts of more complex entities – rather like a series of Russian dolls. In the complex systems I have in mind here, the parts retain their identity and properties as isolated individual entities.

3 See, for example, Arthur Peacocke, *Theology for a Scientific Age: Being and Becoming – Natural, Divine and Human*, 2nd enlarged edn (Minneapolis, MN and London: Fortress Press and SCM Press, 1993), 36–43, 214–18, and figure 1, based on a scheme of W. Bechtel and A. Abrahamson, in their figure 8.1 in *Connectionism and the Mind* (Oxford and Cambridge, MA: Blackwell, 1991).

4 W. C. Wimsatt has elaborated these criteria of 'robustness' for such attributions of reality to emergent properties at the higher levels in his 'Robustness, Reliability and Multiple-Determination in Science', in *Scientific Inquiry and the Social Sciences: A Volume in Honor of Donald T. Campbell*, ed. by M. Brewer and B. Collins (San Francisco: Jossey-Bass, 1981), 124–63.

5 William Bechtel and Robert C. Richardson, 'Emergent Phenomena and Complex Systems', in *Emergence or reductionism?*, ed. by A. Beckermann, H. Flohr, and J. Kim (Berlin: Walter de Gruyter, 1992), 266, emphasis added (page references in the text are to this article).

6 As does Philip Clayton. Note that the term 'monism' is emphatically *not* intended (as is apparent from the non-reductive approach adopted here) in the sense in which it is taken to mean that physics will eventually explain everything (which is what 'physicalism' is usually taken to mean).

7 A dictum attributed to S. Alexander by J. Kim in 'Non-Reductivism and Mental Causation', in *Mental Causation*, ed. by J. Heil and A. Mele (Oxford: Clarendon Press, 1993), 204; and in his ' "Downward Causation" in Emergentism and Nonreductive Physicalism', in *Emergence or Reduction? Essays on the Prospects of Nonreductive Physicalism*, ed. by A. Beckermann, H. Flohr, and J. Kim (Berlin: Walter de Gruyter, 1992), 134–5.

8 D. T. Campbell, ' "Downward causation" in Hierarchically Organised Systems', in *Studies in the Philosophy of Biology: Reduction and Related Problems*, ed. by F. J. Ayala and T. Dobhzhansky (London: Macmillan, 1974), 179–86.

9 For a survey with references, see Arthur Peacocke, *The Physical Chemistry of Biological Organization* (Oxford: Clarendon Press, 1983, 1989).

10 Harold Morowitz, *Emergence* (New York: Oxford University Press, 2002).

11 I. Prigogine and I. Stengers, *Order Out of Chaos* (London: Heinemann, 1984).

12 Terrence Deacon, 'Three Levels of Emergent Phenomena', paper presented to the Science and Spiritual Quest Boston Conference, October 21–23, 2001. Similar proposals are made by him in 'The Hierarchic Logic of Emergence: Untangling the Interdependence of Evolution and Self-organization', in *Evolution and Learning: The Baldwin Effect Reconsidered*, ed. by B. Weber and D. Depew (Cambridge, MA: MIT Press, 2003). See also B. Weber and T. Deacon, *Cybernetics & Human Knowing 7* (2000): 21–43.

13 The physical scales of these levels are, according to P. S. Churchland and T. J. Sejnowski ('Perspectives in Cognitive Neuroscience', *Science*, 242 (1988): 741–5), as follows: molecules, 10^{-10}m.; synapses, 10^{-6}m.; neurones, 10^{-4}m.; networks, 10^{-3}m.; maps, 10^{-2}m.; systems, 10^{-1}m.; central nevous system (CNS), 1m., in human beings.

14 See, for example, the collection of papers in *Mental Causation*.

15 It must be stressed that the 'whole–part' relation is *not* regarded here necessarily, or frequently, as a spatial one. 'Whole–part' is synonymous with 'system–constituent'.

16 The idea of mental states being 'physically realized' in neurones was expanded as follows by John Searle, in *Minds, Brain and Science* (Cambridge, MA: Harvard University Press, 1984), 26 (emphasis added):

> Consciousness ... is a real property of the brain that can cause things to happen. My conscious attempt to perform an action such as raising my arm causes the movement of the

arm. At the higher level of description, the intention to raise my arm causes the movement of the arm. At the lower level of description, a series of neuron firings starts a chain of events that results in the contraction of the muscles … the same sequence of events has two levels of description. … *Both of them are causally real*, and the higher level-causal features are both caused by and realized in the structure of the lower level elements.

What follows in the main text here shows that I am not satisfied with Searle's parallelism between the causality of the mental and physical; it is not enough – and I argue later on for a notion of *joint* rather than parallel causality as being more useful in this context.

17 'Non-Reductivism and Mental Causation', 202–5.

18 Dr Steven D. Crain, in an unpublished paper, kindly made available to me.

19 See, among other papers, Carl Gillett, 'Strong Emergence as a Defense of Non-reductive Physicalism: A Physicalist Metaphysics for "Downward" Causation', *Principia*, 6 (2003): 83–114.

20 Churchland and Sejnowski, 'Perspectives in Cognitive Neuroscience', 743.

21 See 'Emergence, Mind and Divine Action'.

22 This emergentist monist perspective emphasizes that the higher level in this context is real and has causal efficacy in a way that, in general, the purely epistemological assertion of 'dual-aspect monism' (affirming that mind–brain events may be *viewed* from two different perspectives) does not. Talk of two 'aspects' does not imply any *causal* relation between the aspects any more than between the similarly postulated wave and particle 'aspects' of the electron.

23 As I pointed out in my *Creation and the World of Science* (Oxford: Clarendon Press, 1979, repr. 2004), Appendix C; the present text follows some parts of 368–9.

24 Initially, I prescind from any analogy with the mind–brain–body relation or with personal agency.

25 See *Theology for a Scientific Age*, 160–66, and note 2 above, for an elaboration of this move. For the development of this proposal, see my 'God's Interaction with the World: The Implications of Deterministic "Chaos" and of Interconnected and Interdependent Complexity', 263, note 1, in *Chaos and Complexity: Scientific Perspectives on Divine Action*, ed. by R. J. Russell, N. C. Murphy, and A. R. Peacocke (Vatican City State and Berkeley, CA: Vatican Observatory and Center for Theology and the Natural Sciences, 1995), 263–87; and also 'The Sound of Sheer Silence: How does God Communicate with Humanity?', 215, note 1, in *Neuroscience and the Person: Scientific Perspectives on Divine Action*, ed. by R. J. Russell, N. Murphy, T. C. Meyering, and M. A. Arbib (Vatican City State and Berkeley, CA: Vatican Observatory and Center for Theology and the Natural Sciences, 1999), 215–47.

26 For a contemporary discussion of panentheism, see *In Whom We Live and Move and Have Our Being: Panentheistic Reflections on God's Presence in a Scientific World*, ed. by Philip Clayton and Arthur Peacocke (Grand Rapids, MI: Wm. B. Eerdmans, 2004).

27 What passes across this 'interface', I have also suggested (*Theology for a Scientific Age*, 161, 164), may perhaps be conceived of as something like a flow of information – a pattern-forming influence – but one has to admit that, because of the 'ontological gap(s)' between God and the world which must always exist in any theistic model, this is only an attempt at making intelligible that which we can postulate as being the initial effect of God seen, as it were, from our side of the boundary. Whether or not this use of the notion of information flow proves helpful in this context, we do need some way of indicating that the effect of God at this level, and so at all levels, is that of pattern-shaping in its most general sense. I am encouraged in this kind of exploration by the recognition that the Johannine concept of the *logos*, the Word, of God may be taken to emphasize God's creative patterning of the world and so as God's self-expression *in* the world.

28   The same may be said of *human* agency in the world. Note also that this proposal recognizes more explicitly than is usually expressed that the 'laws' and regularities which constitute the sciences usually apply only to certain perceived, if ill-defined, levels within the complex hierarchies of nature.

29   *Creation and the World of Science*, 241ff.

30   In the terminology of information theory; see Arthur Peacocke, 'The Incarnation of the Self-expressive Word of God', in *Religion and Science: History, Method, Dialogue*, ed. by Mark W. Richardson and Wesley J. Wildman (New York: Routledge, 1996), 321–39.

31   Such an emphasis on continuity (immanence) as well as on emergence (incarnation) is vital, in my view, to any account of Jesus that is going to make what he was relevant to what we might be.

32   John 1:1, 3, 4; 10:14 (NRSV).

33   Arthur Peacocke, 'Complexity, Emergence and Divine Creativity', in *From Complexity to Life: On the Emergence of Life and Meaning*, ed. by Niels Henrik Gregersen (Oxford: Oxford University Press, 2003), 187–205.

CHAPTER FOURTEEN

Non-interventionist Divine Action: Robert Russell, Wolfhart Pannenberg, and the Freedom of the (Natural) World

Lou Ann Trost

A significant reason for carrying on the dialogue between theology and the natural sciences is that it offers a coherent and responsible religious basis for ecological ethics. Finding such a basis is imperative. Robert John Russell, along with Ian Barbour, Holmes Rolston, Ted Peters, and others working in the religion and science field, has seen the importance of both a theology that is firmly planted in the world described by the natural sciences and an ecological ethic that can be supported by this type of theology. While many writers have attempted to show a theological basis for ecological ethics by way of the doctrine of creation, incarnation, or a sacramental view of nature, these have been only partially successful. The deeper problem – the history of splitting theology off from the physical world – remains. Therefore many of these attempts have not taken deep root.

Robert Russell's proposal for non-interventionist objective divine action through quantum events can help provide a basis for a theological approach to ecological ethics. If divine action is seen as non-interventionist, God who creates and sustains the world thus upholds the integrity of nature and its laws. The theological approach of Wolfhart Pannenberg supports and aids in interpreting Russell's work in terms of the freedom of the world, the freedom in which it is created and sustained by the love and Spirit of God. Based on these aspects of Russell's and Pannenberg's work, I will show that the whole of the created order and all of its parts – not just humans – are given their freedom and integrity by their Creator and are destined for a future consummation in union with God. This is the basis for human relationships with the rest of nature and for ecological ethics.

The title of this essay refers to the freedom of the '(natural) world'. This includes humans *as part of nature*, as well as the whole cosmos – not just the planet we inhabit, but the rest of the universe and its history. Many ecological and other problems arise because we have split the world into human and other-than-human, and called the latter 'natural'. Humans are part of nature and we cannot, should not, and need not try to get around this fact.

The need for including the entirety of the cosmos and its history in considering divine action is one of the reasons that Robert Russell chooses to focus on a 'bottom–up' approach. Here, God is thought of as acting 'at a lower level of complexity in nature to influence the processes and properties at a higher level'. Although other approaches are also needed, including 'top–down', this does not work for the history of the universe before the rise of consciousness and self-consciousness. If it can be shown that God has acted from the beginning of the universe with and through quantum events, this provides a solid basis for theology and the doctrine of creation.[1]

Of course, 'freedom' usually refers to humans, to consciousness and free will. In this essay, I wish to change the starting-point of the discussion – namely, the freedom given to all creatures by virtue of their being created through the love and freedom of God. Pannenberg speaks of 'independence' of the creatures and generally uses 'freedom' to apply to humans and to God. By using 'freedom' more broadly, I wish to convey the sense of 'independence-in-relation', with the ontological meaning that each creature is free to be according to its own nature and in relation with its Creator and other creatures. One benefit of using 'freedom' in relation to the whole of creation is that it allows us to treat humans as part of the natural world, and consciousness as a special case of the general freedom of creation. It may be possible to develop this along the lines of the discussion about emergence. We might say that human freedom is emergent from the freedom of all creation, that it is freedom 'all the way down'.[2] 'Freedom' here is not meant in an absolute sense; the creation and its parts are 'free' in following the laws of nature, including the indeterminacy of quantum events.

For Pannenberg, the ontological sense of human freedom is linked with a destiny for a future with God. If, from a theological perspective, all creation is promised this *telos* and destiny, then all creatures are endowed with the freedom to be what they are in relation to this future in God. If creatures are in this sense free, this provides a solid theological basis for considering the moral worth of all creatures and thus for ecological ethics.

This, then, leads us to the exploration of a major theme of Robert Russell's work, quantum events and God's non-interventionist action, which makes up the first section of the essay. The second section examines Russell's and Pannenberg's treatment of contingency. The final sections review parts of Pannenberg's work on the doctrine of creation and on trinitarian relations, including the independence of creation and the laws of nature, the trinitarian basis for divine action in the world, and divine action as governance or reign and its relation to the future.

Robert Russell: Quantum Events and Non-interventionist Objective Divine Action

The theme of non-interventionist objective divine action is based on a working typology that the Vatican Observatory/Center for Theology and the Natural Sciences conferences and publications have utilized since 1991. Russell summarizes the approach in the introduction to the *Quantum Mechanics* volume. It is objective because it is not merely *seen as* revealing something special about the character and intentions of God (the subjective, 'liberal' view), but truly reveals something about the way things are. Most who view divine action as objective also assert that, with such action, God intervenes in or suspends the laws of nature (the 'traditional' or conservative view). The non-interventionist position, that divine acts are neither interventions in nor suspensions of the laws of nature, is prevalent in discussions of divine action in the field of theology and science.[3]

The advantages of using this approach are clear. It upholds the integrity of nature and its laws, and that of the natural sciences that investigate them. If discussions of science and theology are guided by a non-interventionist approach to God's action in the world, scientific work is respected for its methodological naturalism. And theology frees itself from the internal contradiction of an interventionist approach that 'pits God's special acts against God's regular action, the latter of which is seen to be the underlying cause of nature's regularities'.[4]

While Robert Russell and the CTNS/VO working group used the approach of non-interventionist divine action for various fields that they explored, for Russell its basis is a particular interpretation of quantum mechanics – ontological indeterminism – found in one form of the Copenhagen interpretation. This involves 'complementarity (e.g., wave–particle duality), inherent indeterminism at the most fundamental level of quantum phenomena, and the impossibility of an event-by-event causal representation in a continuous spacetime background'.[5]

There are other possible philosophical interpretations of quantum mechanics. Even within the Copenhagen interpretation, it is possible to interpret indeterminacy in epistemic or ontological terms. If one goes with the view that quantum indeterminacy is merely epistemic, it is expected that our ignorance of what is really happening will someday be replaced by a better theory. Werner Heisenberg developed a 'realist, indeterministic version of the Copenhagen interpretation in which the measurement process actualizes potential characteristics of the quantum system. His interpretation suggests that the unpredictability that arises during measurement has an ontological basis and is not simply epistemological.'[6] The Heisenberg uncertainty principle states that the position and the momentum of a particle cannot be simultaneously definite. William Stoeger explains it this way:

> Objective uncertainty or indeterminacy describes the fundamental limit on our ability to simultaneously determine – measure – two noncommuting operators specifying a quantum entity (e.g., its position and its momentum, or its energy at a certain time). By using the adjective 'objective' I have already presumed the standard interpretation that this uncertainty or indeterminacy is not due to our lack of knowledge or the imprecision of our measurements, but rather is an underlying indeterminacy in physical reality itself.[7]

Russell chooses this ontological interpretation, that it is indeterminacy 'all the way down'. That is, statistical probabilities are the best explanation. A strictly causal explanation according to classical physics is not possible at the quantum level.

In regard to his choice of theory and interpretation of quantum mechanics for a discussion of divine action, and the problems of historical relativity and multiple interpretability, Russell summarizes his reasoning as follows. First, metaphysics is always underdetermined by science, so concern about choice of quantum mechanics applies to metaphysical interpretation of any theory. Second, *all* interpretations of quantum physics require a reconstruction of our philosophy of nature. Third, his approach is a form of constructive theology with a focus on nature, so a change in science or its interpretation would not challenge the overall viability of a theology of divine action in nature, because its primary warrant and sources lie elsewhere, in scripture, tradition, reason, and experience. Finally, implications of a non-interventionist approach to objective special divine action in the light of a particular interpretation of quantum physics, considering the strengths and weaknesses of the approach, may lead to new insight.[8]

Another aspect of his methodology is worth noting. He uses a 'What if' strategy: approaching a theological conversation with quantum mechanics choosing ontological indeterminism within the general Copenhagen interpretation, stating the choice that is being made; and, though the position may one day prove untenable, proceeding to explore philosophical and theological implications. This strategy exemplifies a strong feature of much of the constructive work being done at the theology–science interface. It is exploratory and willing to take risks in the effort to move the conversation forward.

Russell offers other important clarifications regarding his proposal. Most significant among them is that it does not constitute a 'god-of-the-gaps' argument. Since indeterminism is part of the theory (one interpretation of it), Russell's work does not call on God as an explanation for gaps in the science.

God has created the universe *ex nihilo* such that some natural processes at the quantum level are insufficiently determined by prior natural events. One could say that nature is 'naturally' indeterministic. God does not violate the laws of quantum physics but acts in accordance with them. In essence, God creates the universe such that quantum events occur without sufficient natural cause and acts within these natural processes to bring them about.[9]

Russell's approach does not reduce God to a natural cause. 'God's direct action at the quantum level is hidden in principle from science, supporting the integrity of science ... allowing science to be integrated fully into constructive theology where "God" as an explanation of natural events is appropriately and fully developed.'[10]

God's activity at the quantum level has effects at the macroscopic level. 'God's indirect acts of general and special providence at the macroscopic level arise in part, at least, from God's objective direct action at the quantum level.' Quantum processes underlie and give rise to the general features of the world of ordinary experience and classical physics.[11] Quantum events affect the ordinary world in several ways, including the 'bulk' quantum effects of superconductivity and superfluidity, and mental states resulting from quantum events at neural junctions. A prime example of 'biological amplifiers' is the genotype–phenotype relation, which expresses the effects of quantum mechanics within genetic mutations at the macroscopic level of individual organisms and population'.[12] Russell claims that 'chance in evolution, at the level of quantum mechanics underlying genetic mutation, is a sign ... of ontological indeterminism', a non-interventionist view. Thus,

> God can be understood theologically as acting purposefully within the ongoing processes of biological evolution without disrupting them or violating the laws of nature. God's special action results in specific, objective consequences in nature, consequences which would not have resulted without God's special action. Yet, because of the irreducibly statistical character of quantum physics, these results would be entirely consistent with the laws of science, and because of the (*ex hypothesi*) indeterminism of these processes, God's special action would not entail their disruption.[13]

This insight provides a much-needed contribution to the discussion of evolution and religion, and shows how non-interventionist divine action at the quantum level also applies to this important issue in the religion–science dialogue. The final area of Russell's work that bears relationship with his thesis about quantum mechanics is his work on contingency. I will deal with this in the context of his discussion with Wolfhart Pannenberg.

Robert Russell and Wolfhart Pannenberg on the Contingency of Creation

Robert Russell published a significant paper responding to Wolfhart Pannenberg's focus on the contingency of creation. Russell parses Pannenberg's use of the idea of contingency in terms of global and local contingency, both of which can be either empirical or ontological, and nomological contingency, which refers to the laws of nature and history. A fourth, 'the dependence of the present on the future as the being of God with its reversal of ontological priority', is not within the scope of Russell's paper, but I will touch upon it below.[14]

In the 1980s Pannenberg wrote that any discussion of theology and science should focus on the question of what science, especially physics, can say about the contingency of the world. His fundamental assertion was, 'The existence of the world as a whole and all of its parts is contingent. The existence of the whole world is contingent in the sense that it need not exist at all. It owes its being to the free activity of divine creation. So does every part of the world.'[15] The contingency of creation is central to the theme of this paper. God, in creating and sustaining the world freely, imbues creation with freedom.

I would like to focus on part of the Pannenberg–Russell exchange on contingency that deals with inertia and quantum physics. Pannenberg repeatedly stressed the importance of the principle of inertia for the dialogue between science and theology.[16] He retains his concern over the issue in the second volume of his *Systematic Theology*. This is because 'it took on normative significance for the emancipation of the mechanistic view of sciences in the 18th century from all connections with the theological doctrine of the creation and preservation of the world by divine action.' He admits that because of changes in physics, the theory may now have only historical importance. But he insists that the contemporary 'dialogue between scientists and theologians needs to study the process that led decisively to alienation between the scientific worldview and theology if this alienation is to be permanently overcome.'[17]

Russell's critique includes a summary of the changes that have affected the meaning of inertia in contemporary physics, including special relativity, general relativity, and quantum mechanics. I will focus on the last. With quantum physics,

> the classical meaning of inertia has been left far behind although the outcome is unsettled. Moreover, while controversial, the insights to be gained from quantum physics are indispensable not only for the meaning of mass/inertia but more generally for the meaning of local (and even global) contingency. ... Quantum physics brings a reinterpretation of causality.[18]

Russell concludes that the question remains as to how to relate the changes in physics to one another, or to the concept of contingency, and from there to the doctrine of God.

However, both Russell and Pannenberg state that the ideas of contingency and quantum uncertainty are correlated, and that both are related to the idea of an open future. Although Pannenberg does not develop the correlation between contingency and quantum indeterminacy in depth, he identifies the latter as the place where contingency can be seen in the natural sciences: 'The concept of contingency is marginal in the logic of scientific statements. It is a correlate of regularity and not a general characteristic. It occurs only as indeterminacy.'[19] There is convergence between Pannenberg and Russell on this issue. Russell writes, 'Many would argue that quantum physics is now the paradigm of contingency in physics.'[20] This agreement that contingency is related to quantum indeterminacy could contribute to a new philosophy or theology of nature, especially in relation to Pannenberg's work on the openness of the future, the idea of God as the power of the future, and future-oriented ontology. But we begin here with Pannenberg's treatment of trinitarian action in the creation and preservation of the world.

Wolfhart Pannenberg on the Doctrine of Creation and Trinitarian Relationality

Robert Russell proposes that a trinitarian doctrine of God is the most suitable theological context for his thesis regarding divine action and quantum mechanics. Agreeing with others that an elaborated metaphysics is needed, he suggests that 'the metaphysical framework of Wolfhart Pannenberg and other theologians exploring the doctrine of the Trinity' is a promising option.[21]

Wolfhart Pannenberg is among a group of theologians who, over the past several decades, have taken a new look at trinitarian thought. Many of them put renewed emphasis on the relationships among the persons of the Trinity. For Pannenberg, these relationships are God's essence – they are who and what God is – and this essence is love. This is important for consideration of the status of the creatures because creation is viewed as a trinitarian act. And the goal of creation is the freedom of creatures.

The Independence of the Creatures and the Laws of Nature

That God created and is continuing to uphold the cosmos means that it owes its existence to the creative action of God. In the second volume of his *Systematic Theology*, Pannenberg explores the nature of the relationship between God and the creation. He considers the thought of Alfred North Whitehead and other process philosophers, whose God works by persuasion. According to biblical thought, creatures owe all they are to God's creative action. Yet,

> Once having called them into existence, the biblical God then respects their independence in a way that is analogous to Whitehead's description. There is truth in the contention that to attain his ends in creation, and especially the end of the creature's own fulfillment, God works by persuasion and not by force. But the patient and humble love with which God seeks his creatures are divine in the sense that they do not proceed from weakness. They are an expression of the love of the Creator, who willed that his creatures should be free and independent.[22]

The independence of the creatures includes the uniformity of the laws of nature. This is very close to Russell's emphasis that divine action does not take the form of intervention in the laws of nature. Pannenberg writes:

> The uniformity of events according to law is ... a condition of creaturely independence. ... Hence the regulated order of nature does not conflict with the contingent working of God in the producing of creaturely forms but is, in fact, an important means to this end.
> God has bound his creative action to the laws of nature, which are grounded in his creative action, but this no more excludes the creation of what is new than does the immediacy of each created form to God. ... The idea that God can bring forth what is new and unusual only by breaking the laws of nature has been overruled by the insight that for all their regularity the laws of nature do not have the character of closed (or, better, isolated) systems. At the same time the mediation of all emerging and perishing by the validity of the laws of nature is a condition if creaturely forms are to achieve the independence *vis-à-vis* God that lies in the concept of a creature distinct from its Creator.[23]

God's action in creation which is contingent and upholds the laws of nature comes of God's love and freedom and the link between them. 'The freedom of the divine origin of the world on the one hand and God's holding fast to his creation on the other belong together. The nature of the link may be deduced from the concept of divine love as the world's origin. God's love and freedom are inseparably linked.' Pannenberg explains that the trinitarian explication of God's love avoids misconceptions of this love as caprice or as an emotional force that overpowers creatures' freedom.[24] We now move on to this trinitarian explication.

The Trinitarian Basis for Divine Action in the World

As stated above, for Pannenberg God's essence is love, in the intra-trinitarian relations, and extending to God's relation to the world. Generally speaking, the persons of the Trinity are related to one another in their reciprocal self-distinction. The complexity of these relationships as well as the unity of the one God is explored in Volume One of Pannenberg's *Systematic Theology*.[25] The action of God in the world is trinitarian, and is the basis for the independence of all created things and beings as well as for God's relationship with creation. 'The love of the Father is directed not merely to the Son but also to each of his creatures. ... The self-distinction of the Son, which corresponds to the fatherly address to him and which gives to the Father alone the honor of being the one God, forms the starting point for the otherness and independence of creaturely existence.'[26] Again, 'If from all eternity, and thus also in the creation of the world, the Father is not without the Son, the eternal Son is ... the basis of the distinction and independent existence of all creaturely reality.'[27]

While the above quotations highlight the independence of creatures in relation to God, Pannenberg also states that there is a trinitarian basis for creatures' relationships with God and with one another. This involves the Spirit. 'In his linkage with the Spirit the Son acts in creation as the principle not merely of the distinction of the creatures but also of their interrelation in the order of creation. ... The Spirit is the element of the fellowship of the creatures with God and their participation in his life, notwithstanding their distinction from him.'[28]

Pannenberg reiterates how significant is the Spirit's relation to the world in a section of his chapter on creation in *Systematic Theology* entitled 'The Spirit of God and the Dynamic of Natural Occurrence'. Here he explores the concept of field in physics and how it is connected historically with the idea of spirit. He states that the idea of a field of force goes back by way of Stoicism to pre-Socratic philosophy and the Stoic doctrine of the divine *pneuma*, citing Max Jammer's work on field theory.[29] Robert Russell finds Pannenberg's proposal promising, though he and John Polkinghorne have offered a critique of this part of Pannenberg's work. Russell and Polkinghorne suggest that while Pannenberg's understanding of field is based in the context of classical field theory, quantum mechanics and quantum field theory offer new features that should be considered, including superposition, non-locality, entanglement, and the Copenhagen interpretation.[30] It would be helpful to see how Pannenberg or others might apply quantum field theory.

Pannenberg uses the (classical) idea of field in a general and metaphorical way when he writes that biblical statements about God as Spirit are better thought of as field than as consciousness: 'It is more in keeping with what the Bible says about God as Spirit, or about the Spirit of God, to view what is meant as a dynamic field that is structured in trinitarian fashion, so that the person of the Holy Spirit is one of the personal concretions of the essence of God as Spirit.' The Spirit's work in creation 'relates to the link and movement that connects the creatures to one another and to God.'[31] Thus we see that God's relationship with the world is trinitarian, that God creates and acts in the world through the Son, in whom the creatures' distinction from God and from one another is based, and through the Spirit who connects them with one another and with God. This, then, is the basis for creatures' freedom as independence-in-relation.

Divine Action as Governance: The Reign of God and the Future

God's action in the world is seen in terms not only of creation at the beginning, but also preservation that continues to sustain the world in existence and provide sustenance for the various forms of life. Robert Russell deals with this in terms of general and special providence. I would like to focus on Pannenberg's treatment of governance as a form of God's providence and preservation of the creation.

This part of Pannenberg's work brings us back to the theme of this essay, namely the freedom of the natural world and a theological basis for ecological ethics. Pannenberg repeatedly writes that with the independence of creatures, creation reaches its goal. The world as a whole as well as the relations of the parts to one another is the object of God's governance.

In a reference to Jesus' sayings about God's care for all creatures (Matt. 6:26ff.; 10:29f.), Pannenberg raises a crucial point regarding God's purpose, or end, in the creation and governance of the world. Jesus' sayings 'rule out any creature having less significance for God as just a means to the higher ends of his world government.' He cites Karl Barth, who rejects this idea and says that each creature has '"its own significance and validity, its own value and dignity" (CD, III/3, 173)'. Yet Pannenberg believes that Barth did not go far enough in using this idea to criticize the older doctrine of providence in terms of ends, found especially in Thomas Aquinas, for whom God is the final end of his action. Pannenberg states that 'the idea that God, not creatures, is the final end of his world government has a harsh sound and leaves the impression that his rule is one of oppression.'[32] He states this tersely in the positive, 'Every creature is itself an end in God's work of creation and therefore an end for his world government as well.'[33] That Pannenberg considers creatures as ends in the working of God in creation is connected with his emphasis on their independence, and constitutes their integrity and freedom in relation to this *telos*.

God's governance is the same as the divine reign 'whose imminence Jesus proclaimed and that already came in him', the eternal reign of God being actualized in history and awaited as the future of the consummation of history. Jesus' message has its basis in the statement that this future is near at hand. Providence or world government has a forward reference to creatures' future consummation. The final vindication of God's rule will come only with the eschatological transformation and consummation of the world as the kingdom of God.[34]

Lastly, this future is the 'field of the possible. It is thus the basis of the openness of creation to a higher consummation and the source of what is new, i.e., of contingency in each new event. ... In the creaturely power of the future as the field of the possible, the dynamic of the divine Spirit in creation expresses itself.'[35] In New Testament thought, the Spirit's powerful presence in the person of Jesus indicates that God's eschatological reign is already dawning in him. The Spirit is the origin of the new life of resurrection; the Spirit's working in creation is also linked with the creation of eschatological reality.

This allows us to return to Robert Russell's thesis regarding quantum physics and non-interventionist divine action. If God's action is seen in (as influencing the outcome of) the statistical probabilities of quantum events, does this not have a connection with the idea of the future as the field of the possible? Although Russell might object to Pannenberg's use of 'field' in this context, would not the idea of the Spirit as the source of the contingency of each new event, quantum event, be consistent with Russell's thought?

Russell also sees eschatology as significant in discussions of divine action. 'Hopefully, these discussions [of quantum mechanics and quantum field theory], in turn, will contribute at least indirectly to the central issue of eschatology and scientific cosmology, towards which our focus on divine action and quantum physics has slowly but inexorably led.'[36] Pannenberg makes some promising suggestions based on the work of Hans-Peter Dürr, who related quantum indeterminacy to the concept of possibility. Pannenberg writes of

> the power of the realm of the future being given concrete form by the event that takes place in the present ... If we view occurrence of microevents at each present moment as a manifestation of the future (deriving from the possibility field of future events), this has considerable implications for the philosophy of nature and for theology ... Ontologically the possibility field of future events may be seen as a field of force with a specific temporal structure. ... A constitution of elementary events along such lines also forms the basis for macroevents that take place according to natural law in the classical sense.[37]

Here again there is convergence in the work of Robert Russell on quantum indeterminacy and Wolfhart Pannenberg's reformulations of a philosophy of nature and theology in terms of a future-oriented ontology. I have here only pointed out some areas of convergence in these two thinkers' work, which could lead to new insights into the philosophical interpretation of quantum physics, theological formulations of God's relation to and action in the world, and a possible basis for ecological ethics.

Conclusion

Over the past decades, Robert Russell and Wolfhart Pannenberg have shared the concern that theology should take into account contemporary work in the natural sciences and that the philosophical underpinnings of both should be examined. Robert Russell's proposal for non-interventionist divine action at the quantum level offers insight into issues that Pannenberg raised over the course of his career. I have shown that both see the correlation between quantum indeterminacy and the concept of contingency. Russell sees promise in Pannenberg's thought about divine action in the world as trinitarian. I have shown that Pannenberg's development of a trinitarian-based independence of creatures, as the goal of creation held in relationship by trinitarian dynamics, exemplifies non-interventionist divine action. This led to developing the theme in terms of the freedom of creatures as independence-in-relation. Russell also sees promise in Pannenberg's futuristic ontology. I have suggested that quantum indeterminacy and non-interventionist divine action can be correlated with Pannenberg's metaphysics of the future.

Based on the convergence between these two thinkers' work, there is much that could be done to further develop a philosophy of nature, called for by many working in the theology–science dialogue. I have outlined a few areas that I believe could prove fruitful for this philosophy of nature, particularly as a theological basis for ecological ethics. Of course, this proposal calls for further work. It is my hope that examining Robert Russell's work in the light of several of Wolfhart Pannenberg's themes has offered at least some possibilities for a philosophy of nature and a theological basis for ecological ethics.

Notes

1　Robert John Russell, 'Divine Action and Quantum Mechanics: A Fresh Assessment', in *Quantum Mechanics: Scientific Perspectives on Divine Action*, ed. by Robert John Russell, Philip Clayton, Kirk Wegter-McNelly, and John Polkinghorne (Vatican City State and Berkeley, CA: Vatican Observatory and Center for Theology and the Natural Sciences, 2001), 300–301.

2　For thorough discussion of emergence in relation to theology and sciences see the work of Philip Clayton.

3　Russell, 'Introduction', in *Quantum Mechanics*, ii–v.

4　Russell, 'Divine Action and Quantum Mechanics', 295.

5　James T. Cushing, *Quantum Mechanics: Historical Contingency the Copenhagen Hegemony* (Chicago: University of Chicago Press, 1994), 24. Cited in Robert Russell, 'Divine Action and Quantum Mechanics', 302.

6　Russell, 'Divine Action and Quantum Mechanics', 303. This text offers a more detailed discussion of the Heisenberg uncertainty principle and other interpretations of quantum physics as well as references.

7　William Stoeger, 'Epistemological and Ontological Issues Arising from Quantum Theory', in *Quantum Mechanics*, 88.

8　Russell, 'Divine Action and Quantum Mechanics', 302–5.

9   Ibid., 295.

10 Ibid., 296.

11 Ibid., 293. For a more detailed discussion and references, see 297.

12 Ibid., 299.

13 Russell, 'Special Providence and Genetic Mutation: A New Defense of Theistic Evolution', in *Evolutionary and Molecular Biology: Scientific Perspectives on Divine Action*, ed. by Robert John Russell, William R. Stoeger, SJ, and Francisco J. Ayala (Vatican City State and Berkeley, CA: Vatican Observatory and Center for Theology and the Natural Sciences, 1998), 193.

14 Russell, 'Contingency in Physics and Cosmology: A Critique of the Theology of Wolfhart Pannenberg', *Zygon*, 23:1 (March 1988): 23–4.

15 Cf. Wolfhart Pannenberg, 'The Doctrine of Creation and Modern Science', *Zygon*, 23 (1988): 8.

16 Pannenberg, 'Theological Questions to Scientists', in *The Sciences and Theology in the Twentieth Century*, ed. by Arthur Peacocke (Notre Dame, IN: Notre Dame University Press, 1981), 3–16.

17 Pannenberg, *Systematic Theology*, 3 vols, trans. by G. W. Bromiley (Grand Rapids, MI: Wm. B. Eerdmans, 1998), 2:50.

18 Russell, 'Contingency in Physics and Cosmology', 33.

19 Pannenberg, *Systematic Theology*, 2:70.

20 Russell, 'Contingency in Physics and Cosmology', 41.

21 Russell, 'Divine Action and Quantum Mechanics', 293, 320. Making the choice to explore the explicitly Christian doctrine of God as Trinity may be seen as problematic for dialogue among the world's religions. However, careful elaboration of thought within each tradition is a sound basis for dialogue and can contribute to increased understanding among the traditions.

22 Pannenberg, *Systematic Theology*, 2:16.

23 Ibid., 2:72–3.

24 Ibid., 2:19.

25 Ibid., 1:259–336.

26 Ibid., 2:21–2. Pannenberg retains traditional language and understanding of the trinitarian persons as 'Father', 'Son', and 'Spirit'. For attempts to address the issue of gender in trinitarian thought, see the work of Elizabeth Johnson or Catherine Mowry LaCugna.

27 Ibid., 2:23.

28 Ibid., 2:32.

29 Ibid., 2:80–81. Pannenberg had written about this in the 1980s, in his article 'The Doctrine of Creation and Modern Science'. (See note 14.)

30 Russell, 'Divine Action and Quantum Mechanics', 323. Russell here cites John Polkinghorne's article 'Pannenberg's Engagement with the Natural Sciences', *Zygon*, 34:1 (March 1999): 151–8.

31 Pannenberg, *Systematic Theology*, 2:83–4. Discussion of the history of the idea of Spirit as *nous* is found at 1:372ff.

32 Ibid., 2:53, note 135.

33 Ibid., 2:53.

34 Ibid., 2:54–5, 58–9.

35 Ibid., 2:97–8.

36 Russell, 'Divine Action and Quantum Mechanics', 323.

37 Pannenberg, *Systematic Theology*, 2:99–100.

CHAPTER FIFTEEN

How Many Universes?

Paul Davies

Why Are Things The Way They Are?

It is an honor and a pleasure to dedicate this paper to Robert John Russell. Whenever I think of science and religion in creative synergy, Bob's wide-ranging and incisive contributions come to mind; indeed, it is no exaggeration to say that he is one of the founders of the subject of science and religion as a recognizable discipline, and I personally have benefited enormously from his lucid expositions, his talent for posing the right questions, and his tireless commitment to building bridges between two subjects often presented as mutually hostile.

In what follows, I should like to review a topic of great contemporary interest in the ongoing science–religion dialogue that Bob Russell helped establish, one that is attracting increasing attention beyond the confines of this field. The said topic proceeds from a bold assertion: that what we have all along been calling 'the universe' is in fact nothing of the sort. Rather, it is but an infinitesimal component in a much larger (probably infinite) ensemble of systems which, for want of a better word, has been dubbed the *multiverse*.[1] Such a notion emerges rather naturally from any attempt to explain at least some low-energy physics as the product of particular quantum states combined with a model of the universe originating in a big bang. The multiverse hypothesis is by no means incompatible with the existence of God, but it is increasingly being invoked as a challenge to theism in general, and specifically to refute the argument by design that has re-emerged in contemporary cosmological theory.[2]

The basic question that this issue addresses is the age-old conundrum, why are things the way they are? Why *this* universe rather than some other? First, let me make an obvious but absolutely crucial point. If the physical world could have been otherwise, then there has to be some rule or algorithm that separates the actually existing universe from the set of merely possible but in fact non-existing universes. One may then ask where that rule comes from. And why *that* rule rather than some other? Or, to use Stephen Hawking's evocative metaphor, what is it that 'breathes fire' into the equations describing *this* universe, thereby bestowing upon it the privilege of existing?[3] Given the infinite number of possible rules for picking out one universe and discarding infinitely many others, the application of one particular rule, *reasonlessly*, would be arbitrary and absurd. So it is natural to seek a reason for that rule; that is, to seek an explanation for the *specific nature* of physical existence.

The problem becomes acute when one recognizes that this particular universe is not just any old universe, but one that is remarkably special in a number of ways. For example, most scientists concede that there are features which appear to be felicitously contrived or ingeniously arranged, especially in relation to the existence of life in general, and intelligent observers in particular. I shall call this 'bio-friendliness', or 'biophilicity'. It is normally discussed in connection with so-called fine-tuning of the parameters in the laws of physics, by which is meant that the existence of life seems to depend rather sensitively on the values of these parameters. Since examples of such fine-tuning have been thoroughly discussed over many decades, I make no attempt to review them here.[4]

One possible explanation for why the universe is as it is, and why in particular it is biophilic, is that it has been created with the requisite properties by a loving God who expressly wishes that life and mind emerge at some stage in the evolution of the cosmos. Thus God, in the guise of 'Cosmic Architect', selects a judicious set of laws in order that the universe might eventually host intelligent life. The rule that separates the actually existing universe from the infinite number of possible but non-existing universes is a rule chosen by God, and as a result this universe does not exist reasonlessly, and absurdly, but as part of a rational divine plan. It is, of course, this very appeal to divine action that has provoked some noted cosmologists invoke the multiverse hypothesis to explain cosmic bio-friendliness.

The Multiverse Hypothesis

The multiverse explanation goes something like this. The laws of physics, which we have until now regarded as absolute and universal, might, in fact, be more akin to local by-laws. The familiar laws found in our textbooks are treated as valid in our particular cosmic patch, but it is postulated that these laws vary from one region of space and/or time to another. To take a simple example, it is widely accepted that at least some of the parameters in the standard model of particle physics are not fundamental constants of nature, but assume the values they do as a result of some form of symmetry-breaking mechanism.[5] These parameters include such things as the masses of electrons, quarks, and so on, and the strengths of the forces, for example, the electromagnetic force, that act between them. The observed values of these parameters may not be fixed universally, but may instead reflect *the particular quantum state* in our region of the universe; that is, they would be frozen accidents of history rather than necessary values.

How would this come about? If the universe attained its present state by cooling from a super-hot initial phase, then these crucial symmetries may have been broken differently in different cosmic regions, creating a domain structure. In the standard model, the values that some of the key parameters take on depends on the precise manner in which such symmetries are broken, and the details can vary randomly from place to place.

There is almost no observational evidence for a domain structure within the volume of space accessible to our instruments, but one may imagine that on a much larger scale than a Hubble volume there may exist domains in which the coupling constants and particle masses in the standard model are different, and in particular they are frequently inconsistent with life. Thus the electron mass may be bigger here and smaller there, or the strength of the strong nuclear force might be greater, lesser, and so on, to an extent that would upset the delicate physical processes from which life emerged. It would then be no surprise that we find ourselves located in a, possibly atypical, life-encouraging domain, as we could obviously not be located in one where life was impossible. This appeal to observer selection to explain cosmic biophilicity is sometimes called 'the anthropic principle', though there is no intended implication that human beings as such are a key factor. One can go beyond this simple parameter variation hypothesis and consider the possibility of other spacetime regions – which I shall informally refer to as 'other universes' – that exhibit altogether different physical laws and/or initial conditions, for example, two forces of gravitation, six space dimensions, massless electrons.

A specific mechanism for generating a multiverse comes by combining the popular research themes of string/M theory with eternal inflation. String theory, and its further development as M theory, is an attempt to unify the forces and particles of physics at the Planck scale of energy, $(\hbar c^5/G)^{1/2} \sim 10^{28}$ eV. A seemingly inevitable feature of this class of theories is that there is no unique low-energy limit. In fact, it isn't easy to even quantify the enormous number of potential low-energy ('vacuum') sectors of the theory, but one estimate puts the number of distinct vacuum states at greater than 10^{500}.[6] Each such sector would represent a possible world and possible low-energy physics. (The term 'low-energy' is relative here; it means energies much less than the Planck energy. That includes almost all of what is traditionally called high-energy physics.) The problem arises because string theory is formulated most naturally in ten or eleven spacetime dimensions, whereas the spacetime of our perceptions is four-dimensional. The extra space dimensions are rendered unobservable by a process called compactification: they are rolled up to a very small size. In general, there are very many ways of compactifying several extra dimensions. When additional degrees of freedom in string theory are taken into account, compactification may involve several hundred variables, all of which may vary from one region of the universe to another. These variables serve to fix the low-energy physics, by determining what sorts of particles exist, what their masses might be, the nature and strengths of the forces that act between them, and so on. The theory also permits compactification to spaces with other than three dimensions. Thus string theory predicts myriad possible low-energy worlds. Some might be quite like ours, but most would differ radically.

Although string theory predicts a vast number of alternative low-energy physical worlds, the theory alone does not ensure that all such worlds are physically instantiated. That step comes with the adoption of the now-standard model of the Big Bang, known as inflation. In the popular variant called eternal inflation,[7] our 'universe' is just one particular quantum vacuum bubble within a vast – probably infinite – assemblage of bubbles, or pocket universes, to coin

Susskind's preferred expression (due originally to Alan Guth, one of the originators of the inflation theory). If one could take a god's-eye-view of this multiverse of universes, the overall superstructure would continue to expand, explosively fast – an eternal big bang – and doubling in size in a tiny fraction of a second. But here and there 'bubbles' would pop out, champagne-like, to form universes expanding more sedately, and permitting (in some cases at least) the emergence of complex structures.

When eternal inflation is put together with the complex landscape of string theory, there is clearly a mechanism for generating universes with different local by-laws, that is, different low-energy physics. So the ensemble of physical by-laws available from string theory becomes instantiated as an ensemble of pocket universes, each having its own distinctive low-energy physics. The total number of such universes may be infinite; the total variety of possible low-energy physics finite, but stupendously big.

This by no means exhausts the multiverse possibilities; there are many possible models in which an ensemble of universes can be described. An extreme version has been proposed by Tegmark.[8] Not content to imagine universes with all possible values of the fundamental 'constants' of physics, Tegmark envisages universes with completely different laws of physics, including those described by unconventional mathematics such as fractals. In fact, he suggests that *all* logically possible universes actually exist. The vast majority of such universes would not support life and so go unobserved.

Arguments against the Multiverse Concept

In spite of its simplicity and persuasive appeal, the multiverse/anthropic explanation of cosmic biophilicity is not without some considerable problems. I list a few of them here.

1. It's Not Proper Science

If the other universes can never be observed, their existence cannot be considered a proper scientific hypothesis. However, most scientists and philosophers concede that the prediction of unobservable entities is an acceptable component of a scientific hypothesis if those entities stem from a theory that has *other* testable consequences. At this stage, string theory does not have any clear-cut experimental predictions, but one may imagine that a future elaboration of the theory might produce testable consequences. This would not confirm the existence of other universes, but would lend credibility to that hypothesis.

2. The Blunderbuss Objection

In an infinite universe, anything that can happen will happen. However, this catch-all explanation of a particular feature of the universe is in fact no explanation at all. The issue is to understand the bio-friendliness of *this* universe. To postulate that all possible universes exist does not advance our understanding at all. Like a blunderbuss, it explains everything and nothing. By contrast, a true scientific explanation would be analogous to a single well-targeted bullet.

To illustrate this point, imagine that the universe we observe is divided into minute three-dimensional cells. Each cell may be assigned a finite set of numbers that determines its state; for example, the amplitudes of all fields at that point. Now imagine that the digits of pi are expressed in binary and used to label the state of each cell in sequence, with as many digits as necessary to specify the field amplitudes to any desired precision. When all the cells in the observable universe have been labelled, a state of the entire universe is specified. Imagine repeating the process with the further digits of pi, thus defining another state. This process may be continued for an unlimited number of steps, yielding a 'cosmic history'. Most of that history would be random noise, lacking even the semblance of causal order, because the digits of pi are statistically indistinguishable from a random digit string. But by the very definition of randomness it must be the case that, eventually, the actually observed cosmic history will be generated. So too will *all other* cosmic histories: the digits of pi contain all possible worlds!

Should one be satisfied, therefore, that we have 'explained' our universe, together with all its remarkable features such as biophilicity, merely by declaring that it is 'a manifestation of pi'? Clearly not. Remarking that our world is (by definition) buried in the limitless noise of the digits of pi does not make pi a magic generator of reality. It merely points up the vacuousness of seeking to appeal to everything in order to explain something in particular.

3. Multiverses merely Shift the Problem Up One Level

Multiverse proponents are often vague about how the parameter values are selected across the defined ensemble. If there is a 'law of laws' or meta-law describing how parameter values are assigned from one universe to the next, then we have only shifted the problem of cosmic biophilicity up one level. We still need to explain where the meta-law comes from. Because the set of such meta-laws is infinite, one has merely replaced the problem of 'why this universe?' with that of 'why this meta-law?' Each meta-law specifies a different multiverse, and not all multiverses are certain to contain even one biophilic universe. In fact, on the face of it, most multiverses would *not* contain even a single component universe in which all the parameter values were suitable for life. To see this, note that each parameter will have a small range of values consistent with biology. Only in universes where all the relevant parameters take biophilic values simultaneously will biology be possible. If the several parameters vary independently between universes, each according to its own rule, then for most sets of rules the concurrence of biophilic values will not concur. Thus one needs to explain not only why there is a meta-law, but also why the actual meta-law (that is, the actual multiverse) happens to be one that intersects the requisite restricted region of parameter space that permits life. If the parameters do not vary independently, but are linked by an underlying unified physical theory, then each underlying theory will represent a different track in some multidimensional parameter space. Only in some unification theories would this track intersect the common biophilic region. One must now explain why this particular underlying unified theory, with its felicitous biophilic concurrence of parameter values, is the one that underpins reality ('has fire breathed into it').

4. Teleology Comes Back through the Window

It is ironical that the multiverse theory, which is frequently motivated by the attempt to expunge teleology from cosmology, is actually hoist by its own petard. In a truly general multiverse, there is no reason why the laws that may be instantiated in a subset of universes should always be of the traditional differential equation variety. (Indeed, in Tegmark's multiverse, this is explicitly not so.) One can entertain laws that are constrained by final conditions – teleological laws – in which it would make sense to describe the universe (by analogy with a living organism) as having *a purpose*. Since this entire subject proceeds from the observation that the universe at least *appears* to have a teleological component (that is, it evolves *as if* it has been designed for a purpose) then the application of Occam's razor suggests the simplest explanation is that it does *in fact* have a purpose (or, at the very least, that it belongs to the subset of universes that possess teleological laws). In other words, if there are universes on offer that evolve in a purpose-like manner, what justification is there to suppose that *this* one is actually a non-purpose-like universe cunningly mimicking a purpose-like one?

5. The Fake Universe Problem

The multiverse theory forces us to confront head-on the contentious issue of what is meant by physical reality. Is it meaningful to assign equal ontological status to our own, observed, universe and universes that are *never* observed by any sentient being? This old philosophical conundrum is exacerbated when account is taken of the nature of observation. In most discussions of multiverse theory, an observer is simply taken to mean a complex biological organism. But this is too restricted. Many scientists are prepared to entertain the possibility of conscious machines, and some artificial intelligence (AI) advocates even claim that we are not far from producing conscious computers. In most multiverse theories, although habitable universes may form only a sparse subset among all possible universes, there is still a stupendous number of inhabited universes. It is inevitable that some fraction of habitable universes in this vast set will permit technological communities to develop to the point of creating artificial intelligence and simulated consciousness. It is then but a small step to create engineered conscious beings inhabiting a simulated world. For such beings, their 'fake' universe will appear indistinguishable from reality. So should we include these simulated universes in the ensemble that constitutes the multiverse? Yes, we should, according to a distinguished philosopher[9] and two prominent cosmologists.[10]

The problem that now arises is that any given 'real' universe with world-simulating technology could simulate a vast number of 'fake' universes. Thus, fake universes would proliferate and greatly outnumber the real ones. A randomly selected observer is therefore more likely to inhabit a fake, rather than a real, universe. By implication, our universe is very probably a simulation. But if it is a simulation, then the application of physical theory to unobserved regions/universes is invalid, because there is no reason to suppose that the simulating system will consistently apply the observed physics of our simulation to other, unobserved, simulations. Thus, subject to the assumption that consciousness has a physical basis, the multiverse hypothesis contains the elements of its own invalidity!

More Than Mere Observers

When cosmologists invoke anthropic selection to explain 'fine-tuning' of certain physical parameters, they treat humans as mere observers. That is, it is simply necessary for there to exist observers *of some sort* for their argument to work. The application of anthropic reasoning usually ignores even the conditions necessary for intelligent observers to evolve and restricts attention just to the existence of life as such. Humans, however, are *more* than mere observers of nature. They also have the ability to *understand* the universe through logical reasoning and the scientific method. It is perfectly possible for there to exist a universe that permits the existence of observers who nevertheless do not, or cannot, make much sense of nature. Thus cats and dogs surely qualify as observers, but are not, like humans, privy to the deep mathematical rules on which the universe runs. In a general multiverse scenario, the vast majority of universes that permit the existence of observers with the same intellectual prowess as humans will *not* be comprehensible to those observers. For example, there are many ways that the laws of physics we observe could be more complex without threatening the existence of biology (non-computability of the laws; forces varying with time in a complicated way that leaves chemistry largely unaffected; additional weak forces that do not substantially affect the formation of galaxies, stars, and planets; millions of species of neutrinos ...). In fact, the physics of our universe is *extremely special*, being both simple and comprehensible to the human mind. This 'understandability factor' is left out of anthropic/multiverse explanations.

But one may go beyond this. Humans possess still more qualities than those of being observers and interpreters of nature. They are also *moral agents*. What better authority to address this issue than Robert Russell? Recognizing that the problem of theodicy must be raised to the level of cosmology, Bob poses the question with which I began this essay: 'Why did God choose to create this universe with this particular set of laws and their unfolding consequences?'[11] His answer is unequivocal: 'God created this universe with the evolution of moral agents in mind.' This is a direct challenge to the multiverse explanation for the world. Can the multiverse hypothesis even engage the issue of the moral dimension to human life? Suppose that Tegmark's multiverse is extended to include all possible good universes, all possible evil ones, and so on. Could an argument then be made that universes containing beings with moral purpose are more likely to be observed than those inhabited by evil beings? I seriously doubt it. It seems to me that the existence of a moral dimension to the universe is simply beyond the scope of multiverse/anthropic reasoning.

My conclusion is that some form of multiverse is probably an unavoidable consequence of modern physics and cosmology, but that the hypothesis is a slippery slope that leads ultimately to absurd and contradictory conclusions such as reality being engulfed by fake universes. Anthropic selection does have some limited explanatory power when it comes to certain physical properties of nature, but in the realm of human affairs, and in the moral aspect of being in particular, it is of little value.

Notes

1   Martin J. Rees, 'Numerical Coincidences and "Tuning" in Cosmology', *Astrophysics and Space Science*, 285:2 (2003): 375.
2   Steven Weinberg, *Dreams of a Final Theory* (New York: Vintage Books, 1992).
3   Stephen W. Hawking, *A Brief History of Time* (New York: Bantam, 1988), 174.
4   Brandon Carter, 'Large Number Coincidences and the Anthropic Principle in Cosmology', in *Proceedings of the IAU Symposium 63*, ed. by M. Longair (New York: Reidel, 1974); John D. Barrow and Frank J. Tipler, *The Anthropic Cosmological Principle* (Oxford: Oxford University Press, 1986).
5   For a recent popular review, see Brian Greene, *The Fabric of the Cosmos* (New York: Alfred A. Knopf, 2004).
6   Leonard Susskind, *The Cosmic Landscape: String Theory and the Illusion of Intelligent Design* (New York: Little Brown & Co., 2005).
7   Andrei Linde, *Particle Physics and Inflationary Cosmology* (Chur, Switzerland: Harwood Academic Publishers, 1990).
8   Max Tegmark, in *Science and Ultimate Reality: From Quantum to Cosmos*, ed. by John D. Barrow, Paul C. W. Davies, and Charles L. Harper (Cambridge: Cambridge University Press, 2004).
9   Nick Bostrom, *Philosophical Quarterly*, 53 (2003): 243. For a popular account, see Michael Brooks, 'Life's a sim and then you're deleted' *New Scientist* (27 July 2002): 48.
10 Martin J. Rees, *Edge*, 116 (19 May 2003); John D. Barrow, *New Scientist* (7 June 2004): 44.
11 Robert J. Russell, 'Special Providence and Genetic Mutation: A New Defense of Theistic Evolution', in *Evolutionary and Molecular Biology: Scientific Perspectives on Divine Action*, ed. by Robert J. Russell, William R. Stoeger, SJ, and Francisco J. Ayala (Vatican City State and Berkeley, CA: Vatican Observatory and Center for Theology and the Natural Sciences, 1998), 222.

CHAPTER SIXTEEN

Bodies Matter: A New Fad and a Fallacy in the Name of Science

Noreen Herzfeld

In 1952, Martin Gardiner published a book entitled *Fads and Fallacies in the Name of Science*. In this book he examined a number of pseudoscientific claims. Fifty years later we have an entirely new crop of fads and fallacies in science – in mainstream science, not in the fringe we normally think of as pseudoscience. These fads are promoted by respected scientists who work at respected institutions. What are some of these fads and fallacies, and what have they to do with the occasion of Robert John Russell's sixtieth birthday and the twenty-fifth anniversary of the Center for Theology and the Natural Sciences?

Bob has suggested that both theology and science can benefit from a model of critical mutual interaction. It has become clear that theology can afford to ignore neither the technological advances nor the understanding of the world and of humanity that have arisen as a result of modern science. The data and theories of science necessarily influence our theological understanding of the world and our place in it. Any coherent philosophy of nature and of human anthropology must take scientific data into account. And, in general, the science and religion dialogue has worked in this direction. For example, John Haught does a marvelous job of reinterpreting the theology of creation through the lens of evolutionary theory. Bob Russell himself re-examines divine action in the light of quantum mechanics. However, the interaction between theology and science is asymmetrical in these examples. Science provides the agenda and theology adapts, or gets out of the way.

Yet Bob proposes a model of mutual interaction. What has theology to say to science beyond providing some ethical constraints? I propose in this chapter that theology can provide some necessary corrections when science strays into fads and fallacies. Bob rightly notes that theology can provide criteria for choosing between rival scientific theories. It can provide philosophical assumptions that science can test as well as input into the formation of scientific theories and analogies. On a simpler level, theology can take the role of the child in the story of the emperor's new clothes, who pointed out the wardrobe malfunction that the rest of the populace were either too naive or too enamored to see.

The Invisible Man: Living Without a Body

A single chapter provides the scope for examining only one fallacy. I will focus here on the trend, enabled by computer technology, to view the human person not as an embodied whole, but as a disembodied mind or as the sum of the information stored in such a mind.

Do our bodies really matter? We live in an age that answers this question in an increasingly schizophrenic way. Never before have so many worried so much about their physical appearance. In 2002 the weight loss industry in the United States was estimated at $39 billion and was growing at a rate of 5.6 per cent annually.[1] The $1 billion cosmetic surgery industry is growing at twice that rate (11.2 per cent).[2] Over seven million American women and girls and a million men suffer from eating disorders and at any given time over 50 per cent of American women are on a diet.[3] Clearly, bodies are a major preoccupation in our society.

On the other hand, computer technology allows human interaction in the bodiless world of cyberspace. Many activities that once took place in real space now take place in cyberspace: we communicate via chat rooms and e-mail; we shop, bank, and do research on the internet; we amuse ourselves with video games, MP3s, and streamed videos. We project our minds across vast distances or into fictional realms and have experiences in those places that form us as persons. In cyberspace we don't need bodies; we can conceive of ourselves as pure mind.

Why would one wish to live without a body? First, as the statistics on dieting and cosmetic surgery cited above indicate, many Americans are unhappy with the bodies they have. In cyberspace, we need not present ourselves to the world in one limited visual package. We can present ourselves only in words or we can create avatars that represent us as we would like to be. Neal Stephenson describes the advantage of living in cyberspace in his novel *Snow Crash*: 'If you're ugly, you can make your avatar beautiful. If you've just gotten out of bed, your avatar can still be wearing beautiful clothes and professionally applied makeup. You can look like a gorilla or a dragon or a giant talking penis.'[4] In other words, one can look however one wishes in cyberspace. One can project an image of oneself and that image is utterly malleable, changed at the flick of a bit. Or one may exist without any bodily image. Nicole Stenger describes this experience: 'Cyberspace grafts a new nature of reality on our everyday life. It opens up an infinity of space in an eternity of light ... On the other side of our data gloves, we become creatures of colored light in motion, pulsing with golden particles ... we will be, as in dreams, everything.'[5]

However, the greatest seduction of a bodiless existence lies in the fact that our bodies are mortal. They are subject to sickness, aging, and, ultimately, death. Computer scientist Ray Kurzweil, in *The Age of Spiritual Machines*, suggests that cyberspace provides a place where we can evade the mortality of the body by downloading our brains into successive generations of computer technology. Kurzweil writes,

Up until now, our mortality was tied to the longevity of our hardware. When the hardware crashed, that was it. For many of our forebears, the hardware gradually deteriorated before it disintegrated ... As we cross the divide to instantiate ourselves into our computational technology, our identity will be based on our evolving mind file. We will be software, not hardware ... As software, our mortality will no longer be dependent on the survival of the computing circuitry ... [as] we periodically port ourselves to the latest, evermore capable 'personal' computer ... Our immortality will be a matter of being sufficiently careful to make frequent backups.[6]

Kurzweil suggests we might achieve this new platform within the next fifty years. He is not the sole holder of this expectation, though he may be among the more optimistic in his timeline. In *The Physics of Immortality*, physicist Frank Tipler conjectures that the universe will cease to expand and at some point end in a contraction which he calls the 'omega point'. Tipler sees this omega point as the coalescence of all information, including the information that has made up every person who ever lived. Thus this point can be seen as corresponding to the omniscient and omnipotent God referred to in religious traditions. At such a point, the information making up any given individual could be reinstantiated, resulting in a form of resurrection for that person. Tipler is vague as to how such a reinstantiation might come about.[7]

Both Kurzweil and Tipler believe that cybernetic immortality is consonant with the physical world. In that world all things can be thought of as merely matter or, alternatively, as merely information. This is a seductive worldview for the computer scientist who sees the world in terms of zeros and ones. And to the scientific materialist, those parts of our being that seem the least material – consciousness, soul, or spirit – can be thought of as qualities that emerge as matter evolves or self-organizes into a sufficiently complex system. Molecular biologist Francis Crick describes this emergence as follows: 'You, your joys and your sorrows, your memories and your ambitions, your sense of personal identity and free will, are in fact no more than the behavior of a vast assembly of nerve cells and their associated molecules ... You're nothing but a pack of neurons.'[8] The 'you' that Crick speaks of here arises from the workings of the material brain. Without such a material basis, 'you' cease to exist. But what we identify as 'you' is not the material basis itself, but the information stored on that basis, the collection of sorrows, memories, ambitions, feelings, and experiences that Crick describes. According to Kurzweil or Tipler, this information could be stored on a computer system.

The problem with living a bodiless existence is that ultimately it is a lie. Common sense tells us that, no matter how real a disembodied experience in cyberspace may seem, one will sooner or later need to leave the computer terminal or virtual reality helmet to eat, sleep, or go to the bathroom. Even promoters of virtual reality understand it to be 'a habitat of the imagination', where one engages in 'consensual hallucination'.[9] That one cannot, and simply does not, live a bodiless existence is consonant with Christian theology. The biblical tradition is clear that the human being is an integrated whole, one that is human precisely in being both body and spirit.[10] Nor is a bodiless reinstantiation consonant with the Christian understanding of immortality. The Nicene Creed states that our resurrection is one 'of the body'. Reinhold Niebuhr sees our inability to accept our bodily finitude as the source of sin:

> Man is ignorant and involved in the limitations of a finite mind; but he pretends that he is not limited. He assumes that he can gradually transcend finite limitations until his mind becomes identical with universal mind. All of his intellectual and cultural pursuits, therefore, become infected with the sin of pride.[11]

Our finite bodies are an integral part of who we are. The essential nature of the human being always contains two inseparable elements, self-transcending mind and finite creaturely being. The denial of the latter leads to a denigration of both the natural environment and of women. For, if we could live in the bits of a computer, of what use is the natural world? Nor do intelligences that can replicate themselves through back-up copies need sexual differentiation. Here I note, however, that, while it serves no reasonable purpose, proponents of cybernetic immortality are loath to give up sexual experience itself. Tipler waxes eloquent on the possibility of fulfilling all our sexual desires at his omega point; Kurzweil is equally enthusiastic about the possibilities of disembodied sexual experience.[12] But these experiences are viewed only in terms of self-gratification, not as truly relational, with all the complexity that true relationship entails. In the Christian tradition, being in relationship with that which is by nature other to ourselves, whether that be a human of the other gender, a non-human part of nature, or God's self, is an integral part of our creation in the image of a triune God.[13]

Cybernetic immortality denies the importance of the body while at the same time tying immortality to the material world. Niebuhr does the opposite. He acknowledges our dependence on our bodily nature in this life, a dependence that is concomitant to a yearning to transcend the finitude of the world. This paradox is not resolvable within history; to try to do so leads humans into the dual trap of either denying God and living totally within our created nature, like animals, or denying our created nature and trying to be as God (an attempt that is acknowledged occasionally within the computer technology community). We escape this paradox only when we leave the historical time–space continuum through death and resurrection.[14] As Bob Russell once put it, 'immortality does not just mean a long time'.[15] Yet, for those putting their hope in cybernetic immortality, more time on this earth is precisely what they have in mind. No matter what physical platform is used to instantiate information, it remains within a finite universe. Even scientists agree that 'heaven and earth will pass away' (Mark 13:31).

The Disembodied World of Video Games

So no one can live full time in cyberspace, nor can it offer us immortality. Attempts to live in cyberspace, either now or in some reinstantiated future, seem a bit silly, but ultimately harmless. However, many live there part time, and herein lies a darker side. First, the time we spend in cyberspace can cut us off from the real world, distancing us from nature and from each other. Second, when we see ourselves and our world through the lens of the unreal and disembodied existence of cyberspace, we form a worldview and a view of the self that is distorted. And we proceed to act on the basis of this worldview. I will conclude this chapter by examining each of these propensities in the most common virtual experience today, one experienced by over three quarters of our children on a frequent basis, an experience that is forming their view of themselves and the world – the video game.

Video games are a major factor in the lives of our young people. In a report issued in December 2003, the National Institute on Media and the Family noted that, in a survey of 778 students in grades four through twelve, 87 per cent of all students and 96 per cent of the boys reported playing video games regularly.[16] Today's games are visually stunning, challengingly complex, and deeply immersive. They have come a long way from the days of Pong and Pac-Man. There are role-playing games, puzzles and strategy games, simulations, and sports games. The largest category of games, and the ones my college-aged computer science students report that they prefer, are 'first-person shooter' games, in which the player faces down other players, monsters, or characters. My students' favorite games sport names like Street Fighter, Vice City, Doom, America's Army, and Manhunt. How do these games affect the frequent player's view of the self in relationship to the natural world and to others?

The world of video games isolates a player from the natural world. The laws of cyberspace need not conform to the laws of the real world. New possibilities open up: one can move in three dimensions, into and through objects, which can be made to appear and disappear. This can be a mind-expanding imaginative experience. However, it can also distance a child from the real world. Hours spent in front of a screen are hours not spent messing around outdoors. Carl Pope describes what is lost:

> In losing our contact with the natural world we are losing something precious. In a way, we are losing part of what it means to be human. We evolved in nature, dependent on its rhythms, inextricably connected to other living things ... Playing outside every evening until called home by parents and falling darkness, we develop a sense of our human community as part of the wider, natural world. American children are losing that connection.[17]

Nature and a sense of place are lost in the virtual world.

Some parents may see the virtual world as a physically safer place than the real world precisely because it is a world that does not involve physical bodies. But is it safer? Virtual bullets don't kill, but continued exposure to violence can change the way a child views the world and, hence, how that child acts in the real world. Several recent studies show growing evidence that playing violent video games results in increased aggressive behavior. A Japanese study of fifth and sixth graders showed a clear correlation between the amount of time spent on video game playing early in the year and later physical aggression.[18] Two other studies, reported at the 2003 conference of the Society for Research in Child Development, found a similar link between violent game playing and aggressive thoughts and behavior, even after controlling for innate temperament and exposure to violence through other sources, such as movies and television.[19]

The results of these studies should be no surprise. Video games reward the player for mastering violence. Moreover, they teach that violence is an appropriate response to threat. That is why these games are used by the military as recruiting and training devices. America's Army, a first-person shooter game, is both distributed on CD by Army recruiters and downloadable from the Army's website. Dune has been used by the Marine Corps as a training device. Lt David Grossman, retired Professor of Psychology at West Point, notes that these games provide a script for the rehearsal of the act of killing: 'Video games teach children the skill and the will to kill. ... We are teaching children to associate pleasure with human death and suffering. We are rewarding them for killing people and we are teaching them to like it.'[20]

Perhaps the most disturbing thing about the relationship between the military and video games, however, is not that games like America's Army imitate war, but that war seems to increasingly imitate video games. The Bush administration's policy of pre-emptive attack is a given in the video game world, a world in which the 'bad guys' must be killed before they kill you. Video games teach quick reaction, not reasoned response. A focus on the immediate is another characteristic of video games. General Wesley Clark, in an article for the *New York Review of Books*, notes the almost exclusive focus on the initial conflict in Iraq, to the exclusion of planning for the post-war stage. Clark describes Secretary Rumsfeld's vision for Operation Iraqi Freedom as simplistic, merely the detection and destruction of enemy forces with minimum risk to one's own forces. In the words of one senior officer, 'Imagine a box of enemy territory 200 kilometers wide and 200 kilometers deep; we should be able to detect every enemy target there, and to strike and kill any target we want.'[21] This is war understood through the lens of the virtual world, as an operation in striking targets and only as such. Immersion in such a world, even for training, affects how one thinks and acts in the real world.

There are obvious reasons to be concerned about the increased prevalence of violent and graphic video games. Exposure to simulated violence and death can desensitize, lowering inhibitions and making it easier to commit violence in the real world. Violence is romanticized and equated with personal power and achievement. Many games include a 'back story' that explains the characters and their motivations. Revenge is a common feature in these stories, fostering the notion that violence as payback is justifiable. Nick Yee, a doctoral student in Communications at Stanford, notes, 'It's hard to have an in-game and out-game moral compass. I think it's the same thing, and when you play the game, your moral compass gets influenced and impacted by your decisions.'[22] Though one does not kill real people, one gets used to the concept of killing. From a Kantian or utilitarian ethical perspective one has neither hurt nor used another person. But virtue ethics warns us that one's character is formed by one's habits. First-person shooter games are designed to present the world in adversarial terms and to inure the player to violence.

Even video games that are not violent depend upon the ability of the player to exercise choice. The emphasis is on defeating adversaries, whether violently or not, besting opponents, designing functional tools or worlds – in other words, in all ways showing oneself to be master of one's environment. Consider, for example the class of games called 'God games', in which one builds and controls a virtual environment.[23] Simulations and role-playing games, while generally less violent than first-person shooters, still call on the player to assert herself, to exercise her will in manipulating the virtual world. Though not as obviously as in the first-person shooters, the player is still the actor and holds her power not jointly with others, but alone. God games allow the player to try out different scenarios, to see how things interact within the world of the game. Adventure, or quest, games are a third category of games with a large following. In these the vision of what it means to be fully human remains a skill-based vision, one that presents each person as an autonomous agent. Whether shooters, simulations, or adventures, games are all about individual control, a control that is not far from the human will-to-power that, according to Reinhold Niebuhr, lies at the root of the Christian concept of sin. Niebuhr notes, 'There is a pride of power in which the human ego assumes its self-sufficiency and self-mastery.'[24] To see the self only in terms of mastery is risky.

A larger problem is that all these games present the human person as lone actor. For most Christians, being fully human always entails being in relationship. Karl Barth notes that humans are created in the image of a trinitarian God, a God that embodies relationship in God's very self. Thus, to be fully human is to be in relationship with others. Barth's vision of humanity places face-to-face encounter and mutual aid at the center. Is this vision a part of the video game world? Some multi-player games do require interaction and cooperation between players. However, cooperation is rare in the video game world. Most games demand that the player act alone. Even in multi-player games, the players must often make decisions too quickly for them to be in any real sense collaborative. In the end, the cyberworld of video games is a very lonely place.

As an occasional pastime, video games seem harmless enough. But when the average American child spends nine hours per week playing these games, we need to ask what sort of worldview the games are furthering. What do these games teach our children about what it means to be fully human, about having a body, about social roles, about living in the real world? Eugene Provenzo, Professor of Education at the University of Miami, considered these questions in his testimony before a Senate committee hearing on interactive violence and children as follows:

> [These games] are the cultural equivalent of genetic engineering, except that in this experiment, even more than the other one, we will be the potential new hybrids, the two-pound mice. It is very possible, that the people killed

in the last few years as the result of 'school shootings' may in fact be the first victims/results of this experiment.[25]

In the end, the disembodied world of cyberspace could end up endangering the very bodies of our children. That is why it is important for theology to engage this fad, to point out that we are truly embodied beings, in a real physical world where death is final and rarely neat or clean.

Bodies matter. In the end we are more than the information in our brains, more than lone actors in either the real or the virtual world. We are finite, imperfect, and subject to a death that is not a game but very real. To think otherwise is to be caught in a pernicious fallacy, a fad of the early twenty-first century. Our physical and fallible bodies, our limited minds, give us our chief joys as well as our many sorrows. We relate to others and to our world through our embodied selves. The promise that a similarly relational existence will continue after death is found in the Christian concept of the resurrection of the body, where ultimate security lies 'beyond all the securities and insecurities of history'.[26]

Notes

1   'US Weight Loss and Diet Control Market', Market Data Enterprises Study, October 2002.
2   'Cosmetic Surgery Products to 2007', The Fredonia Group, February 2004.
3   K. Schneider, 'Mission Impossible', *People Magazine*, June 1996, 64–73.
4   Neal Stephenson, *Snow Crash* (New York: Bantam, 2000), 33.
5   Nicole Stenger, 'Mind is a Leaking Rainbow', in *Cyberspace: First Steps*, ed. by Michael Benedikt (Cambridge, MA: MIT, 1991), 53–4.
6   Ray Kurzweil, *The Age of Spiritual Machines: When Computers Exceed Human Intelligence* (New York: Penguin, 1999), Chapter 6.
7   Frank Tipler, *The Physics of Immortality: Modern Cosmology, God, and the Resurrection of the Dead* (New York: Doubleday, 1995).
8   Francis Crick, *The Astonishing Hypothesis: the Scientific Search for the Soul* (New York: Charles Scribner's Sons, 1994), 3.
9   Michael Benedikt (ed.), *Cyberspace: First Steps* (Cambridge, MA: MIT, 1991), 122.
10 See Joel Green, 'Bodies – That Is, Human Lives: A Re-Examination of Human Nature in the Bible', in *Whatever Happened to the Soul*, ed. by Warren Brown, Nancey Murphy, and H. Newton Malony (Minneapolis, MN: Fortress, 1998), 155–9.
11 Ibid., 178–9.
12 Tipler, *The Physics of Immortality*, 255. While this is not the place for an extended feminist critique, one can't help but notice that the proponents of cybernetic immortality and artificial intelligence are overwhelmingly male. Women remain in their speculations as objects of desire, yet are stripped of their reproductive role. Disembodied sexual experience, in the form of pornography, is, of course, a staple of the internet.
13 This understanding of the image of God is fundamental to the thought of Karl Barth and explicated in *Church Dogmatics*, volume 3. *The Doctrine of Creation*, part 1, ed. by G. W. Bromiley and T. F. Torrance, trans. by J. W. Edwards, O. Bussey, and Harold Knight (Edinburgh: T. and T. Clark, 1958).
14 Reinhold Niebuhr, *The Nature and Destiny of Man: A Christian Interpretation*, volume 2, *Human Destiny*, Library of Theological Ethics (Louisville, KY: Westminster John Knox, 1996), 75.

15 Robert Russell, personal interview, May 2001.

16 'Seventh Annual MediaWise Video Game Report Card', National Institute on Media and the Family, December 2002.

17 Carl Pope, 'The Forgotten Family Value', *Sierra*, November/December 2000, 16–18.

18 N. Ihori, A. Sakamoto, K. Kobayashi, and F. Kimura, 'Does Video Game Use Grow Children's Aggressiveness?: Results from a Panel Study', in *Social Contributions and Responsibilities of Simulation and Gaming: Proceedings of the 34th Annual Conference of the International Simulation and Gaming Association*, ed. by K. Arai (Tokyo: Japan Association of Simulation and Gaming, 2003), 221–30.

19 See D. A. Gentile, J. R. Linder, and D. A. Walsh, 'Looking Through Time: A Longitudinal Study of Children's Media Violence Consumption at Home and Aggressive Behaviors at School', and Craig Anderson and Kevin Buckley, 'Effects of Exposure to Violent Video Games'. Papers presented at the Society for Research in Child Development Biennial Conference, April 2003, Tampa, FL.

20 Interview on 20/20, March 2003.

21 Wesley Clark, 'Iraq: What Went Wrong', *New York Review of Books*, October 23, 2003: 54.

22 Heather Wax, 'In a Virtual World, What Happens When the Bad Guy Wins?', *Research News and Opportunities in Science and Theology*, October 2003: 35.

23 Examples of God games include SimCity, in which cybercharacters go about their daily lives; Tropico, in which you can run a banana republic, or RollerCoaster Tycoon, in which you build and run your own theme park. One can even simulate an ant colony with SimAnt.

24 Reinhold Niebuhr, *The Nature and Destiny of Man: A Christian Interpretation*, volume 1, *Human Nature*, Library of Theological Ethics (Louisville, KY: Westminster John Knox, 1996), 188.

25 Eugene Provenzo, *Testimony before the Senate Commerce Committee Hearing on the Impact of Interactive Violence on Children*, March 21, 2000: 5.

26 Ibid., 320.

Published Works of Robert John Russell

With F. A. Bais, 'Magnetic–monopole solution of non-Abelian gauge theory in curved spacetime', *Physical Review D*, 11 (1975), 2692.

With Frank Bridges, 'Isotope Effect on the Paraelectric Resonance of $KBr:Li^+$', *Bulletin of the American Physical Society*, 21 (1976), 265.

With Frank Bridges, 'A New Paraelectric Center in Lithium-Doped KBr', *Solid State Communications*, 21 (1977), 1011.

With Frank Bridges, 'Suppression of the Paraelectric Resonance of $KBr:Li^+$ by OH^-', *Bulletin of the American Physical Society*, 22 (1977), 332.

With Frank Bridges, 'A New Paraelectric Center in $NaCl:Li^+$', *Bulletin of the American Physical Society*, 23 (1978), 18.

'Relative Magnitude of Tunneling Parameters Versus Energy Levels in Paraelectric Models', *Bulletin of the American Physical Society*, 26 (1981), 30.

'Energy and Values', *New Catholic World*, 224 (May/June 1981), 1341.

With Frank Bridges, 'Unusual Paraelectric System, $KBr:Li^+$', *Physical Review B*, 26 (1982), 6.

'Systematic Approach for Comparing Paraelectric Tunneling Models to Resonance Data', *Physical Review B*, 26 (1982), 6.

Ed., 'Computers: Altering the Human Image and Society Edited Transcripts', *Computers & Society*, 13:1 (1983).

'Entropy and Evil', *Zygon: Journal of Religion and Science*, 19:4 (December 1984), 449–68. Also *CTNS Bulletin*, 4:2 (Spring 1984).

With Andrew J. Dufner, SJ, 'Foundations in Physics for Revising the Creation Tradition', in Philip N. Joranson and Ken Butigan (eds), *Cry of the Environment: Rebuilding the Christian Creation Tradition*, Santa Fe, NM: Bear & Co. (1984), 163–80.

'How Does Modern Physical Cosmology Affect Creation Theology?', *Pacific Theological Review*, 18:3 (Spring 1985), 33–42.

'A Critical Appraisal of Peacocke's Thought on Religion and Science', *Religion and Intellectual Life*, II:4 (Summer 1985), 48–58.

With Ian G. Barbour, 'The Thought of David Bohm: Introduction', *Zygon: Journal of Religion and Science*, 20:2 (June 1985), 107–10.

'The Physics of David Bohm and its Relevance to Philosophy and Theology', *Zygon: Journal of Religion and Science*, 20:2 (June 1985), 135–58.

'A Response to David Bohm's "Time, The Implicate Order and Pre-Space"', in David R. Griffin (ed.), *Physics and the Ultimate Significance of Time*, Albany, NY: State University of New York Press (1986), 209–19.

'How Does Scientific Cosmology Shape a Theology of Nature?', *CTNS Bulletin*, 6:1 (Winter 1986), 1–12.

With Christoph Wassermann, 'Kerr Solution to Whitehead's Theory of Gravity', *Bulletin of the American Physical Society*, 32:90 (1987), p. 90.

'The Meaning of Causality in Contemporary Physics', in Viggo Mortensen and Robert C. Sorensen (eds), *Free Will and Determinism*, Aarhus, Denmark: Aarhus University Press (1987), 13–31.

'Science and Theology Today: A Fresh Appraisal of Peacocke's Thought', *Religion & Intellectual Life*, V:3 (Spring 1988), 64–9.

'Contingency in Physics and Cosmology: A Critique of the Theology of Wolfhart Pannenberg', *Zygon: Journal of Religion and Science*, 23:1 (March 1988), 23–43.

'Technology, Ethics and Education in a Global Perspective', in Guy Fitch Lytle (ed.), *Theological Education for the Future*, Cincinnati, OH: Forward Movement Publications (1988), 76–80.

'Whitehead, Einstein and the Newtonian Legacy', in George V. Coyne, SJ, Michael Heller, and Jozef Zycinski (eds), *Newton and the New Direction in Science*, Citta Del Vaticano: Specola Vaticana (1988), 175–92.

With William R. Stoeger, SJ, and George V. Coyne, SJ (eds), *Physics, Philosophy, and Theology: A Common Quest for Understanding*, Vatican City State: Vatican Observatory Publications (1988).

'Quantum Physics in Philosophical and Theological Perspective', in Robert John Russell, William R. Stoeger, SJ, and George V. Coyne, SJ (eds), *Physics, Philosophy, and Theology: A Common Quest for Understanding*, Vatican City State: Vatican Observatory Publications (1988), 343–74.

'Evolutionary Understanding of Humanity and the Problem of Evil: Biological Evolution, Thermodynamics and the Problem of Evil', in Hans May, Meinfried Striegnitz, and Philip Hefner (eds), *Kooperation und Wettbewerb*, Rehberg-Loccum, West Germany: Evangelische Akademie Loccum (1988), 307–12.

'Bread of Life: A Communion Meditation', *CTNS Bulletin*, 9:3 (Summer 1989), 3–6.

'Cosmology, Creation and Contingency', in Ted Peters (ed.), *Cosmos as Creation*, Nashville, TN: Abingdon Press (1989), 177–209.

'Agenda for the Twenty-First Century', in John Mangum (ed.), *The New Faith–Science Debate*, Minneapolis, MN: Fortress Press and Geneva: WCC Publications (1989), 91–105.

'The Thermodynamics of "Natural Evil"', *CTNS Bulletin*, 10:2 (Spring 1990), 20–25.

'Christian Discipleship and the Challenge of Physics: Formation, Flux, and Focus', *Perspectives on Science and Christian Faith*, 42:3 (September 1990), 139–54. Also *CTNS Bulletin*, 8:4 (Autumn 1988), 1–16.

With William Stoeger, SJ, and George Coyne, SJ (eds), *John Paul II on Science and Religion: Reflections on the New View from Rome*, Vatican City State: Vatican Observatory (1990).

'Theological Implications of Physics and Cosmology', in James B. Miller and Kenneth E. McCall (eds), *The Church and Contemporary Cosmology*, Pittsburgh, PA: Carnegie Mellon University Press (1990), 247–72.

'Contemplation in the Vibrant Universe: The Natural Context of Christian Spirituality', *CTNS Bulletin*, 11:4 (Autumn 1991), 5–17.

'Theological Lessons from Cosmology: Two Case Studies', *Cross Currents: Religion & Intellectual Life*, 41:3 (Fall 1991), 308–21.

'The Theological–Scientific Vision of Arthur Peacocke', *Zygon: Journal of Religion and Science*, 26:4 (December 1991), 505–17.

'Theological Implications of Artificial Intelligence', in C. Wasserman, R. Kirby, and B. Rordorff (eds), *The Science and Theology of Information*, Geneva: Editions Labor et Fides (1992), 245–60.

'Cosmology', in Donald W. Musser and Joseph L. Price (eds), *A New Handbook of Christian Theology*, Nashville, TN: Abingdon Press (1992), 101–5.

With Ted Peters, 'The Human Genome Project: What Questions Does It Raise for Theology and Ethics?', *Midwest Medical Ethics*', 8:1 (Summer 1992), 12–17.

'Finite Creation Without A Beginning', *The Way: Contemporary Christian Spirituality*, 32:2 (October 1992), 268–280.

'Contemplation: A Scientific Context', *Continuum*, 2:2 and 3 (1992/1993), 135–53.

With Nancey C. Murphy and Chris J. Isham (eds), *Quantum Cosmology and the Laws of Nature: Scientific Perspectives on Divine Action*, Vatican City State: Vatican Observatory Publications and Berkeley, CA: The Center for Theology and the Natural Sciences (1993).

'Introduction', in Robert John Russell, Nancey C. Murphy and Chris J. Isham (eds), *Quantum Cosmology and the Laws of Nature: Scientific Perspectives on Divine Action*, Vatican City State: Vatican Observatory Publications and Berkeley, CA: The Center for Theology and the Natural Sciences (1993), 1–32.

'Finite Creation without a Beginning: The Doctrine of Creation in Relation to Big Bang and Quantum Cosmologies', in Robert John Russell, Nancey C. Murphy and Chris J. Isham (eds), *Quantum Cosmology and the Laws of Nature: Scientific Perspectives on Divine Action*, Vatican City State: Vatican Observatory Publications and Berkeley, CA: The Center for Theology and the Natural Sciences (1993), 293–329.

'Cosmology: Evidence for God or Partner for Theology?', in John Marks Templeton (ed.), *Evidence of Purpose: Scientists Discover the Creator*, New York: Continuum (1994), 70–90.

'Cosmology from Alpha to Omega', *Zygon: Journal of Religion and Science*, 29:4 (December 1994), 557–77.

'Theistic Evolution: Does God Really Act in Nature?', *CTNS Bulletin*, 15:1 (Winter 1995), 19–32.

With Nancey C. Murphy and Arthur R. Peacocke (eds), *Chaos and Complexity: Scientific Perspectives on Divine Action*, Vatican City State: Vatican Observatory Publications and Berkeley, CA: The Center for Theology and the Natural Sciences (1995).

'Introduction', in Robert John Russell, Nancey C. Murphy and Arthur R. Peacocke (eds), *Chaos and Complexity: Scientific Perspectives on Divine*

Action, Vatican City State: Vatican Observatory Publications and Berkeley, CA: The Center for Theology and the Natural Sciences (1995), 1–31.

With Wesley J. Wildman, 'Chaos: A Mathematical Introduction with Philosophical Reflections', in Robert John Russell, Nancey C. Murphy and Arthur R. Peacocke (eds), *Chaos and Complexity: Scientific Perspectives on Divine Action*, Vatican City State: Vatican Observatory Publications and Berkeley, CA: The Center for Theology and the Natural Sciences (1995), 49–90.

't = 0: Is it Theologically Significant?', in W. Mark Richardson and Wesley J. Wildman (eds), *Religion and Science: History, Method, Dialogue*, New York: Routledge (1996), 201–24.

'Religion and the Theories of Science: A Response to Barbour', *Zygon: Journal of Religion and Science*, 31:1 (March 1996), 29–41.

'Philosophy, Theology and Cosmology: A Fresh Look at their Interactions', in Padre Eligio, Guilio Giorello, Gioachino Rigamonti, and Elio Sindoni (eds), *Scienze, Filosofia e Teologia di Fronte alla Nascita dell'Universo*, Como, Italy: Edizioni New Press (1997), 215–43.

'How should Religion and Science be Creatively Related? A Christian Perspective', *Hindu–Christian Studies Bulletin*, 10 (1997), 28–35.

'Cosmology and Eschatology: The Implications of Tipler's "Omega Point" Theory to Pannenberg's Theological Program', in Carol Albright and Joel Haugen (eds), *Beginning with the End: God, Science, and Wolfhart Pannenberg*, Chicago: Open Court (1997), 195–216.

'Does the "God Who *Acts*" Really *Act*? New Approaches to Divine Action in Light of Science', *Theology Today*, 54:1 (April 1997), 43–65.

'Does Creation Have a Beginning?', *Dialog: A Journal of Theology*, 36:2 (Summer 1997), 180–87.

'The God Who Infinitely Transcends Infinity: Insights from Cosmology and Mathematics into the Greatness of God', in John Marks Templeton and Robert L. Herrmann (eds), *How Large is God?*, Philadelphia, PA: Templeton Foundation Press (1997), 137–65.

With William R. Stoeger, SJ, and Francisco J. Ayala (eds), *Evolutionary and Molecular Biology: Scientific Perspectives on Divine Action*, Vatican City State: Vatican Observatory Publications and Berkeley, CA: The Center for Theology and the Natural Sciences (1998).

'Introduction', in Robert John Russell, William R. Stoeger, SJ, and Francisco J. Ayala (eds), *Evolutionary and Molecular Biology: Scientific Perspectives on Divine Action*, Vatican City State: Vatican Observatory Publications and Berkeley, CA: The Center for Theology and the Natural Sciences (1998), i–xxxiv.

'Special Providence and Genetic Mutation: A New Defense of Theistic Evolution', in Robert John Russell, William R. Stoeger, SJ, and Francisco J. Ayala (eds), *Evolutionary and Molecular Biology: Scientific Perspectives on Divine Action*, Vatican City State: Vatican Observatory Publications and Berkeley, CA: The Center for Theology and the Natural Sciences (1998), 191–223.

'Does the "God Who Acts" Really Act in Nature?', in Ted Peters (ed.), *Science and Theology: The New Consonance*, Boulder, CO: Westview Press (1998), 77–102.

'Causality', in Hans Dieter Betz, Don S. Browning, Bernd Janowski, and Eberhard Jüngel (eds), *Religion in Geschichte und Gegenwart (RGG⁴)*, 8 vols, Tübingen, Germany: Mohr Siebeck (1998–2005), Vol. 4:90.

'Complementarity', in Hans Dieter Betz, Don S. Browning, Bernd Janowski, and Eberhard Jüngel (eds), *Religion in Geschichte und Gegenwart (RGG⁴)*, 8 vols, Tübingen, Germany: Mohr Siebeck (1998–2005), Vol. 4:1539.

'Contingency', in Hans Dieter Betz, Don S. Browning, Bernd Janowski, and Eberhard Jüngel (eds), *Religion in Geschichte und Gegenwart (RGG⁴)*, 8 vols, Tübingen, Germany: Mohr Siebeck (1998–2005), Vol. 4:1646.

'Relativity', in Hans Dieter Betz, Don S. Browning, Bernd Janowski, and Eberhard Jüngel (eds), *Religion in Geschichte und Gegenwart (RGG⁴)*, 8 vols, Tübingen, Germany: Mohr Siebeck (1998–2005), Vol. 7:262.

With Nancey Murphy, Theo C. Meyering, and Michael A. Arbib (eds), *Neuroscience and the Person: Scientific Perspectives on Divine Action*, Vatican City State: Vatican Observatory Publications and Berkeley, CA: The Center for Theology and the Natural Sciences (1999).

With Lindon J. Eaves, Katherine M. Kirk, and Nicholas G. Martin, 'Some Implications of Chaos Theory for the Genetic Analysis of Human Development and Variation', *Twin Research*, 2:1 (March 1999), 43–8.

With Lindon J. Eaves and Brian D'Onofrio, 'Transmission of religion and attitudes', *Twin Research*, 2:2 (June 1999), 59–61.

'How the Heavens Have Changed!', *Ad Astra: The Magazine of the National Space Society* (November/December 1998), 16–20 and *CTNS Bulletin*, 19:3 (Summer 1999), 3–10.

'What are Extraterrestrials Really Like?', in Russell Stannard (ed.), *God for the 21st Century*, Philadelphia, PA: Templeton Foundation Press (2000), 64–6.

'Time in Eternity: Special Relativity and Eschatology', *Dialog: A Journal of Theology*, 39:1 (Spring 2000), 46–55.

'Did God Create Our Universe? Theological Reflections on the Big Bang, Inflation, and Quantum Cosmologies', in J. B. Miller (ed.), *Annals of the New York Academy of Sciences*, vol. 950, *Cosmic Questions*, New York: New York Academy of Sciences (2001), 108–27.

'The Relevance of Tillich for the Theology and Science Dialogue', *Zygon: Journal of Religion and Science*, 36:2 (June 2001), 269–308. Also in Frederick J. Parrella and Raymond F. Bulman (eds), *Religion in the New Millennium: Theology in the Spirit of Paul Tillich*, Macon, GA: Mercer University Press (2001), 261–311.

'Life in the Universe: Philosophical and Theological Issues', in Julian Chela-Flores, Tobias Owen, and François Raulin (eds), *First Steps in the Origin of Life in the Universe*, proceedings of the Sixth Trieste Conference on Chemical Evolution, Dordrecht, Netherlands: Kluwer Academic Publishers (2001), 365–75.

'Dialogo Science–Teologia, Metodo e Modelli', Italian translation of Part 1, 'Theology and Science: Current Issues and Future Directions', in Giuseppe

Tanzella-Nitti (ed.), *Dizionario Interdisciplinare di Scienze e Fede*, Città del Vaticano: Urbaniana University Press (2002), Vol. 1:382–94.

With Ted Peters and Michael Welker (eds), *Resurrection: Theological and Scientific Assessments*, Grand Rapids, MI: Eerdmans (2002).

'Bodily Resurrection, Eschatology, and Scientific Cosmology: The Mutual Interaction of Christian Theology and Science', in Ted Peters, Robert John Russell, and Michael Welker (eds), *Resurrection: Theological and Scientific Assessments*, Grand Rapids, MI: Eerdmans (2002), 3–30.

'Eschatology and Physical Cosmology: A Preliminary Reflection', in George F. R. Ellis (ed.), *The Far-Future Universe: Eschatology from a Cosmic Perspective*, Philadelphia, PA: Templeton Press (2002), 266–315.

With Kirk Wegter-McNelly, 'Science and Theology: Mutual Interaction', in Ted Peters and Gaymon Bennett (eds), *Bridging Science and Religion*, London: SCM Press and Minneapolis, MN: Fortress Press (2002), 19–34.

With Kirk Wegter-McNelly, 'Natural Law and Divine Action,' in Ted Peters and Gaymon Bennett (eds), *Bridging Science and Religion*, London: SCM Press and Minneapolis, MN: Fortress Press (2002), 49–68.

With Philip Clayton, Kirk Wegter-McNelly, and John Polkinghorne (eds), *Quantum Mechanics: Scientific Perspectives on Divine Action*, Vatican City State: Vatican Observatory Publications and Berkeley, CA: The Center for Theology and the Natural Sciences (2001).

'Introduction', in Robert John Russell, Philip Clayton, Kirk Wegter-McNelly, and John Polkinghorne (eds), *Quantum Mechanics: Scientific Perspectives on Divine Action*, Vatican City State: Vatican Observatory Publications and Berkeley, CA: The Center for Theology and the Natural Sciences (2001), i–xxvi.

'Divine Action and Quantum Mechanics: A Fresh Assessment', in Robert John Russell, Philip Clayton, Kirk Wegter-McNelly, and John Polkinghorne (eds), *Quantum Mechanics: Scientific Perspectives on Divine Action*, Vatican City State: Vatican Observatory Publications and Berkeley, CA: The Center for Theology and the Natural Sciences (2001), 293–328.

'The Doctrine of Creation out of Nothing in Relation to Big Bang and Quantum Cosmologies', in *The Human Search for Truth: Philosophy, Science, Theology*, International Conference on Science and the Faith, Philadelphia, PA: Saint Joseph's University Press (2002), 108–29.

With W. Mark Richardson, Philip Clayton, and Kirk Wegter-McNelly (eds), *Science and the Spiritual Quest: New Essays by Leading Scientists*, London: Routledge (2002).

'Special Providence and Genetic Mutation: A New Defense of Theistic Evolution', in Keith B. Miller (ed.), *Perspectives on an Evolving Creation*, Grand Rapids, MI: William B. Eerdmans Publishing Company (2003), 335–69.

'Bridging Theology and Science: The CTNS Logo', *Theology and Science*, 1:1 (April 2003): 1–3.

'Five Attitudes towards Nature and Technology from a Christian Perspective', *Theology and Science*, 1:2 (October 2003): 149–59.

'Sin, Salvation, and Scientific Cosmology: Is Christian Eschatology Credible Today?', in Duncan Reid and Mark Worthing (ed.), *Sin and Salvation: Task of Theology Today III*, Adelaide, Australia: Australian Theological Forum Press (2003), 130–54.

With Kirk Wegter-McNelly, 'Science', in Gareth Jones (ed.), *The Blackwell Companion to Modern Theology*, Oxford: Blackwell Publishing (2004), 512–56.

Ed., *Fifty Years in Science and Religion: Ian G. Barbour and His Legacy*, Aldershot, UK: Ashgate (2004).

'Introduction', in Robert John Russell (ed.), *Fifty Years in Science and Religion: Ian G. Barbour and His Legacy*, Aldershot, UK: Ashgate (2004), 1–16.

'Ian Barbour's Methodological Breakthrough: Creating the "Bridge" between Science and Theology', in Robert John Russell (ed.), *Fifty Years in Science and Religion: Ian G. Barbour and His Legacy*', Aldershot, UK: Ashgate (2004), 45–59.

'Barbour's Assessment of the Philosophical and Theological Implications of Physics and Cosmology', in Robert John Russell (ed.), *Fifty Years in Science and Religion: Ian G. Barbour and His Legacy*, Aldershot, UK: Ashgate (2004), 145–61.

'Spirituality and Science', in Philip Sheldrake (ed.), *The New Westminster Dictionary of Christian Spirituality*, London: SCM Press (2005), 55–61.

'Natural Sciences', in Arthur Holder (ed.), *Blackwell Companion to Christian Spirituality*, Oxford: Blackwell Publishing (2005), 325–44.

Index

243